# MADAM PRESIDENT

# MADAM PRESIDENT

## THE SECRET
## PRESIDENCY OF
## EDITH WILSON

## WILLIAM HAZELGROVE

REGNERY
HISTORY

Regnery History™ is a trademark of Salem Communications Holding Corporation; Regnery® is a registered trademark of Salem Communications Holding Corporation

Cataloging-in-Publication Data on file with the Library of Congress

ISBN 978-1-62157-475-0

Published in the United States by
Regnery History
An imprint of Regnery Publishing
A Division of Salem Media Group
300 New Jersey Ave NW
Washington, DC 20001
www.RegneryHistory.com

Manufactured in the United States of America

10 9 8 7 6 5 4 3 2 1

Books are available in quantity for promotional or premium use. For information on discounts and terms, please visit our website: www.Regnery.com.

Distributed to the trade by
Perseus Distribution
250 West 57th Street
New York, NY 10107

*Once again
for Kitty, Clay, Callie,
and Careen*

# CONTENTS

*Do one thing every day that scares you.*

—Eleanor Roosevelt

# PROLOGUE

**SHE WAS FROM THE SOUTH, HAD TWO YEARS OF FORMAL SCHOOLING,** and had the penmanship of a child. She married a quiet man from Washington and had a baby who died after just three days. Her husband then died and left her with a failing jewelry company that was severely in debt. She took almost no salary and turned the company around. She bought an electric car and was issued the first driver's license given to a woman in the District of Columbia. She married a president who had been recently widowed. In four years, the president would have a severe stroke and leave her to run the United States government and negotiate the end of World War I. She was our first woman president.

# ONE

# THE COVER-UP

PRESIDENT WOODROW WILSON LAY WITH HIS MOUTH DROOPING, unconscious, having suffered a thrombosis on October 2, 1919, that left him paralyzed on his left side and barely able to speak. The doctors believed the president's best chance for survival was in the only known remedy for a stroke at the time: a rest cure consisting of total isolation from the world.

His wife of four years, Edith Bolling Wilson, asked how a country could function with no chief executive. Dr. Dercum, the attending physician, leaned over and gave Edith her charge: "Madam, it is a grave situation, but I think you can solve it. Have everything come to you; weigh the importance of each matter, and see if it is possible by consultations with the respective heads of the Departments to solve them without the guidance of your husband."

From there, Edith Wilson would act as the president's proxy and run the White House and, by extension, the country, by controlling access to the president, signing documents, pushing bills through Congress, issuing vetoes, isolating advisors, crafting State of the Union addresses, disposing of or censoring correspondence, and filling positions. She would analyze every problem and decide which ones to bring to the president's attention and which to solve on her own through her own devices. All the while she had to keep the fact that the country was no longer being run by President Woodrow Wilson a guarded secret.

A few guessed at the real situation. A frustrated Senator Albert Fall from New Mexico pounded the senatorial table when he demanded a response from the White House: "We have a petticoat government! Wilson is not acting! Mrs. Wilson is President!"

Some saw it as a power grab when Edith Wilson kept Vice President Thomas R. Marshall from seeing the president and preventing the constitutional transfer of power. But Edith believed the doctor's warning that any stress would kill her husband. To keep her husband alive, she would have to shield him from the world—and that meant running the country herself.

Even before her husband's stroke, Edith, as first lady, had participated in the Wilson administration to an extraordinary degree. She and Woodrow resembled a twenty-first-century political power couple. President Wilson kept her close by his side and clearly valued his wife's input, making her a partner in many political decisions. In this way, he had given her hands-on training for her "stewardship."

"I tried to arrange my own appointments to correspond with those of the President, so we might be free at the same times," she would later write. Woodrow gave Edith presidential access to all his work, and she often spent all day with him. As she later wrote, "Breakfast at eight o'clock sharp. Then we both went to the study to look in The Drawer and possibly, if nothing had 'blown up' overnight, there was time to put signatures on commissions or other routine papers. These

I always placed before my husband, and blotted and removed them as fast as possible..."

Edith's participation in the Wilson White House gave her—a woman, who just four years before had been a widow living alone in Washington—the capacity to deal with the demands of running the United States while nursing her husband. The impact of the president's death was profound and broad-ranging: domestic problems were on the rise; foreign policy initiatives ground to a virtual standstill; and the League of Nations, first proposed by Wilson, failed to get approved. At a point, the White House had begun to cease to function.

Edith Wilson, a woman with only two years of formal education, had to step in. She had to make it up as she went along, approving appointments, making foreign policy and domestic policy decisions, orchestrating the cover-up, and restricting access to her husband, who at times was totally "gone." When looking through *The Papers of Woodrow Wilson*, one is struck by how much correspondence from 1919 to 1921 was directed toward Edith. She was on the front lines of issues ranging from the recognition of diplomats to America's entry into the League of Nations.

The correspondence of the Edith Wilson years was voluminous. As she wrote to Colonel Edward House, the president's unofficial advisor, "My hands now are so full that I neglect many things. But I feel equal to everything that comes now that I see steady progress going on..."

Americans wouldn't see their president for five months. Appointments remained unfilled and correspondence piled up. Years later, essential communications to the president that had never been opened in the White House were found in the National Archives. Like someone who didn't have time to get to her bills, Edith had simply thrown them in a pile.

The cover-up has persisted to the present day; in part, because of Edith Wilson herself. In her memoir, written in 1939, she called her presidency a "stewardship," effectively downplaying the true significance of her role. But historians have been complicit in the cover-up, as well. While many concede that Edith Wilson was almost the president, they also insist that Woodrow Wilson remained in charge. And while some go so far as to claim she acted as president for six weeks, *at most*, they go no further in acknowledging the extent of her presidency.

Many Americans are still surprised to learn that President Wilson suffered a massive stroke while in office, but what they find totally inconceivable is that his wife, Edith Wilson, was the acting president for almost two years. To acknowledge this would be to diminish Woodrow Wilson's legacy.

Power is given to those who can wield it, and President Wilson, who remained in bed only to be wheeled out for movies and some fresh air, was virtually powerless.

The question then is: who was Edith Bolling Wilson? Was she a woman singularly gifted enough to run the country and nurse her husband back to health? Or was she a woman doing the best she could in a world in which women were seen as little more than second-class citizens? Now, almost a hundred years later, we again ponder the impact of our first woman president.

To do so, we must first go back to a train car outside of Pueblo, Colorado, in the Indian summer of 1919. It is here in the heat and dust on September 25 that Edith Wilson's presidency began.

# TWO

# A BAD DAY

## 1919

**"EDITH, CAN YOU COME TO ME? I AM VERY SICK."**

A woman stood in the darkness with the desert wind blowing in the open windows. The train car shifted from side to side as she grabbed the handle to the president's bedroom. Somewhere outside of Pueblo, Colorado, in the stifling heat of September 14, 1919, Edith Bolling Wilson opened the door from her train compartment and found the twenty-eighth president of the United States with his forehead against a chair just a half hour before midnight. Pressing against the cranial thump of blood gave some relief to President Wilson, but his condition was quickly deteriorating.

The steel presidential car, the *Mayflower*, was stifling hot as Wilson moaned and inhaled the lingering scent of smoke from forest fires they had passed through earlier. The president had found few remedies for the excruciating headaches caused by hypertension, a result, perhaps, of his years of campaigning for the League of Nations, which had left him physically exhausted.

The League was already under attack by Henry Cabot Lodge and other isolationist Republicans. Lodge saw the League as a threat to America's sovereignty. And he loathed Wilson, whom he viewed as an arrogant dreamer with no gift for realpolitik. The Brahmin from Boston, who wore spats and sported a Vandyke beard, thought Wilson inept in war and peace; it didn't help that Wilson had defeated Lodge's lifelong friend Teddy Roosevelt in the 1912 presidential race and that the League had become the barefoot child of the peace negotiations in Paris.

President Wilson feared the defeat of the League would lead to another war, perhaps one even greater than "The War to End All Wars." So the president had gone on the road to take his case to the American people. But there was no Air Force One; there was only the presidential train car, the *Mayflower*, basically a steel tube hauled by a steam locomotive that belched coal smoke. Edith described the presidential accommodations this way in her memoir: "Entering the car from the rear one came first to a sitting room, fitted with armchairs, a long couch and a folding table on which we dined. Next came my bedroom and then the President's, with a door connecting. Each room had a single bed and dressing table. Beyond this was a room which my husband used as an office. There was placed his typewriter, without which he never traveled..."

A whistle-stop tour would be a grueling event for a healthy, young man, and the sixty-two-year-old Wilson was neither of these. They passed through the scorching temperatures of the West without the comfort of air conditioning. They had been traveling for twelve days, and the last two had been brutal. As Edith later wrote in her memoir: "The weather was warm and enervating. These two days would have taxed the vitality of one who was rested and refreshed. My husband took them on top of twelve days and nights of travel..."

Hypertension and a hardening of the arteries had begun to take a toll on Wilson. His latest relief-seeking technique was to press his head against a chair. Many times the headaches would drive the president to darkened bedrooms where Edith would pull the curtains.

Edith immediately called Dr. Grayson. She had been married to the president for four years but had been apprehensive about accepting his proposal of marriage. Born in a small town in Virginia and widowed at twenty-three, Edith had been an independent woman before she met the president. Wilson, who was a recent widower, immediately started wooing her with Victorian love letters, launching a campaign to win over the younger woman with the flashing wit and buxom figure.

Grayson examined his patient and noticed that the president's face was twitching and that he was gasping from an asthmatic attack. As Grayson later recorded in his diary, "The strain of the trip had at last taken its toll from him and he was very seriously ill.... For a few minutes it looked as if he could hardly get his breath." The headache screwed into his forehead and was getting worse. The president of the United States was suffering the early symptoms of a stroke.

The doctor moved him to the larger "office" car, where Wilson tossed and turned most of the night. "The Doctor and I kept the vigil while the train dashed on and on through darkness," Edith would later write in her memoir. "About five in the morning a blessed release came, and, sitting upright on the stiff seat, my husband fell asleep. I motioned to the Doctor to go on to bed, and I sat opposite scarcely breathing..."

The next morning, Wilson emerged clean-shaven, but Grayson argued against continuing on. They had completed only 3,500 miles of a 10,000-mile trip. The president pointed out his problem: "Don't you see that if we cancel this trip, Senator Lodge and his friends will say that I am a quitter, that the [Western] trip was a failure. And the Treaty will be lost."

Grayson advised against continuing on and then bluntly predicted that the tour would kill him. Edith urged her husband to cancel the rest of his speeches. When Joe Tumulty, his personal secretary, came in, the president admitted, "I don't seem to realize it, but I have gone to pieces. The Doctor is right. I am not in condition to go on." He then turned and looked out the window with tears coming to his eyes. Wilson would later call it "the greatest disappointment of my life."

The train started back East. Edith sat up watching her husband with the steam locomotive chugging toward Washington. Edith had begun to make the psychological shift that would allow her to run the United States. She had married Woodrow Wilson four years before, knowing her life would change forever. Now her life would change again. Edith reflected twenty years later that she "would have to wear a mask, not only to the public but to the one I loved best in the world; for he must never know how ill he was and I must carry on."

Edith was devoted to the president. She rose early to help make his meals and monitored who saw him. She took long drives with Woodrow, believing this would help remedy his exhaustion, occasional depression, and chronic hypertension. Edith had tried for years to protect her husband from stress. An election in 1916, a world war, then a year in Europe fighting for the League of Nations had taken everything Wilson had.

The president believed the League would give meaning to the sacrifice of millions of young men who had died in the hollowed-out hell of trench warfare in France. At the very least he would be able to look American mothers in the eye and say their sons helped to prevent future wars. Wilson saw American boys who came over "as crusaders, not merely to win the war, but to win a cause." That cause was the

League of Nations, but without approval by the United States, the League would mean nothing.

The train ran back on a specially cleared track with the blinds lowered. People gathered at stations to watch the speeding *Presidential Express*. The press was told "nervous exhaustion" was the reason for the cancellation of the speaking tour. Wilson sent a telegram from Wichita, Kansas, to his daughter, Jessie Woodrow, trying to stem alarm. "Returning to Washington. Nothing to be alarmed about. Love from all of us. Woodrow Wilson."

A news report in the *Denver Post* on September 26 ran: "President Is Ill and Cancels his Tour." In what would become a precedent, Dr. Grayson reported physical exhaustion as the reason the Western speaking tour had been cancelled. The article speculated that the ordeal of parades "seemed to be most trying on [the president's] nerves" and that "the trip had also been very tiring to Mrs. Wilson." The press respected privacy in 1919 in a pact between the White House and the reporters who covered the president.

Edith knitted while the president tossed in the agony of extreme hypertension. On September 27, Grayson issued another press bulletin from the train: "The president's condition is about the same. He has had a fairly restful night." The *New York Times* headline on Saturday, September 27 announced, "The President Suffers Nervous Breakdown" and connected it to an attack of influenza in Paris.

Grayson requested the train run at half speed to keep from jarring the president. The train slowed to twenty-five miles per hour while Wilson writhed from the intense cerebral pressure. When they reached Washington, the president managed to walk from the presidential car and then was ordered to bed by Admiral Grayson. The next day he and Edith took a two-hour drive in the Pierce-Arrow presidential limousine. It was a cool autumn day, and Wilson seemed to improve. But the headaches never abated, and upon his return, Grayson ordered him back to bed.

The doctor then issued several mandates that would guide Edith Wilson over the next two years. In his diary he wrote, "I took steps to put into effect the rest cure which I had planned and which I realized was the only thing that would restore him to health." The only cure was total isolation from the pressures of his job: he "shouldn't be bothered with any matters of official character....It was to be a complete rest, not partial rest...and nothing was to be allowed to interfere with the President's restoration to health if possible."

Any pressure on the president could now be fatal. If Edith's husband were to survive, she must insert herself between him and the United States government. No cabinet meetings. No meetings of any kind.

Edith Wilson started to fill in for her ailing husband. The secretary of war, Newton Diehl Baker, sent her the first official telegram. "Dear Mrs. Wilson, If anything comes to the White House in the next few days which you think I could do and so save the President having to give it attention...feel free to send it to me..." Edith then stepped in by entertaining ten journalists from the Western tour. Her first duty of state was when Sir William Wiseman of the British government said he had an urgent message for the president, which Edith conveyed to her husband. But the president waved it off, and Sir William Wiseman received no response. Edith would write in her memoir, "This was the only instance that I recall having acted as an intermediary between my husband and another on an official matter..." The real Edith starts to bleed through her prose when she comments, about Wiseman, "I had never liked this plausible little man." Edith was liable to make snap judgments that dictated who got an answer and who didn't. Sir William Wiseman would never get one.

On the third day, Wilson improved and even played some pool. He was eating more and taking his daily drives. But nothing could alleviate the lurking thrombosis caused by pressured arteries. Medical science had years earlier told another future president that he would have to live the life of a recluse because of an abnormality in his heart. But Teddy Roosevelt did not take his doctor's advice and would become the most vigorous president America ever had.

The *New York Times* reported on September 30, "President Wilson seems to be getting better...at 10:30 tonight Rear Admiral Grayson issued the following bulletin. The President spent a fairly comfortable day and is improving." The *Times* then reported on October 1, "President is Again Jaded After Another Restless Night..."

On the night of October 2, Edith looked into the president's bedroom and found her husband sleeping soundly. She stopped back a half hour later and found him sitting up in his bed. "I have no feeling in that hand," he murmured, gesturing to his left. Edith sat on the bed and started rubbing the president's hand, then helped him to the bathroom.

"I'm going to call Dr. Grayson," she told him and left her husband in the bathroom.

Edith hurried down to the White House switchboard and told the operator to contact Dr. Grayson immediately. She then heard a thump that sounded like a body falling to the floor. Edith ran back upstairs and found the president of the United States bleeding and unconscious on the hard white tiles of the bathroom floor.

# THREE

# THE FIRST
# MRS. WILSON

1883

**THE GAWKY YOUNG LAWYER ATTENDING THE CHURCH IN GEORGIA**
was ill at ease. He didn't have the easy affability of the salesman. He
lived in his head a good deal and had a professorial air. His heart was
in turmoil, for he had just seen a woman he was certain he would
marry. As a Calvinist, he believed that God's plan was preordained.
He believed it was ordained that he should meet Ellen Axson and
marry her.

Her mother had died four weeks after giving birth to her fourth
child, and her father, a pastor of the First Presbyterian Church of
Rome, Georgia, suffered from depression that would later turn into
mental illness. Twenty-one-year-old Ellen Louise Axson had to raise
her three siblings. Woodrow Wilson had come down to settle the estate
of his father, and he went to church that morning and saw a woman
in a veil with "splendid, mischievous, laughing eyes" and reddish hair
parted in the middle with curly bangs.

Wilson called on the reverend, and Ellen came to the parlor. He fell in love and returned home to begin composing love letters, a skill he would master when addressing Edith Bolling Galt twenty years later. "I am quite conscious that young ladies generally find me...tiresome, and often vote me a terrible bore—and that I have not the compensating advantage of being well-favored and fair to look upon."

Wilson had long wanted to marry, but he feared he'd never find his true match. "I had longed to meet some woman of my own age who had acquired a genuine love for intellectual pursuits without becoming bookish, without losing her feminine charm; who had taken to the best literature from a natural, spontaneous taste for it, and not because she needed to make any artificial additions to her attractiveness...I had about given up expecting to make her acquaintance."

Ellen seemed to fit the bill. She had studied art at Rome Female College and was a graduate of New York's National Academy of Design. A bronze medal had come to her at eighteen for her paintings at a Paris International Exposition. Ellen wasn't a wilting Southern belle painting on the porch while the magnolias bloomed. She already had an agent, and she was selling. She was a well-read, educated young woman with a real talent in the arts. "From Mrs. Wilson," Woodrow later wrote, "not only have I learned much but have gained something of a literary reputation. Whenever I need a poetic quotation she supplies it, and in this way, I acquire the fame of possessing a complete anthology of poetry."

Unlike Edith Wilson, Ellen was Wilson's intellectual equal. Woodrow kept coming to Rome, Georgia, for buggy rides and picnics with Ellen. They rode in a hay wagon together and ended up in a meadow where Wilson recited poetry. In a hammock, he told Ellen she was the only woman who could "open his heart." Wilson believed a bachelor was "an amateur at life," and took Ellen to meet his family. Soon after,

Ellen Axson accepted his proposal and they kissed for the first time. They married in Savannah, Georgia, on June 21, 1885.

Ellen pledged to forgo art in favor of a life with Woodrow. She justified her decision to him saying, "As compared with the privilege of loving and serving you and the blessedness of being loved by you, the praise and admiration of all the world and generations yet unborn would be lighter than vanity."

Ellen saw something great in Wilson and hitched her wagon to a star. And, in turn, Wilson needed Ellen Axson. He had a retiring, academic disposition that made him lose confidence in social settings. As George Viereck wrote in *The Strangest Friendship in History*, "Wilson's instinctive timidity made him falter before every audience and made every speech an ordeal. He gave up his law career and became a teacher in a ladies' seminary because he could not face the odds against him in a trial court...he could not have overcome his temperamental weakness without his first wife, Ellen Axson...he would have remained a teacher in an all-girls school."

Wilson revealed his deepest secret and said, "I do feel a very real regret that I have been shut out from my heart's *first*—primary— ambition and purpose, which was to take an active, if possible a leading, part in public life." So Wilson revealed that he wanted to lead the world and Ellen revealed that she would give up her life for him. They honeymooned in North Carolina, then headed for New York to see Woodrow's parents. Ellen was two months pregnant and the wife of a professor.

Their first daughter was named Margaret, after Ellen's late mother. Woodrow had decided he didn't care for law and after returning to school took a job teaching history at Bryn Mawr College for girls. Ellen questioned the advisability of taking the position.

"Do you think there *is* much reputation, to be made in a *girls school*...?" she wondered.

Wilson said he would rather teach men, but this was all that was open to him. Another daughter soon followed. Woodrow continued to write books and pursue his career in academia. Ellen and Woodrow experienced some hard times in the early years of their marriage. After each pregnancy Ellen suffered from post-partum depression and a third baby brought kidney damage. After her second child, Ellen spilled hot lard on her feet and was confined to bed for five weeks. Woodrow did much of the cooking and cleaning and bathing of his daughters. He then took a job teaching at Princeton and they moved to New Jersey.

The Wilson family had a stable period in which Woodrow doted on his daughters and played games. "A deep happy peace permeated the household," Nell, one of his daughters, would later recall. Ellen homeschooled the children in history and literature and the Bible with her easel set up by the window for light. Woodrow told a friend he thought Ellen "in all senses my literary partner."

The love letters never ceased. "I am madly in love with you…I live upon your love," he wrote in 1895. "[I]…would die if I could not win and hold your admiration: the homage of your mind as well as your heart." Ten years into their marriage, their sex life had remained constant. "When you get me back you'll smother me, will you, my sweet little lover?" Wilson wrote on one overnight trip. "And what will I be doing all the while—simply submitting to be smothered?…Are you prepared for the storm of love making with which you will be assailed?"

A cloud then appeared in 1891. While writing a letter, Wilson's hand froze. Pain shot down his right arm and his fingers became numb. He consulted a doctor who diagnosed writer's cramp. But this was probably the result of high blood pressure from work and the financial strain of a new home and a growing family.

The upshot was Woodrow would go to Europe while Ellen stayed home with the kids. Wilson protested, but Ellen pushed him out the door. "I am counting so much on the sea voyage," she wrote to him, "and after that on mental refreshment, the *rest* without ennui, the complete change from all the trains of thought that have been making such exhausting demands upon you for so long.... I simply can't have you give it up, darling."

A refreshed Woodrow Wilson returned to Princeton and was asked to give a speech during its sesquicentennial celebration. He was known as a powerful orator and Ellen helped him with his speech. She found the problem quickly: "It does not end well. It ends too abruptly. It needs something to lift it and to lift your audience up to the highest plane of vision." Ellen suggested a few sentences and Wilson made the changes. The speech was "the most brilliant, *dazzling*, success from first to last," Ellen would later write her cousin.

The professor's literary career continued to flourish. In 1902 he was offered the presidency at Princeton. Ellen had misgivings about her husband becoming a public figure: "this was the end of the simple, ideal life," she wrote. Like Edith Galt, she knew the value of a private life and the cost of losing it.

Wilson threw himself into his new life as university president and took Ellen to Europe on a two-month vacation. When they returned, tragedy struck when Ellen's brother along with his pregnant wife and their child drowned in a freak accident on the Etowah River. Their horse had bolted while boarding a ferryboat, plunging the young family into the swirling river. Ellen mourned her brother and his family but tried to deal with the loss by staying busy with her own family.

Wilson made a speech to the Lotos Club of New York, which several newspapers reported on. The papers also reported that Democratic operative Colonel George Harvey had nominated Wilson for president of the United States. Ellen stared at her husband.

"Was he joking?" she asked.

Wilson paused. "He did not seem to be."

On May 28, 1906, Woodrow woke up and couldn't see out of his left eye. He went to Philadelphia with Ellen to see ophthalmologist Dr. George deSchweinitz, who said he had suffered a blood clot and possible rupture in the eye. The weakness and the numbness in his hands made the doctor suspect arteriosclerosis; a hardening of the arteries. Wilson's father had died of the disease. In what would become a mantra, the doctor told Ellen her husband needed rest.

"[We] are making every effort to keep him free from anxiety and worry and above all to keep things quiet for him." Ellen's words of concern would be echoed by second wife Edith ten years later: "He is of course *very* nervous—annoyed by things he usually enjoys…"

The conventional medical wisdom of the day said that only complete rest could restore his damaged heart and heal the neurological trauma. The rest cure did help him recover his vision, but it could do nothing for his diseased arteries.

The Wilsons went on vacation to Great Britain, where Woodrow was given a clean bill of health by two doctors. Still, Ellen knew his hardened arteries wouldn't heal and privately called it "dying by inches." When they returned to the United States, Woodrow Wilson's name was floated as candidate for the U.S. Senate. Colonel Harvey was still at work behind the scenes, but Wilson said his duty was to Princeton.

The Princeton president became embroiled in a struggle to take on the caste system of privilege at Princeton. Ellen saw the same danger signs of overwork and stress and insisted that he take another vacation. Bermuda in 1907 was what the Left Bank in Paris would become in the 1920s. It was a haven for leftists, writers, dilettantes, socialites—even Mark Twain and Rudyard Kipling frequented the islands. It was six hundred miles east of the Outer Banks of North Carolina and offered long white beaches and beatific days of crystalline blue water.

Wilson checked into the Hotel Hamilton and spent his days reading and working on a speech on government. The mayor and his wife held a small luncheon in his honor and invited an American who spent her winters in Bermuda. She had been born in Grand Rapids, Michigan, and grew up in Duluth, Minnesota, marrying mining engineer Thomas Hulbert. When Hulbert died, he left her with an infant son and a determination to marry up. She married a textile executive, Thomas Dowse Peck, who had been recently widowed himself.

The marriage went cold and Mary Peck began to live her own life. An accomplished pianist, she was cultured, she smoked, and she traveled on her husband's money. She was the type of smart woman Wilson enjoyed bantering with—and she was sexy. Mary Peck became Wilson's Bermuda friend for lack of a better word. In 1908, Wilson and Ellen were facing an empty nest after their daughters moved out. Like many husbands in long marriages, Wilson was toying with a midlife crisis, and what better way to dispel the angst than to hang in the bohemian salon of Mrs. Peck.

He ate lunch and dinner in Paget, the fashionable area of the island, and went for long walks with Mary along the shore. Woodrow spent time in her home, which had become a salon with writers and artists holding court over long dinners. Mary introduced him to Mark Twain and they played golf. She and Wilson spent a lot of time together and he left her a note upon his departure, saying, "It is not often that I can have the privilege of meeting anyone whom I can so entirely admire and enjoy."

When he returned home, Woodrow entered into the fight of his life in trying to reform Princeton by abolishing its eating clubs. The alumni fought back and threatened to cut off funding. In a showdown, a trusted friend, Professor Jack Hibben, turned against him and supported the opposition that wanted the social clubs to remain.

Wilson's health declined again with the same numbness and pain. Ellen, in a very Edith-like statement, would say, "Mr. Hibben can thank himself for this illness.... Nothing else has caused it but the fact that his heart is broken."

Woodrow went back to Bermuda alone. This second trip does call into question the nature of the Wilsons' marriage. With her daughters grown, Ellen spent a lot of time at home by herself. Ellen had also taken to inviting over witty female friends for Wilson to converse with. Ellen, while confident of her own intellect, didn't have the vivacity her husband often craved.

The minute Wilson got off the boat, he sought out Mary Peck. They took a walk on the beach and had a conversation that shows the depth of their affair. "I stand a very good chance of being the next President of the United States," Wilson told her. "Shall I, or shall I not, accept the opportunity they offer?"

Mary Peck looked at him.

"Why not? Statesmanship has been your natural bent, your real ambition all your life and, God knows, our country needs men like you in her national life!"

Wilson pointed out that he didn't come from money.

Mary replied, "If I know anything of your wife and daughters they would rather scrub to earn their bread than have you do less than your best work in life." She added that she knew he would rather "die in harness" than fail to live up to his destiny.

What is fascinating about this conversation is that Mary Peck seems to know Woodrow Wilson very well. He is on a beach with a beautiful woman, away from Ellen, and asking her if he should run for president of the United States. At the end of the conversation, Wilson made his decision and told Mary Peck, "Very well. So be it."

There is something of Edith Wilson about Mary Peck: a woman who has broken boundaries and who lives outside the parameters of the feminine ideal of that day and age. Wilson was longing for a confidant and he had gone all the way to Bermuda to find one. Woodrow would write Mary Peck hundreds of letters from 1908 to 1910. Ellen eventually did find out and there was a confrontation, but somehow they agreed to put it behind them.

Later, Woodrow Wilson would refer to the period as one of "folly and gross impertinence," where he violated the benchmark of "honorable behavior." Ellen Wilson would say that the "Peck affair" was the only unhappiness her husband had ever caused her. It is interesting to speculate that Mary Peck prefigured Edith, who would arrive years later under very different circumstances.

Ellen had become a politician's wife after Woodrow Wilson won the governorship of New Jersey in 1911. Immediately people began talking about her husband running for president. Ellen began clipping articles having anything to do with the future presidential campaign. She proved her political savvy when she invited William Jennings Bryan to dinner at their home, realizing Wilson would need his support to get the nomination. Bryan was charmed and Woodrow got the nomination.

Joseph Patrick Tumulty, who would become Wilson's personal secretary as president, said Ellen had a much better political nose than her husband. Edith Galt possessed the same political savvy and Wilson would rely on both women as sounding boards. In a close election, Woodrow ran on a progressive platform called New Freedom, fighting for the "little man." Teddy Roosevelt, who ran as a third-party candidate, considered using a Mary Peck letter against Wilson, but ultimately decided Wilson looked like "an apothecary's clerk" and Roosevelt didn't want people to think Wilson was a passionate man.

In 1912, "the druggist" became president of the United States and brought about the "New Freedom" of progressive change with the formation of the Federal Reserve to give more working families loans, an eight-hour workday, and the first child-labor laws. He was the first president to address a joint session of Congress in person and said he wanted to "humanize" the presidency.

Ellen used her position as first lady to take on humanitarian causes and social injustices. This would become a benchmark for all subsequent first ladies. She did not, however, cease caring for her husband. In *Wilson*, A. Scott Berg describes Ellen's spousal role this way: "She catered to all [Wilson's] needs, still serving as his most discriminating editor and adviser, and encouraging the professorial evenings of old, during which he might study and write and then recite poetry or sing around the piano with his daughters. She maintained Sunday as his day of observance, filled only with family and a restorative ride by automobile or on horseback. In accordance with Dr. Grayson's advice, she kept his meals simple—plain fish and meat courses, a vegetable and potatoes, a salad, and ice cream..."

But in the summer of 1912, Wilson sent her from Washington to the shore. Washington in summer was empty as everyone tried to get away from the heat. Ellen returned in midsummer and endured the heat that continued to weaken her. She had felt exhausted and tired for some time. On March 1, 1914, Ellen slipped on the bathroom floor, an incident that seemed to usher in a period of deteriorating strength. Her brother Stockton was shocked at how fragile his sister looked. The president believed it was the exhausting social season, but by June 1914, Ellen was losing strength, though Doctor Grayson couldn't determine the cause. "There is nothing at all the matter with her organically," Wilson wrote.

The president often sat by her in the middle of the night to make sure she was still breathing. Grayson finally determined what was robbing Ellen Wilson of her health. His report read: "The chief cause of Mrs. Wilson's present critical condition is a chronic kidney trouble...developed as one of the results of a nervous breakdown." As

Ellen declined, Dr. Grayson brought in three more doctors who diagnosed an inflammation of the kidneys or Bright's disease.

The symptoms were excruciating back pain, high fever, puffiness, and bloody urine. It was a fatal disease and it was up to Grayson to tell Wilson. When he told him, the president said, "Let's get out of here," and they walked on the South Lawn of the White House. Beside himself, Wilson didn't know if he could carry on.

He returned to Ellen's bedside, never leaving except when required by the duties of his office. On June 28, 1914, Archduke Ferdinand was assassinated in Sarajevo by a Bosnian Serb. This was the catalyst for the alliances formed by the European powers that would begin World War I. As the countries mobilized, the president sat holding Ellen's hand. The press was told nothing and all discussion of her illness and care was restricted to the second floor. In this respect it foreshadowed the way the White House would handle Woodrow Wilson's debilitating stroke.

Ellen knew she was dying and pulled Dr. Grayson close, "Please take good care of Woodrow, Doctor." The doctor summoned the family. Woodrow and his daughters kept vigil as the guns of World War I were uncovered and men rushed into position. A telegram arrived at the White House announcing that Germany had declared war on Russia.

On August 6, 1914, Ellen Axson Wilson stopped breathing. She was fifty-four years old. Wilson folded her hands upon her chest and then went to the bedroom window. He wept and would later be heard by the servants walking through the gloom of the White House crying, "My God, what am I to do?"

# FOUR

# "THE PRESIDENT IS PARALYZED!"

## 1919

EDITH RAN FRANTICALLY AFTER SEEING THE PRESIDENT OF THE United States on the bathroom floor with blood painting the white tiles. She rushed to the Lincoln bed and grabbed the comforter. "My first thought was to keep him warm," she wrote years later in her memoir. "From his bed I snatched a blanket, and while I was arranging it over him he stirred and asked for a drink of water. I got it, and also got a pillow for his head. I did these things automatically, for I was utterly devoid of feeling."

Edith allowed Dr. Grayson to squeeze into the bathroom. They put the blanket around the president, pulled him into the hallway, and, with the White House valet, Ike Hoover, lifted Wilson into his bed. Hoover noticed blood on his face and then Grayson performed a quick examination. He left the bedroom and walked briefly into the hallway, saying out loud, "My God, the President is paralyzed!"

How bad was it? In *Woodrow Wilson: A Medical and Psychological Biography* Edwin Weinstein writes, "The symptoms indicate that Wilson suffered an occlusion of the right middle cerebral artery, which resulted in a complete paralysis of the left side of his body, a loss of sensation on that side, and a left homonymous hemianopia— a loss of vision in the left half fields of both eyes.... he had clear vision only in the temporal (outer) half field of his right eye. The weakness of the muscles of the left side of his face, tongue, and jaw and pharynx accounted for his difficulty in swallowing and the impairment of his speech."

Admiral E. R. Stitt of the Naval Medical Corps and the nurse who had been Ellen Wilson's attendant arrived and were joined by Dr. Francis Dercum from Philadelphia's Jefferson Medical College, Edith's family physician, Sterling Ruffin, and an eye specialist, George deSchweinitz.

Dr. Dercum, a pioneer in nervous and mental diseases, found Wilson's left leg and arm "in a condition of 'complete flacced paralysis,' with the lower half of the left side of the face drooping.... [and] his left eye responded feebly to light." Dercum knew what had occurred: a thrombosis or an ischemic stroke, a blood clot in an artery of the brain. It hadn't burst yet, but any extra pressure could set it off. Edith sagged at the sound of the words. This was a time when strokes were considered a death sentence. As Ike Hoover remarked when he saw the president, "He looked as if he were dead."

Dr. Grayson suggested making a statement to the press but Edith shut him down. The orders went out that no one was to tell the public anything. This moment would be interpreted many ways, but the truth was that Edith had known for a long time that her husband was ill. Secrecy had become routine. The word "stroke" or "paralysis" wouldn't be spoken again. No one, including the vice president, was to be informed that President Woodrow Wilson was now a low-functioning invalid.

Dr. Grayson would later insist that Wilson's mind was still clear. This wasn't true. As Dr. Bert E. Park wrote in "The Aftermath of Wilson's Stroke," "During the first phase of Wilson's illness he was unable to do much more than react to events.... Others were obliged to think and act for him." The cover-up had begun and would be maintained all the way to the day Wilson left office. It is incredible to think that the leader of the United States was struck down and that no one was told.

Dr. Dercum explained to Edith that the president must not be disturbed so nature could repair the damage. Edith wrote years later of the conversation. "'How can that be,' I asked the doctors, 'when everything that comes to an Executive is a problem? How can I protect him from problems when the country looks to the President as the leader?'"

Dr. Dercum leaned toward Edith and said, "Madam, it is a grave situation, but I think you can solve it. Have everything come to you; weigh the importance of each matter, and see if it is possible by consultation with the respective heads of the Departments to solve them without the guidance of your husband. In this way you can save him a great deal."

Dr. Dercum then piled on the pressure saying, "every time you take him a new anxiety or problem to excite him, you are turning a knife in an open wound. His nerves are crying out for rest, and any excitement is torture to him."

There it was: assume the reins of power or your husband will die. Edith couldn't believe what she was hearing. Was she really to be at the center of a grand conspiracy in which she would act as president for an ailing man who could be told nothing but good things?

But what about the vice president? Thinking of Vice President Marshall, who by the Constitution should assume the reins of power, she said "had he better not resign, let Mr. Marshall succeed to the Presidency and he himself get that complete rest so vital to his life?"

Edith had just exposed the elephant in the room. Legally speaking, this should have been the moment that ushered in constitutional succession, thus relieving Edith and Woodrow Wilson of their burden. But this was not to be. Dr. Dercum sealed her fate.

> No, not if you feel equal to what I suggested. For Mr. Wilson to resign would have a bad effect on the country, and a serious effect on our patient. He has staked his life and made his promise to the world to do all in his power to get the Treaty ratified and make the League of Nations complete. If he resigns, the greatest incentive to recovery is gone; and as his mind is clear as crystal he can still do more with a maimed body than anyone else. He has the utmost confidence in you. Dr. Grayson tells me he has always discussed public affairs with you; so you will not come to them uninformed.

A different person might see a setup. Some historians have suggested Edith created this "baton" of power through her edict to keep the president's illness from the public. What is more likely is that the doctors had decided that the only person who could "stand in" for the president was his wife. Vice President Marshall had been added to the ticket for regional reasons. He was a man who spent his time on paid speaking tours and the Wilsons never included him in their inner circle. Marshall would become best known for his quip, "What this country really needs is a good five-cent cigar." He was never without one.

This is probably a good point at which to address Dr. Dercum's comment about the League of Nations. This point of light in the Wilsonian universe had become a holy grail that the president had sacrificed his health for. He had never accepted the slaughter of war and had justified it by attaching the carnage to something higher. If the League failed, Wilson's driving force would be lost. What Edith didn't know was that Grayson had told Dr. Dercum that the president had kept her in the loop in the White House. They had their president, and Dercum inaugurated her with "He has the utmost confidence in you."

"So began my stewardship" is the way Edith would refer to this moment. But even writing twenty years after the fact, she used the parlance of the time. She was a woman and women did not stand in for presidents. But she could act as a steward, one ready to serve until the commander got back on his feet. But this commander would never get back on his feet. Ike Hoover summed it up this way: "The President," he said, "was simply gone."

The men around President Wilson were concerned with preserving the status quo. The United States has a spoils system; and beside the high purpose of maintaining the country's "health" there was the more terrestrial concern of keeping one's job. Patronage is a powerful weapon, and the vice president had been out of the loop for years. Marshall would never be included in the conspiracy but there were some who considered the vice president stepping in. Secretary Lansing recorded in his diary, "Conferred with Tumulty and Grayson in Cabinet room.... Discussed V.P. acting as Pres.... Hood on precedents as to V.P. acting as Pres. None..."

Grayson put out a bulletin on October 3, which was run by *Washington Post*. "The President is a very sick man. His condition is less favorable today and he has remained in bed throughout the day.... The President's illness is diagnosed as 'nervous exhaustion.'" Grayson issued another bulletin on October 4 that said, "Admiral Grayson said that the President's mind was alert and clear, that his physical condition was fairly good."

Then on October 7 another bulletin from Grayson: "The President had a fairly comfortable day with a slight improvement." But at the same time, Breckinridge Long recorded in his diary on October 7, "I talked to Admiral Grayson...he said the President is still in grave danger and will be for some days, possibly weeks..."

Dr. Grayson was telling the public that the president was recovering from exhaustion, when the truth was he was tending to a man who had suffered a devastating stroke. In a telegram from William Phillips to Peter Augustus Jay dated October 9, Phillips quotes Dr. Grayson, "President is seriously ill and Grayson does not expect him to be able to handle any business for a minimum of at least six weeks." Then in a telling statement in the Associated Press on October 11, the idea that the president would recover was dealt another blow: "Hope that President Wilson soon might regain his normal health and resume fully the duties of his office was swept away today by his physicians, who announced it would be impossible for him to leave his bed for an extended period."

Grayson knew he couldn't keep blaming the problem on nervous exhaustion when the president might well die in office. Senator Moses wrote a letter, published in the *New York Times*, saying that President Wilson "may live...but he will not be any material force or factor in anything.... He suffered some kind of cerebral lesion either during his speech at Pueblo or immediately thereafter..." An unnamed source to the *Times* is quoted saying, "What we have been afraid of is that something might snap, and for that reason the treatment prescribed for the President is absolute rest, both mental and physical."

What snapped of course was a blood vessel in his brain. On October 13, Grayson went back on the offensive and said in a bulletin "that the President's mind is 'clear as a bell' and there is nothing in his condition that renders it impossible for him to act." This assertion would become Grayson's standard line: the president, while physically devastated, had a clear mind that could run the United States government. In this way, Dr. Grayson could pitch the idea of "a cerebral Presidency."

The cover-up included Edith's assuming the reins of power. In her memoir, Edith claimed to have never made a decision but she quickly belies this. "I studied every paper, sent from the different Secretaries or Senators, and tried to digest and present in tabloid form the things that, despite my vigilance, had to go to the President. I myself never made a single decision regarding the disposition of public affairs."

Here we have in 1939 a woman saying what is palatable to the male-driven world. The fact was that the president was on his back, paralyzed, unconscious, almost vegetative, and unable to do anything. He was a shadow of himself. And it is Edith Wilson's next sentence that shows how she began to govern. "The only decision that was mine was what was important and what was not, and the *very* important decision of when to present matters to my husband."

As A. Scott Berg wrote in *Wilson*, "In insisting that she never 'made a single decision regarding the disposition of public affairs,' Mrs. Wilson failed to acknowledge the commanding nature of her role, that in determining the daily agenda and formulating arguments thereon, she executed the physical and most of the mental duties of the office."

Berg goes on to say, "Edith Bolling Wilson did not become, as some have asserted, 'the first female President of the United States.' But she came close. She considered herself more of a lady-in-waiting to her husband than an executive; *but she was in a position to act, while he could only react* [emphasis added]."

This is really just semantics; close or not, the proof will be revealed in how Edith Wilson governed the United States. The Constitution, Berg notes, provided for "'the Case of Removal, Death, Resignation or Inability' of the President with the ascension of the Vice President, 'until the Disability be removed or a President shall be elected.'" But there is no clear definition of the "inability of the President." The fact that President Wilson's illness was kept secret suggests everyone knew they were skirting the lines when it came to constitutional law.

After that, there was one simple mandate Edith Wilson was compelled to follow: to make sure her husband survived. The only medicine was the rest cure and the rest cure must be administered with constancy and discipline. Better the country should suffer than her husband. A little signature here, a gentle nudge there, a decoding of a message from an embassy, a State of the Union address, appointments of cabinet members, bills not signed, vetoes, ambassadors not seen, an encoding of a message to an embassy, letters not opened, staged meetings, a few signatures no one would suspect as coming from an entirely different hand.

Edith and Dr. Grayson had to keep up the charade for sixteen months. Deception was their arsenal. The fine line between making executive decisions and doing what was best for Woodrow Wilson was crossed immediately, for where does love end and duty begin? At its most basic level, Edith and Woodrow's relationship was a love affair between a surprisingly passionate president and a modern career woman who had had no interest in being his wife. It was a matter of muddy shoes, a golf game, and tea five years before that changed the life of Edith Bolling Galt.

# FIVE

# A MODERN WOMAN

## 1915

IN MARCH OF 1915, THE PRESIDENT SAT IN THE BACK OF THE PIERCE
Arrow with the slight scent of unburned gasoline whipping up. He and
Cary Grayson had left the dark and gloomy White House for a drive.
Wilson had been depressed since the death of his wife the previous
August and stared moodily at the passing brownstones in the glaring
March sun. He noticed two women on the sidewalk. One of the
women had a buxom figure, a wide smile, and bright blue eyes. The
president craned his neck and turned to the doctor, who was waving
at the two women. He obviously knew them.

"Who is that beautiful woman?"

"Edith Galt," Grayson replied.

Grayson was surprised. It had been eight months since Ellen's
death and Wilson was depressed to the point that he had considered
resigning the presidency. But love had recently bloomed for Grayson
and he hoped it might for the president again too. Cary Grayson had
recently fallen in love with Alice Gertrude Gordon, a young heiress

looked after by Edith Galt. It is hard to know if Wilson saw the younger woman from Virginia (Edith was forty- three to Wilson's fifty-nine) as a possible match, but they had more in common than one might think.

She was from the South. Edith Bolling Galt was born in Wytheville, Virginia, to William Holcombe Bolling and Sarah Spiers née White on October 15, 1872. Edith was the seventh of eleven children and counted the Indian princess Pocahontas as one of her ancestors. The Bolling family had prospered up to when their Rose Cottage plantation was lost to taxes after the Civil War, forcing William Bolling to migrate to Wytheville and settle on his father's property, where he practiced law and eventually became a circuit court judge. Money was tight and Edith's father made her brothers' education a priority. Edith had only two years of schooling, but her father read to the young girl at every opportunity. "So Father kept the watch at night, and if we were not going out he would read aloud to us—Dickens, Shakespeare or some book of the day."

Edith's real education came from Grandmother Anne Wiggington Bolling, a strict dressed-in-black matriarch who rarely left the home because of a riding accident. She homeschooled Edith in reading and writing, French, the Bible, and crochet and knitting, and instilled in young Edith a bright sensibility and strong views. "If you basked in the light of Grandmother Bolling's approval—no inconsiderable asset when compared to her displeasure—you were given access to all she had, physical, material or spiritual. For myself I can truly say she taught me nearly everything I know," Edith would later write.

Her two years of formal schooling came when she was fifteen at the Martha Washington College, a finishing school for girls. Edith didn't thrive there and suffered from poor food and the unheated rooms. She came back home and didn't go back to school until she was seventeen, eventually attending the Powell's School for Girls in

Richmond, Virginia. She liked the school, but it closed when the headmaster suffered an accident.

Edith became a self-taught woman. She said she could remember something by reading it just once. But she was never happy with her handwriting, which would come to be a problem during Wilson's presidency. Photographs do not do Edith's beauty justice. She had dark brown hair, a heart-shaped face, and a spark in her blue eyes. From her pictures, she would seem more earthy than refined. She was twenty-two years old when she met Norman Galt, a lonely bachelor in Washington. Galt must have thought the world brightened quickly when Edith walked in with her Junoesque figure and quick wit. Edith became the center of Norman's world and he pursued her to Wytheville, where the young owner of the family jewelry business persuaded Edith to marry him.

"We were the best of friends, and I liked him immensely, but I did not want to marry anyone. However, his patience and persistence overcame me," she noted in her memoir.

Norman was a decade older, but for a twenty-four-year-old girl he was a key to a bigger world. Edith probably married for money and to escape from Wytheville, for there seemed to be little passion. But this would not have been looked down upon at the time. Position was obtained by birth and money, and she endured her mother-in-law's house as Norman built up the jewelry business.

They married in 1896, and almost immediately suffered through a period of death and illness. Edith writes later: "when we had been married less than two years, death claimed first Norman's brother-in-law...then, in twenty-four hours, his father.... Then my own adored father died very suddenly... " In 1903, Edith had a son who died after three days and left her unable to have more children. Later, the couple moved into a larger house as the business improved and Norman bought Edith her first electric car.

In 1906, Edith went down with an attack of appendicitis. She was due to leave for Europe, but six weeks later she had not improved. She was operated on in her home. As Alden Hatch described it in *Edith Bolling Wilson*, "The library was fitted out as an operating room with clean sheets covering the floor and furniture, and an operating table brought in. The anesthetist required no more paraphernalia than a gauze cone and a bottle of ether; and the instruments were boiled in dishpans. The surgeon and nurses wore white but no face masks. Edith came through nicely."

Norman, on the other hand, died from a liver infection on January 28, 1908, at their home in Washington. After twelve years of marriage, Edith remembered Norman as "a most immaculate person, he never wore the same suit two consecutive days. He took two baths and wore at least two clean shirts every day." One gets the feeling that Edith regarded her husband as a very good "friend."

But now she owned a jewelry business and "was immediately faced with the decision of whether to continue the business alone, take on a partner, or close it up." Edith decided to keep the jewelry business and grow it. She was not someone who gave up easily.

Edith took a very small salary and put the day-to-day management operations in the hands of Henry Christian Bergheimer, who had worked for Norman and his father. In short, she delegated. "I made him manager, without bond, and tried to learn from him, instead of interfering with his authority," she later noted. Edith used a family friend, lawyer Nathaniel Wilson, as an advisor, and the triumvirate successfully ran the jewelry business for three years.

Edith didn't just let the two men run the business. She proved to be a hardheaded businesswoman with the grit and tenacity to keep the small business afloat. "My own part was small, for it consisted chiefly in holding up the hands of my advisors. But we had long and technical conferences and I was kept in touch with the conduct of everything…with all we made and all we owed; I set for myself the minimum amount I could live on and never exceeded it, in order to leave every cent in the business until we had paid for it."

By the time she was forty, Edith was a well-to-do widow. She traveled to Europe and went to the theatre and bought an electric car. She was the first woman to get a driver's license in the District of Columbia. She would eventually sell the jewelry business in 1918 for $80,000.

President Wilson didn't know any of this when he saw Edith for the first time. After he and Dr. Grayson drove past her, Grayson swung into action. He called Edith to suggest she come to the White House to cheer up Woodrow's cousin, Helen Bones, who desperately needed companionship. "My dear Doctor," Edith wrote in reply, "I am not a society person. I have never had any contacts with official Washington, and don't desire any."

The doctor then called Edith and asked if he could stop by. He pulled up to her home with Nell McAdoo (Wilson's daughter) and Helen Bones. They all went for a ride and Edith hit it off with Helen. There were stories of "cousin Woodrow" that Edith found fascinating. They went out several times together, then Helen had the White House limousine pick up Edith. They went for a walk along muddy trails in the park.

"We are not going to your house," Helen announced after they had finished their walk. "I have ordered tea at the White House this afternoon, and you are to go back with me."

"Oh, I couldn't do that; my shoes are a sight, and I should be taken for a tramp," Edith protested.

"Yes, you can" Helen replied, "for there is not a soul there. Cousin Woodrow is playing golf with Dr. Grayson…"

Edith reluctantly agreed and they went to the White House.

The trap was set.

# SIX

# LESS IS MORE

## 1919

WALL STREET WAS IN A PANIC. A RUMOR IN NEW YORK HAD SENT the stock market into free fall. The rumor was that the president of the United States had died. The White House dispelled the rumor, but the country was still on pins and needles. The pivotal question remained: How sick was President Woodrow Wilson?

In *Woodrow Wilson: A Medicinal and Psychological Biography*, author Weinstein writes, "Some of the symptoms of a thrombosis in the human brain are violent stomach upsets...insomnia, twitching of the face, difficulty in using a pen, headaches, great weakness, and paralysis of one side of the body.... The victim often becomes unreasonable, apprehensive, irritable. He may become violently emotional—the most common characteristic is frequent crying spells..."

President Wilson would at one time or another exhibit all of these symptoms. The blood clot hadn't burst, but no one knew what was next. As Dr. Dercum put it, "He might live five minutes, five months or five years." Grayson knew Wilson needed at least six weeks of complete rest. The *New York Times* reported: "All sorts of rumors have been running the gamut of gossip in the capital regarding the exact nature of the President's illness.... One of the most insistent reports has had it that the President's real trouble has been a slight abscess of the brain."

The *Times* reported that the president was "very urgent that he be permitted to leave bed." The *New York Herald* picked up the story and reported that Wilson was "restive...[and] particularly anxious to see several Democratic Senators." But then the *Times* ran a story on October 14 headlined, "Details of Illness Kept from Cabinet." Particularly illuminating was an interview with Attorney General Mitchell Palmer. When asked about the president's condition, he replied, "You read the newspaper don't you?"

"Don't you know any more than that?"

"I do not," he said.

"Does any cabinet member know any more about it than what he reads in the newspapers?"

"No," Palmer answered.

Wilson's guardians, Dr. Grayson and Edith, guarded the sick room and the truth about the condition of the man inside. Grayson directed all information away from Wilson. "Under instructions from Admiral Grayson, all dispatches concerning the Treaty situation and other public questions were withheld from the President."

Dr. Grayson issued another bulletin: "The President is a very sick man. His condition is less favorable today and he has remained in his bed throughout the day. After consultation with Doctor F. X. Dercum of Philadelphia, Doctor Sterling Ruffin and Doctor E. R. Stitt of Washington, in which all agreed as to his condition, it was determined that absolute rest is essential for some time."

Grayson would later say that he wanted to give a full accounting of Wilson's real situation, "but in the view of the wishes of Mrs. Wilson this was deferred." Ike Hoover, the president's valet, recorded in his diary, "Never was deception so universally practiced in the White House as it was in those statements being given out from time to time." The president's mind was not clear, as Grayson stated repeatedly. When Wilson was conscious, he had little ability to focus. Still, on October 15, Grayson released another bulletin, this one announcing, "The President had a restless and uncomfortable day, but he is better tonight." From this bulletin one might think that the president was suffering from nothing but a bit of insomnia.

Edith, Grayson, and Secretary Tumulty (later to become chief of staff) came to believe in the policy of "less is more." Grayson and Edith were Southerners and shared a distrust of journalists and an abhorrence of anything of a personal nature being released to the press. This was a time when a political figure's personal life was considered off limits. At a meeting with journalists in 1914, President Wilson had entered the room and berated the assembled journalists for publishing disparaging stories about his ill wife and daughter. The president said that if he read another one, he would find the man who wrote it and "thrash him."

But there were leaks in the dam. On October 10, the Associated Press painted a picture that contradicted the one coming from the second floor of the White House. The article speculated on constitutional succession, and Secretary Lansing felt compelled to deny a story claiming that another cabinet member was discussing the possibility of Vice President Marshall taking the reins of power. The *New-York Tribune* wrote at the same time, "Democratic leaders are seriously discussing the possibility of Vice President-Marshall assuming the duties of the Presidency."

For a month after the stroke, Edith Wilson's husband could do nothing but try to get better. He was unconscious the first week. The doctors began suggesting that Edith interview people for appointments and meet with senators and cabinet members. No one should disturb the president. Total rest was the order of the day. Edith and Grayson agreed on this and as David Lawrence writes, "Together they carried the secrets of the sick room while Private Secretary Tumulty played the role of everything-as-usual in the Executive offices.... But those were topsy-turvy days and many an old friend who had served Mr. Wilson in the past was turned away."

On October 6, Edith was handed a request from Congress for clarification about a newspaper report of sailors landing on the Dalmatian coast. Edith wrote a ragged note to the secretary of the navy, Josephus Daniels. The note, composed on White House stationery, was supposedly from the president, but it had Edith written all over it: "If the Congress should ask questions concerning the employment of our nava[l] forces in the Adriatic and the Meditarea [sic] please refer the questions to me at once informing the Congress you have done so by my direction and that the replys [sic] will be forth coming in the due course unless indeed the Executive should find that it was not compatible with the public interest to convey to the [public crossed out] Congress at this time the particular information desired."

She then called Daniels and told him a memorandum was coming from the president but that it was unsigned. Daniels told Edith he would handle it from here and sent a letter to the presiding officer of the senate. Edith had performed one of her first duties as president. On the heels of this came another problem with the Bolshevik capture of Petrograd and the challenge of feeding the Russian people.

Robert Lansing wrote "Memorandum to be Read by the President" concerning the Russian embassy's request to buy twenty-nine thousand tons of wheat flour for $3.7 million from the United States Grain Corporation. A draft letter was created by the State Department giving authority to Julien Barnes, wheat director, to make the transaction occur. The letter was copied on White House stationery with a signature purported to be the president's. When the Polish government made a similar request, Edith shortened the process by writing a note beginning with what would become a standard salutation: *The President says…*

In this case she instructed Tumulty to "tell Mr. Barnes to draw up the proper form of authorization and send it for the President's signature." This was initialed *EBW.* Tumulty later complimented Edith's ability to govern: "Her high intelligence and her extraordinary memory enabled her to report…in lucid detail, weighty matters of state brought to her by officials for transmission to him."

Meanwhile, the press started to put together the pieces. The *New-York Tribune* ran another story on October 14, "Cabinet Decides to Act." The article speculated that the cabinet was meeting without a chief and that "if the President is kept to his bed for months to come it is highly improbable that the Government will continue to go along without an actual head…It is not questioned that eventually something will be done to appoint a successor."

Dr. Grayson fought back with another bulletin released on October 15 in the *New York World.* Grayson didn't know "any disease that had not been included in the rumors about the President," and he "would be glad to be as sick as Mr. Wilson if he could also be as alert mentally!"

An Associated Press dispatch took a stab in the dark. "With the exception of the news furnished him by Mrs. Wilson, the President has learned very little of national and international developments." And then another story appeared in the *New York Times*, saying the president performed an executive function by appointing Owen D. Young to a vacant position in the Industrial Conference going on in Washington.

The *Times* then came even closer to the truth. "It was learned at the White House that during the day the President had occasion to send for some papers of an official character which he went over with Mrs. Wilson. Mrs. Wilson does most of the President's reading for him, as the physicians do not wish to have him do his own reading at the time."

That same day, it was reported that four bills had become laws without the president's signature. There was a ten-day time limit after which bills that the president didn't sign or veto became laws. Between September 30 and November 18, 1919, twenty-eight acts would become law because of the president's failure to respond within the requisite ten days. This included acts pertaining to "Cincinnati, New Orleans and Texas Pacific Railway company, to the authority of the secretary of war, to the Idaho National Forest, to national security and defense, to the Treasury appropriations, and to the granting of citizenship to certain American Indians."

The *Times* put it this way: "It is explained that…these bills…were not presented to him under the policy of keeping as much business as possible from him." What the story doesn't say is that Edith intercepted legislation and pushed it back toward Congress. Nothing would go to the president that did not pass through her first. This applied to people as well. For months, people didn't see President Woodrow Wilson; they saw the new regent of power, Edith Wilson.

Colonel House recorded in his diary, "The President's condition is such that no one is seeing him outside of his physician and Mrs. Wilson.… There is much discussion in Washington and elsewhere as to whether the President has suffered a stroke." Grayson released another cheery bulletin on October 16: "The President had a satisfactory day.… The President had a good night's rest, enjoyed his breakfast, and aside from a slight headache, continues to make improvement."

The audacity of the lie is amazing. Colonel House, chafing from not seeing the president, asked Edith what the real story was in a letter dated October 22: "The fact that you have not told him of my return indicates that he is much sicker than I had thought."

In his book *The Strangest Friendship in History*, George Viereck puts it this way: "While Wilson was on his back, [Edith] exercised the functions of the President.... No Senator, no member of the Cabinet, not the President's own secretary, could gain a glimpse of Wilson without her permission. Her whim decided whether a king or an ambassador was to be received, whether a bill awaiting the President's signature would become law or not.... No act of Woodrow Wilson, from this period until the end of his life, was undertaken without the knowledge and consent of Edith Bolling Wilson."

Woodrow Wilson could sign nothing in the first month. Edith claimed to have helped his hand, but many knew she signed the documents. As one reporter noted, "It was she who acted as personal secretary, taking notes and writing memoranda and messages to the various Cabinet officers and officials of the Government generally. Even the Private Secretary Mr. Tumulty refrained from entering the bed chamber except when sent for."

Tumulty's telling of one particular event illustrates Edith's view of her obligations to the country and her husband. One day, during "an acute period of his illness, certain officials insisted that they must see him because they carried information which it was 'absolutely necessary that the President of the United States should have.'"

Edith stared the men down and quietly responded, "I am not interested in the President of the United States. I am interested in my husband's health."

One cannot discount the power of the League of the Nations in the machinations of Edith, Tumulty, and Grayson. To Edith and others, the League of Nations *was* Woodrow Wilson. On October 21, Henry Fountain Ashurst recorded in his diary, "I was informed that Senator Hitchcock, Democrat leading the fight for Treaty Ratification, had gone to the White House, to inform Dr. Grayson, who in turn is to tell W.W. that Treaty cannot be ratified without vital reservations."

Senator Lodge and the twelve to eighteen senators bitterly opposed to the treaty—labeled the Irreconcilables—were trying to kill the League of Nations. To expose Wilson as an invalid would give red meat to these men. Meanwhile, the public had gone wild with rumors. *The president had gone mad. He was a drooling insane man talking gibberish. Bars had been put on the White House windows to keep Wilson from throwing himself to his death.* In fact, the bars had been installed during Teddy Roosevelt's administration to keep his children from falling out. But the lack of information had created a vacuum, and into that vacuum went innuendo, rumor, and slander.

The White House had changed dramatically. Edith had all tours suspended and padlocks put on the gates. The curtains were drawn and the windows darkened as the somber air of a Tyrolean haunted house fell over the Executive Mansion. The invalid's hospital was the center of power of the United States and the first real consequence was a grinding halt to all business. No proclamations were issued, no pardons granted, no bills signed. The cabinet members met, but with no chief they were powerless. The president was incapacitated and in his place was a woman who was doing the best she could.

# SEVEN

# TEDDY AND WOODROW

## 1912

**TEDDY ROOSEVELT FINISHED DINNER AT THE GILPATRICK HOTEL** in Milwaukee and walked toward his car to give a speech in the Milwaukee Auditorium. The election of 1912 had been vitriolic with Roosevelt bolting the Republican Party and forming his own Bull Moose Party. Roosevelt was sure he could beat his own handpicked incumbent, William Howard Taft, and the Democratic candidate, the former Princeton president Woodrow Wilson. The fifty pages of his speech inside his coat pocket were folded twice behind his steel glasses case.

John Schrank, a psychotic former New York saloonkeeper, approached Roosevelt. Schrank stepped in front of the former president and raised a black .38 caliber pistol and fired. Roosevelt felt the bullet enter his chest after piercing his fifty-page speech and steel glasses case. He immediately took out a handkerchief, dabbing his mouth to see if his lungs had been hit. He then proclaimed he wouldn't go to the hospital, but would instead deliver his scheduled speech.

People were in shock and tried to dissuade him but Theodore Roosevelt went to the auditorium and spoke for more than ninety minutes while bleeding under his coat, thundering to the crowd the immortal line, "It takes more than a bullet to stop a Bull Moose!" The crowd loved it and when Teddy Roosevelt went to the hospital the doctors opted to leave the bullet in his chest.

People were astounded that a man shot at point blank could give a speech for an hour and a half. But they expected no less from Teddy Roosevelt. He was the cowboy who had taken over the White House once before and planned to do it again. The Bull Moose Party was created when he threw his hat in the ring against his old friend and successor, President William Howard Taft. The Republicans balked at nominating the Rough Rider for president this time, so he took his spurs and left the convention hall to form a new party.

Woodrow Wilson couldn't have been more pleased. The former schoolmaster didn't have a chance against a unified Republican Party but a split party made his chances very good. Thomas Woodrow Wilson was born in Staunton, Virginia, on December 29, 1856. The son of a minister, Wilson was a Calvinist Presbyterian who as a boy saw the former president of the Confederacy, Jefferson Davis, paraded through Georgia in handcuffs. His Calvinism would see him advance as one of God's anointed all the way to the White House.

At ten years old he still couldn't read and what was probably dyslexia kept him from excelling in school. It wasn't until his father tutored him rigorously that he discovered that he "had a mind." He went to Princeton and changed his name from "Tommy" to his middle name "Woodrow," thinking it sounded more distinguished.

Theodore Roosevelt was from a patrician family in New York. The closest he came to the Civil War was seeing Lincoln's funeral procession from his grandfather's house. His father had hired a substitute to go in his place to the Civil War; something that bothered the young Roosevelt, who made it his life mission to test himself in battle. But the Roosevelt family's wealth allowed him to do whatever he wanted and after graduating from Harvard he dabbled in law, then immediately went into politics and became an assemblyman in Albany, taking on the Tammany Hall crowd.

Woodrow meanwhile would graduate from Princeton and pursue a law degree, returning to school to take a degree in political science. He lectured at Cornell before marrying and becoming a professor at Bryn Mawr College. Both Theodore and Woodrow were sickly as young men. At boarding school, Wilson had to withdraw because of health problems. Along with chronic indigestion and headaches, he would fight depression his whole life.

Roosevelt was a sickly asthmatic who suffered from chronic diarrhea and was often confined to bed. He traveled to the West after his wife and mother died on the same day in 1883 and in his twenties lived the life of a cowboy. He came back the barrel-chested Teddy Roosevelt who embodied the "vigorous life."

Wilson taught history at Wesleyan University after leaving Bryn Mawr and coached the football team and created a debating club. Roosevelt returned from the West to jump into the political fray and run for governor of New York as a reforming Republican. Woodrow started teaching at Princeton and moved slowly into the administration. Roosevelt became secretary of the navy and left his position to charge San Juan Hill in Cuba, making him a national hero. Wilson became the president of Princeton.

Teddy Roosevelt then took the presidency when an assassin's bullet cut down President McKinley. Wilson gained fame by trying to push through social reforms in the privileged world of Princeton clubs and eventually left to run for governor in New Jersey. Roosevelt built the Panama Canal, carried a Big Stick, set aside millions of acres for national forests, gave the presidency to William Howard Taft, then realized he wanted to run again.

Wilson served as governor of New Jersey and secured the Democratic nomination for president. Roosevelt created the Bull Moose Party, split the ticket, and laughed at the prospect of a man like Wilson, "a druggist," beating him.

But Woodrow Wilson saw their differences and defined them this way: "[Roosevelt] appeals to their imagination; I do not. He is a real vivid person, whom they have seen and shouted themselves hoarse over and voted for, millions strong; I am a vague, conjectural personality, more made up of opinions and academic prepossessions than of human traits and red corpuscles."

President Taft was out of the race after his vice president, James Sherman, died. It was between Theodore Roosevelt and Woodrow Wilson. They both campaigned hard and in a presentiment of his final stroke, Wilson complained often of chronic headaches and indigestion. He summed up his campaign as a classic grassroots crusade against the interests of big business: "The pygmy hasn't any chance in America; only the giant has. And the laws give the giant free leave to trample down the pygmy. What I am interested in is laws that will give the little man a . . . chance to show these fellows that he has brains to compete with them . . . "

In the end the split party undid the Republicans and Woodrow Wilson took 41 percent of the vote to Roosevelt's 27 percent. The schoolmaster had prevailed and the Wilsonian era had begun. It would be only a matter of time before the man with the childhood memory of the South in ruins would have to take America to war.

When Edith met him, President Woodrow Wilson was fifty-nine years old, five-foot-ten, and 170 pounds. He kept his hair short and parted to the side, sported a pince-nez that became his trademark, and led with his jaw. Women found this lanky man attractive in 1915. He was witty, indulged in minstrel humor, liked to sing, could dance a jig, and could even kick up his heels.

But he had been in a dark depression and living in another world since his wife died. "There is nothing but the work for me now," he would later write. Lacking his wife's bolstering presence, Wilson was now deflated, a mere shadow of his former self, despondent and reading detective novels "as a man would get drunk."

Dr. Grayson was worried about his health and the corrosive effect of grief and depression on his spirit. The White House had begun to feel like a prison to him, and he and Grayson took to motoring in the countryside. Grayson was determined to have the president find love again. It was his prescription for getting him back into life. He was able to put his plan into action when the president's cousin Helen befriended Edith Galt and managed to get her to the White House just as he and the president were returning from golf. When they emerged from the second-floor elevator, there was Helen with an attractive brunette with startling blue eyes. Edith Galt and Woodrow Wilson would now get a chance to talk.

# EIGHT

# ATTACK FROM WITHIN

## 1919

**IF PRESIDENTIAL POWER WAS A RIVER THAT FLOWED TO WOODROW** Wilson's bedroom door then Edith had erected a cofferdam to redirect the flow away from him. Edith was making decisions by addressing a simple question: will this problem be the death of my husband? The answer was no, because the problem wouldn't reach him.

Edith quickly developed a system to govern: "Every paper, letter or document that the members of the Cabinet and the senators sent to the President was given to her. She read them with the greatest care. If they seemed at all important she would send for the official concerned and confer with him directly to see if he himself could solve the problem. Whenever she felt something must be decided by the President she made a brief digest of the situation."

How did she know what was worthy of the invalid's attention? Edith responded, "I just decided." Then she added, "I had talked with him so much that I knew pretty well what he thought of things." Edith was besieged by people who "must see" the president. "Mrs. Wilson" was the ticket to access, but few tickets were given. Few still knew the real condition of the president.

Navy Secretary Daniels was informed of the president's true condition by Tumulty and Grayson. He couldn't tell his wife without fear of breaking down. Secretary of Agriculture Houston also learned the truth and called it one of the tragedies of the ages. Then Senator Houston saw Vice President Marshall at the Shoreham hotel. Marshall begged him for information, but Houston could tell him nothing. Marshall said it would be a tragedy for him to assume the duties of the presidency. According to Houston, Vice President Marshall seemed terrified at the thought.

A Thanksgiving Proclamation was expected from the president. On November 5, Secretary of State Lansing surmised that Edith Wilson had signed the proclamation he had written and sent over.

> Yesterday I sent over to the White House a Thanksgiving Proclamation which I had drafted on the evening of the 3rd. Today it was returned to me signed by the President.... The Proclamation as drafted was not changed in a single word. This fact caused me much concern as to the physical condition of the President, since it showed either that he was not permitted to read the document or that, if he did read it, was not in a mental state to do so critically.... His signatures were shocking manifestations of his serious physical state.... *Woodrow* could not have been deciphered, *Wilson* was better written but shaky and uneven, while the flourish at the end looked quite unnatural.... Both signatures were written with a lead pencil...after seeing this Proclamation with its pitiful signature.... I cannot see how he can really conduct the Government....

The first assault on Edith Wilson's presidency came from Secretary Lansing. He requested a cabinet meeting to consider whether the president was fit to lead. Lansing was brought in after Wilson asked for William Jennings Bryan's resignation over the sinking of the *Lusitania*. Secretary Lansing had helped Wilson craft notes to Germany forming the basis for declaring war but had fallen out of favor during the negotiations of the Treaty of Versailles. He didn't view the League as essential and for this Edith saw him as disloyal to the president.

She would later write, "Mr. Lansing should have retired long before. In Paris he had been a hindrance rather than a help. The same situation continued after we reached home and my husband was expending the last ounces of his strength for the Treaty. As soon as the President became ill, Mr. Lansing started agitation to put his Chief out of office."

Lansing had spoken with Vice President Marshall about taking over the presidency and then requested a meeting with Joseph Tumulty on October 3. When he met with Tumulty, he brought in *Jefferson's Manual*, the parliamentary procedure for the Senate. He read the section regarding the succession of power. Secretary Tumulty frowned and snapped, "Mr. Lansing, the Constitution is not a dead letter with the White House. I have read the Constitution and do not find myself in need of any tutoring at your hands..."

Secretary Lansing persisted. He wanted to know who would declare the president incapable of performing the duties of his office.

Tumulty replied that neither he nor Dr. Grayson would do it. "You may rest assured that while Woodrow Wilson is lying in the White House on the broad of his back I will not be a party to ousting him. He has been too kind, too loyal, and too wonderful to me to receive such treatment at my hands."

Just then, Dr. Grayson appeared. Tumulty turned to him and asked, "And I am sure that Doctor Grayson will never certify to this disability. Will you Grayson?"

He said he would not.

Tumulty then said he and Grayson would fight anyone who tried to certify that the president wasn't capable to lead. The secretary pointed out that if the president knew what Secretary Lansing was up to, he probably would be fired.

Lansing wasn't going to back down. He came from a political family and had married Eleanor Foster, the daughter of Secretary of State John W. Foster. He called a cabinet meeting and declared that it was up to them to decide if the government was going to carry on. Someone pointed out that this was impossible without knowing the president's exact condition. Dr. Grayson was sent for, and while they waited, Lansing read the same passages on constitutional secession he had read to Tumulty. Grayson then arrived and Lansing played his card.

"Dr. Grayson, we wish to know the nature and extent of the President's illness and whether he is able to perform the duties of his office, so that we may determine what shall be done to carry on the business of the Government."

Grayson replied that the president was suffering from a nervous breakdown, indigestion, and a depleted system, and that he must be left alone to heal. The doctor then said the president wanted to know by whose authority the cabinet was meeting and what their intent was. The secretary of war said they were meeting to handle any business that should arise and asked for Dr. Grayson to express their sympathy to the president. Lansing was boxed in and short of impeaching the president he could do nothing.

Meanwhile Grayson kept the press at bay with short bulletins. "The President had a good night and if there is any change in his condition it is favorable.... " Some historians have opined that Dr. Grayson was violating the Hippocratic oath. Kenneth R. Crispell and Carlos Gomez write that, "while one might excuse Mrs. Wilson's actions on the grounds of wifely loyalty, Grayson's behavior during these days exceeded the bounds of physician responsibility." Grayson had more influence with the president than any physician in history. He might have been the son Wilson never had. As Josephus Daniels later wrote, "[Wilson's] paternal regard embraced the younger physician. They rode and walked and played and talked together. Dr. Grayson knew his constitution, knew how he must take care of himself and conserve his strength. He was the skilled physician who studied to keep the President fit.... But he was much more than that: he was the true and trusted friend..."

The president's cabinet had demanded to know more and received less from Dr. Grayson. Traffic was routed away from Pennsylvania Avenue and it was reported that a band playing at a hotel a block away was asked not to play loud numbers. No reason was given. Then Woodrow Wilson's health took a turn for the worse.

# NINE

# THE ARDENT LOVER

## 1914

**THE ELEVATOR SLIDING DOOR ON THE SECOND FLOOR OF THE WHITE** House opened to a man flushed with color from playing golf, his pince-nez lenses reflecting light. It wasn't unlike a staged entrance with the president and Dr. Grayson appearing in the afternoon light and the two women as the deer in the headlights. Woodrow Wilson surely was taken with the woman standing in front of him. At forty-two, Edith Galt was sixteen years younger than the president and living the life of a liberated woman. She played golf, attended the theater and concerts, traveled widely, liked high fashion, and had means. She was stylish and independent and not looking to be tied down to anyone.

Enter the president with his muddy golf shoes. Helen Bones, the longtime White House hostess and the president's cousin, was now Edith's friend. She had wrangled to get her to the White House, assuring Edith the president was out playing golf. They had just arrived when the elevator opened and out stepped the president with Dr.

Grayson. "This was the accidental meeting which carried out the old adage of 'turn a corner and meet your fate,'" Edith wrote in her memoir. Most people would be overwhelmed by bumping into a sitting president, but Edith Galt's initial impression was that the men weren't well dressed. "The two gentlemen, I am sorry to say, were not so well attired. Their golf suits, as I found out later, were made by a cheap tailor the President had known years before and whom he was trying to help by giving an order. They were *not* smart."

After the men had changed out of their golf clothes, they had tea around a roaring fire on the second floor. Wilson was taken with Edith's tart humor, her buxom figure, and her dazzling smile. He immediately invited her to stay for dinner but she declined. Another dinner was arranged with Helen Bones and Grayson on March 23. The doctor was called away, leaving the president alone with Helen and Edith.

The president entertained the women with stories and recited poems. The next day, the big Pierce-Arrow presidential touring car rolled up to Edith's home and she got in the back with Helen and a Secret Service agent. The president sat up front with the chauffeur as they took a drive in the country.

"The President seemed very tired and desirous of rest. Though Helen and I chatted like magpies," Edith later wrote. Helen and the president persuaded Edith to dine with them and they ended up in front of a fire where Wilson read and relayed stories of growing up in the South. "That night he told me of the unusual relationship between him and his father, and of the infinite pains the latter took with his training and education, saying that even when he was a very young boy his father made him a partner in his thoughts and would discuss every subject with him, elucidating as he went.... the admiration he had for his father, immediately established a bond of sympathy between us, for I had so exactly the same reverence for my own father."

The president and Edith talked about being raised by former slaves who had been freed in the war and the poverty after the war. "All Southern children were taught to call the old slaves 'uncle' or 'aunt,'" Edith later wrote. "The Civil War had ended less than fifty years before and for the children of that time this great conflict colored their world and certainly it was a bond among those who lived through it."

Finally the night wound down. Edith wrote, "The evening ended all too soon, for it was the first time I had felt the warm personality of Woodrow Wilson. A boylike simplicity dwelt in the background of an official life.... Thereafter I never thought of him as the President of the United States, but as a real friend."

The president began picking up Edith for long drives with the Secret Service trailing in a car behind. Many times he would confide in her about the war in Europe and looming political issues. "When problems confronted him," Edith said later, "which they did in every hour of those tragic years, it seemed to clarify things for him to talk as we sped along in the cool April night through the darkness with faithful Murphy [the chauffeur] and the Secret Service car close behind us."

President Woodrow Wilson was an ardent lover and began to ramp up his courtship of Edith. On April 30, he sent her the book *Round My House* by Philip Hamerton and a dozen golden roses with the president's card. The car appeared at 7:45 to take Edith to dinner at the White House again. The president was taken with her black charmeuse dress. "She's a looker," the doorkeeper remarked to Colonel Edmund Starling, Wilson's personal bodyguard. "He's a goner," replied the president's valet, Arthur Brooks.

The rides increased and so did the dinners. Wilson was moving quickly and it culminated on May 3 when the president, Helen, Edith, Grayson, and two dinner guests retired to the south portico for coffee. Everyone suddenly left and for the first time it was just the president and Edith. "Almost as soon as they were gone," she later wrote, "he brought his chair nearer to mine and, looking directly at me with those splendid, fearless eyes that were unlike any others I have ever seen, he said: 'I asked Margaret and Helen to give me an opportunity to tell you something tonight that I have already told them.' Then he declared his love for me, speaking quietly but with such emotion the very world seemed tense and waiting."

People were often proposed to after a few dates, but this came as a shock to Edith. She stared at the president and cried out, "Oh, you can't love me, for you don't really know me, and it is less than a year since your wife died." An apropos response to a Victorian gentleman, but the ardent lover wasn't to be put off.

"Yes," he said, " I know you feel that; but, little girl, in this place time is not measured by weeks, or months, or years, but by deep human experiences; and since [my wife's] death I have lived a lifetime of loneliness and heartache. I was afraid, knowing you, I would shock you; but I would be less than a gentleman if I continued to make opportunities to see you without telling you what I have told my daughters and Helen: that I want you to be my wife."

The two lovers talked for another hour and Edith finally said that for now the answer was no. It was a precipitous proposal and Edith was in shock. She had been enjoying the drives and dinners and roses and books, but now there was the president asking her to marry him. The freedom Edith cherished was in the balance and she knew her simple life was about to vanish. It wouldn't have been surprising for her to get in her car and keep driving for the hills. Her first marriage had been to a passionless businessman. Now she had a president with the sexual energy of a man half his age asking to marry her.

Edith went home early and couldn't sleep. She got up and sat in a chair by the window and wrote the president a letter, opening with the lines:

*Your dear love fills me with a bliss untold,*
*Perfect, divine*
*I did not know the human heart could hold*
*Such a joy as mine.*

These are hardly the words someone writes who doesn't want to enter into a marriage. She followed up, writing, "Ever since you went away my whole being is awake and vibrant!...I am a woman—and the thought that you have *need* of me—is sweet."

Helen arrived that morning, and they went for a walk in Rock Creek Park. "Cousin Woodrow looks really ill this morning," she began, and then she burst in to tears. "Just as I thought some happiness was coming into his life! And now you are breaking his heart." Dr. Grayson appeared on a big white horse and asked what was wrong. Helen said nothing and he rode on, but guilt descended on Edith.

"I was beginning to feel like a criminal, and guilty of base ingratitude," Edith wrote in her memoir. She went on to explain to Helen that she thought of the president as a friend. "Of course," I told Helen, "there is a glamour around the man as President. There is the deep admiration I feel for the man himself.... But I am sure I am right in standing off from all these and trying to sift my own feeling free of each circumstance. To do this I must see him and I am honest enough to say I *want* to see him... "

Thus began the love letter campaign of Woodrow Wilson with Helen as the messenger. Wilson led off on the morning of May 7, "Ah, my precious friend and comrade, what happiness it was to be with you last night! While your hand rested in mine I felt as if I could stand up and shout for the strength and joy that was in me.... I knew where I could get the solace that would ease the strain and felt fit for any adventure of the spirit."

Wilson had flooded Ellen with love letters but they were a pittance compared with the epistolary onslaught of missives to Edith. "Here stands your friend, a longing man, in the midst of the world's affair—a world which knows nothing of the heart he has shown you...but which he cannot face with his full strength or with the fullest of keen endeavors unless you come into that heart and take possession..."

President Wilson would often lock himself in his study and write letters like a poet possessed. He imagined her by him and would "dream that her dear, beautiful form is close beside me." He told Edith he loved her "with a sort of fierce devotion compounded of every masculine force in me." Despite the purple prose and typical Victorian restraint, we can't help but sense the heat of his passion.

And at the same time, Edith showed she was interested in her lover's work as president. "Much as I love your delicious love letters, that would make any woman proud and happy, I believe I enjoy even more the ones in which you tell me of what you are working on—the things that fill your thoughts and demand your best efforts, for then I feel I am sharing your work."

Wilson obliged her by talking about the impending war and his lack of confidence in his secretary of state William Jennings Bryan. Edith wished she could do more for him. "How I wish I could really help you—I mean in a practical way—but that is where I am so useless."

Then the ardent lover got his world rocked again. On May 7, 1915, a German U-boat shot a torpedo into the idyll of the Victorian generation forever. President Wilson had to deal with the world once again.

# TEN

# "THE WHOLE BODY WILL BECOME POISONED"

## 1919

DR. GRAYSON STARED AT EDITH AND GAVE HER THE BAD NEWS. "Well, Mrs. Wilson, all agree there is no alternative but an operation, and I feel sure the President can't stand one. Since we came to this conclusion, I went out and walked around the block trying to get myself together before coming to you."

The gates to the White House were closed. The gloom of early winter pushed down on the cupola. People who had come for a tour stared in from Pennsylvania Avenue. Most of the windows were dark. The suffragettes moved silently with their signs past the padlocked entrance. Up on the second floor was a yellow window where the president lay. People whispered that that was the president's bedroom. Little did they know that the life of the president was in danger and it was up to Edith Wilson to decide his fate.

The reassuring bulletins on the president's progress continued, but Irwin Hoover's memoir—written twenty years after the fact—describes the real situation behind the Grayson bulletins. "He was physically almost incapacitated; could articulate but indistinctly and think but feebly.... During his illness everything in the way of business came to a standstill. ... He was lifted out of bed and placed in comfortable chair each day.... Mrs. Wilson would read to him.... Some matters of importance requiring his signature were read to him and with a pencil, his hand steadied and pointed, he would sign where the hand had been placed. He was changed in every way.... He could not talk plain, mumbled more than he articulated, was helpless and looked awful."

For the first month, no one saw the president except nurses, doctors, servants, and Wilson's daughters, Margaret, Jessie, and Nell. Even Secretary Tumulty didn't see him until November, and that was only through Edith. Hoover, the president's personal valet, again wrote what he saw firsthand: "He had changed from a giant to a pygmy in every wise.... He just lay helpless...all his natural functions had to be artificially helped and relieved and he appeared just as helpless as one could possibly be and live." Ray Stannard Baker recorded in his diary a meeting with Edith and Grayson during this time. "I had a hard time getting through the gates as the president has been ill and has no visitors. Mrs. Wilson looks worn and tired after her long vigil.... I spent the entire afternoon talking with Grayson and he went into every phase of the case and read me his secret report...the substance of which I cannot even put down here.... The President will be much longer in getting up and about than any one knows...he may never get up."

Then Baker expands on his impression of Edith Wilson, and in a very illuminating conversation he marvels that she had only two years of formal education. "Mrs. Wilson is of much stronger character than people realize. She has no great education. Yesterday she spoke of the 'decisive vote of California,' shortening the i and then said, I mean decisive—Mr. Wilson is always correcting me!"

Business in the White House was transacted through letters and documents and the tremendous flow to the president continued. Edith began intercepting the documents and putting them aside. Secretary Tumulty walked the halls picking up papers and putting them back down as a period of stasis settled in. A mail clerk asked Dr. Grayson what should be done about the mail that was piling up. He had no answer. The same clerk buttonholed Dr. Grayson the next day and said an important letter had arrived for the president.

"I don't think anyone else can handle it."

Grayson paused.

"I'll talk to Mrs. Wilson and see what I can do."

He took the letter and it disappeared. Another time, a letter came from the Bureau of Investigation, the agency that would later become the FBI. The letter contained charges of graft against a high-ranking official. Tumulty saw the clerk ask the presidential stenographer, Charles Swem, what he should do with the letter.

"Let me have those," Tumulty said, taking the letter from Swem, who continued to hang on.

"No, I'm handling this," Swem protested.

Eventually, Tumulty tore it from Swem's hand, making sure it was routed to Mrs. Wilson. The charges were never brought and the letter disappeared. One can't blame Edith Wilson for losing track of correspondence. Her husband was still in mortal danger. The president had developed an infection in his prostate gland that blocked his urinary tract. Grayson released a bulletin to the press on October 15, "The President did not have a restful night last night. His restlessness was caused by a swelling of the prostate gland, a condition from which he has suffered in the past and which has been intensified more or less by his lying in bed."

A manual attempt to relieve the blockage failed. The doctors went to another room while Edith waited by the president's bedside. Dr.

Grayson beckoned her into her bedroom and stood by the window, staring at the Washington Monument. "This is the situation: Drs. Young and Fowler, who are specialists, agree that this condition cannot be relieved without an operation. I think the others are of the same opinion. I feel an operation will be the end. Therefore, while I hate to put the responsibility on you, there is nothing else, but for you to decide."

Edith was now the sole arbiter of her husband's fate. She had four doctors telling her that they must operate. Edith wrote that she "felt that another chasm had opened at my feet." She looked the doctor in the eye. "Then we will not operate," she told Grayson. "You know more than anyone else of the real chances of recovery. So go down and tell them I feel that Nature will finally take care of things, and we will wait."

Admiral Grayson returned with Dr. Young. "Dr. Young followed me into my dressing room," Edith later wrote, "and taking pencil and paper from his pocket, he proceeded to draw diagrams which my blinded eyes could hardly see. His arguments were supplemented by Dr. Ruffin, my personal physician.... But something kept me steady and I would not agree."

Edith was flying in the face of medical opinion, but at an early age she had learned to test everything against her own experience, intuition, and cold logic. These faculties had served her well before and now they were telling her that surgery would mean death.

Still, the doctors weren't finished.

The president called to her, and as she started to his room Dr. Young called after her, "You understand, Mrs. Wilson, the whole body will become poisoned if this condition lasts an hour, or at the most two hours, longer." Edith went into the room with "this note ringing in my ear like the tolling of a funeral bell." She went back and took the president's hand, and he greeted her with a thin smile.

Edith stayed with her husband for the next three hours as nurses came and went and his temperature rose. "My own life seemed suspended; even Nature herself seemed listening." The "local treatment" was given again which consisted of hot packs put against his lower abdomen. Finally, the president was able to urinate. His temperature began to fall and eventually he slept. Edith Bolling Wilson had gone her own way when all was against her.

# ELEVEN

# CHRISTMAS ON THE BOTTOM OF THE OCEAN

## 1915

**THE GERMAN SUBMARINE SM *U-20* HAD DECIDED TO HEAD HOME.** Commander Walther Schwieger had been dealing with incessant fog that prevented him from surfacing and getting a clear shot. He had only three torpedoes left and his fuel was running low. The isolation of a U-boat is hard to imagine today. But in 1915 the wireless telegraph worked only up to 250 miles from shore; after that, a U-boat commander was on his own. As Erik Larson wrote in *Dead Wake*, "The isolation made the U-boat distinct among Germany's naval forces. Surface ships could travel in groups and, given the height of their masts, could stay in contact with their bases; U-boats traveled solo and lost contact sooner, typically after sailing only a couple hundred miles. Once at sea, a U-boat captain was free to conduct his patrol in whatever manner suited him, without supervision from above. He alone determined when and whether to attack..."

The British hadn't cracked the German code until a codebook had washed up with a dead sailor. From then on, the British knew exactly where the German U-boats were once they checked in. The problem was that Marconi's marvelous invention of wireless telegraph depended very much on the size of the transmitting and receiving stations and the relative location of the U-boat. Once the U-boat passed out of range, not only did the Germans not know where their own submarine was, neither did the British.

World War I had become a war of attrition. Germany's Schlieffen Plan called for launching a massive attack against France before the Russians and British could mobilize. France fought back and held her ground, and the Schlieffen Plan quickly devolved into trench warfare along a 440 mile Western Front as Britain declared war and Russia quickly mobilized. For the Germans the war became a matter of cutting off supplies crossing the seas to the Allies. Submarines were best suited to accomplishing the mission but their attacks lacked accuracy. President Wilson had declared America neutral in the stalemate of 1915 as both sides were seeking an advantage. War materiel was making its way across the Atlantic under the flags of neutral ships and the Germans knew it.

Most Americans assumed the two oceans would isolate them from the world's problems. A British journalist at the time pointed out, "The United States is remote, unconquerable, huge, without hostile neighbors, or any neighbors at all of anything like her own strength, and lives exempt in an almost unvexed tranquility from the contentions and animosities and the ceaseless pressure and counter-pressure that distract the close-packed older world."

Few people among the Allies understood submarine warfare. It wasn't until the destruction of the British cruisers *Aboukir*, *Hogue*, and *Cressy* by a single U-boat that the British realized naval warfare had changed. Fourteen hundred sailors died and three large British cruisers vanished. The German U-boat was never even seen. The rulers of the sea now belonged to the murky depths where submarine commanders struck at will and disappeared.

Germany declared an "area of war" around the British Isles and warned that any ship entering the war zone would be sunk. She knew England needed the lifeline of imported goods and since the British had taken to flying flags from other countries on her own ships, the Germans felt they had no choice but to sink all ships.

President Wilson declared that he would hold the Germans to strict accountability if any American ship were sunk or any Americans killed. The president promised to "take any steps it might be necessary to take to safeguard American lives and property." Many in the German government believed they could knock Britain out of the war before America could get any troops across the ocean. Kaiser Wilhelm concurred and gave tacit approval to submarine commanders to sink any French or British ship.

The problem was that a U-boat commander peered through a tiny lens that posed a very black and white question; fire your torpedo or don't. To any young U-boat commander, the answer was obvious: sink the damn ship and take credit for the tonnage sent to the bottom of the ocean. In 1915 the *Falaba* was sunk with a loss of 104 people, including one American, Leon C. Thrasher. The president, who had just met a very charming woman named Edith Galt, thought about raising the issue with the Germans. But Secretary of State William Jennings Bryan, who was a pacifist, said Thrasher knew what he was doing. He had been warned not to travel on British merchant ships. The president went back to writing love letters.

Commander Schwieger of the SM *U-20* had recently celebrated Christmas on the bottom of the ocean. It was a trick submariners could pull off, as there was no sonar detection yet. Schwieger simply flooded his tanks and let the submarine drift down to a nice landing on the sandy bottom. Then after listening for any sounds of leaks, the crew of the U-boat knew they were safe. No one knew they were down there and for a while the war ceased to exist. Schwieger pulled out some Christmas wreaths and schnapps and if someone had had sonar gear they would have heard the chorus of "O Tannenbaum" floating up from the depths. Then the tanks were flushed and the SM *U-20* floated to the surface and was on its way again.

A U-boat could travel 5,200 nautical miles on a tank of diesel fuel, and on the surface the sleek black ship could make fifteen knots. This was fast enough to overtake most conventional ships. The problem was that once submerged and on battery power, the U-boat slipped to a phlegmatic nine knots and could go only eighty miles under water.

By comparison, the British liner *Lusitania* was one of the fastest ships afloat and could make an easy twenty-five knots. There was no way for Schwieger to catch up to a ship that fast and many times steamers simply outran U-boats. The commander hadn't had much luck until now. His "tonnage" of sunken ships was low, and he would have to turn back soon as his diesel fuel was getting low.

And now Schwieger was in the pea-soup fog that made life for U-boats miserable. Then the fog began to lift; he took to his periscope and thought he saw a trawler headed toward him. Schwieger gave the order to dive and let the ship pass over him. The heavy thrum of the screws and the engine told the U-boat commander that this was no trawler. He surfaced and saw a British destroyer he didn't want to tangle with. The U-boat continued on for some time, then surfaced to take another look. On the horizon came a three-funnel steamer and through the lens Schwieger saw "a forest of masts and stacks.... At first I thought they must belong to several ships. Then I saw it was a great steamer coming over the horizon. It was coming our way."

The *Lusitania* was about to enter the annals of history.

# TWELVE

# "A Small-Caliber
# Man"

## 1919

VICE PRESIDENT THOMAS MARSHALL LOOKED AT HIS WATCH IN THE
luxurious hotel. The cigar smoke angulated over the rich upholstery.
A bellboy asked if he might be of some assistance. He could not. Marshall wanted a drink but as a recovering alcoholic he dared not.
Besides, he and his wife had unofficially adopted a boy and he must
set an example. He was waiting to hear about the president of the
United States who some said was near death. He looked at his watch
again. The man he was to meet would tell him the truth about the
commander in chief.

The man appeared and sat down next to Marshall. He was a
newspaper man from the *Baltimore Sun*. Secretary Tumulty and Dr.
Grayson had decided someone should tell Marshall about the president
and picked Fred Essary to deliver the news. The vice president forgot
to ash his cigar as the man described a president who had become an
invalid. He couldn't move. He couldn't speak. The man finished up

and then he left, leaving Vice President Marshall in shock. He dropped his cigar and covered his face with his hands.

Thomas Riley Marshall was the son of a doctor who opened a law practice in 1876 in Columbia City, Indiana. He was only 124 pounds, walked with a limp, and chomped on an ever-present cigar. He was a great contrast to the austere and tall president who would ask him to join his ticket years later. In 1880 he ran as the Democratic candidate for his district's prosecuting attorney. He lost and became engaged to Kate Hooper, who died the day before they were to be wed. Marshall began to drink and continued as a lawyer, meeting Lois Kimsey in her father's law office, a girl nineteen years his junior. They married but his alcoholism began to affect his professional life. Lois locked him in their house for two weeks to dry him out.

It worked and after serving four years in the state Democratic Central Committee, Marshall successfully ran for governor of Indiana, becoming the state's first Democratic governor in two decades. He had a progressive agenda and pushed through child labor laws and anti-corruption legislation. In 1912 his name was put in to run for the presidential nomination at the Democratic National Convention in Baltimore. Indiana was an important swing state and he was given the chance to be Woodrow Wilson's running mate.

At first Marshall didn't want the job, seeing the vice presidency as a powerless position. But Wilson promised he would keep him busy with important responsibilities. Marshall and Wilson soon disagreed over bills allowing merchant ships to arm prior to World War I. Isolationist senators filibustered the bills and the president demanded that Marshall put a gag order in place to cut off debate. Marshall refused and the bills failed. Wilson never forgave him, the president later remarking that Vice President Marshall was "a small-caliber man."

Wilson immediately took his vice president out of the loop by moving his office away from the White House. Wilson then began meeting personally with the Senate. This was a job usually reserved for the vice president and Marshall saw this as another sign of Wilson's lack of faith in him. In his memoir, the vice president would describe their relationship as "functioning animosity."

During the war the vice president gave speeches across the country in support of bond drives. Marshall was well-paid as a speaker. He never turned down an engagement and viewed it as an extra source of income. Edith and Woodrow regarded him as a crass man of little intelligence. Edith didn't care for Marshall's demeanor or his lowbrow humor. Many encouraged Wilson to dump him for Newton Baker in the 1916 election.

The president stuck with Marshall because vice presidents just didn't matter very much back then, and Marshall, who didn't have any dealings with the White House, didn't matter at all. When President Wilson went abroad to work out the peace, Marshall complained to his wife that Wilson hadn't let him know he was leaving the country. When Marshall went to welcome the king and queen of Belgium, the secretary of state was given a private compartment while the vice president ended up in coach.

Wilson may have viewed Marshall as an insignificant man, but two prominent Democrats and four Republican senators urged him to demand the presidency. Marshall equivocated, then paid a call to the White House. He was intercepted by Edith outside the family quarters. Marshall knew the president was very ill. Constitutionally, the vice president could have brushed the first lady aside and demanded what was his by right of succession. If there was to be a confrontation or a power play, it should have occurred here.

Edith barred Vice President Marshall from seeing President Wilson and after a few minutes she sent him on, saying that "she would let him know if she should think of anyway he might help the President." Clearly, Edith Wilson outranked the man who would be king.

But others saw it differently. Marshall's secretary, Mark Thistlethwaite, thought Marshall should be ready if the president died.

The cigar-chomping vice president grudgingly went over the ground with his secretary. Thistlethwaite believed he should prepare a statement saying he would continue Wilson's policies. Marshall protested that he wouldn't say it because he would have new policies as president.

"All right," said his secretary, "change later but first announce a continuation of the previous policies."

Marshall said no.

Thistlethwaite asked if he would become president if Congress deemed President Wilson incapable of holding office.

"No," said Marshall. "Such a move would be illegal unless the President assented to it or until it had a two-thirds vote and a two-thirds vote is impossible.'"

But what if the Supreme Court declared Wilson unable to fulfill the duties of president?

The vice president shook his head and said the court would never do it. Thistlethwaite was frustrated. He saw himself as serving a potential president, but his boss was a man who didn't want the reins of power.

He then demanded what it would take then for him to be president.

Marshall said a congressional resolution approved in writing by Cary Grayson and the first lady. He then added, "I could throw this country into civil war...but I won't."

His secretary pressed him for more.

"I am not going to seize the place and then have Wilson—recovered—come around and say, 'Get off, you usurper!'"

Vice President Marshall knew Edith would be the one to take him off the throne. As he later told Arthur Knock of the *New York Times*,

"No politician ever exposes himself to the hatred of a woman, especially if she's the wife of the President of the United States."

Marshall's greatest fear almost came to pass. He was speaking in Atlanta when a policeman ran up and told one of the men that the president had died. The news was passed to Marshall who halted his speech. He then said to the audience, "I cannot continue my speech. I must leave at once to take up my duties as Chief Executive of this great nation."

The vice president asked the people to pray for him as everyone broke into "Nearer My God to Thee." Marshall was off to his hotel where he found out the telephone call was a hoax. He returned to his speaking circuit where the real money was. He was still smarting from not being reimbursed for giving the king and queen a dinner with his own funds. The vice president would never see Woodrow Wilson again, save for a moment at the inauguration of President Warren Harding.

One reason Edith Wilson was able to assume the presidency was that the vice president simply didn't want the job. If someone had been waiting in the wings to take power, it is fair to ask if the presidency of Edith Wilson would have occurred. A competent vice president would have joined forces with members of Congress and there would have been little Edith could do. When Thomas Marshall died, in 1924, the *New York Times* said, "We liked him better than we have liked some greater, but less hospitably human persons."

Edith Wilson thought so little of Vice President Marshall that twenty years later she didn't think even to mention him in her memoir.

# THIRTEEN

# "WE SHALL BE AT WAR WITH GERMANY WITHIN A MONTH"

## 1915

IN LONDON A FEW DAYS BEFORE U-BOAT COMMANDER SCHWIEGER stumbled on the *Lusitania*, Colonel House had met with Edward Grey, Britain's foreign secretary. They discussed the submarine war. House later wrote, "We spoke of the probability of an ocean liner being sunk and I told him if this were done, a flame of indignation would sweep across America, which would in itself probably carry us into the war." House would later see King George V, who out of the blue asked, "Suppose they should sink the *Lusitania* with American passengers aboard?"

Commander Schwieger ordered the SM *U-20* to submerge and intercept the steamer. He could go only nine knots on battery power and the steamer was clipping along. He couldn't surface and use his faster diesels and risk being seen. So he trailed the steamer and waited; then the miracle happened. The great steamer turned to starboard and came right toward him.

*Lusitania*'s Captain Turner faced a dilemma. He knew there were U-boats directly in front of and behind him. He was only 250 miles from Liverpool but he had to pass over Mersey Bar at high tide. At his current speed he had the problem of arriving too early, yet he couldn't meander in the Irish Sea while U-boats skulked around. He needed to take some bearings and turn the big ship to starboard so his navigator could line up with the coast.

On board the *Lusitania* were 949 British citizens, seventy-one Russians, fifteen Persians, eight French, six Greeks, five Swedes, three Belgians, three Dutch, two Italians, two Mexicans, two Finns, and 108 Americans. When fully loaded the ship weighed forty-four thousand tons and could travel almost thirty miles an hour across the water. No ship that large had ever gone that fast.

This was due to the immense engines and the insatiable appetite for coal, which was loaded from bunkers lining the sides of the ship. The ship needed 5,690 tons of coal for a crossing and even in dock she burned 140 tons a day. One thousand tons of coal daily went into twenty-five boilers to spin the giant turbines that propelled the screws. The thought was that a ship of this size and speed could never be caught in the crosshairs of a U-boat. That crosshair view was very small for a U-boat captain who watched with water slopping across his vision. It was sheer luck to find a ship like the *Lusitania* out on the Atlantic. It was like striking the mother lode in a vast desert.

Schwieger ordered *U-20* put on a course to confront the liner. He then ordered the torpedo depth set for three meters and the tubes flooded. His crew armed the torpedo. He watched the *Lusitania* become larger in his periscope lens and calculated her speed around twenty-two knots with a range of about a half-mile. The torpedo was a dead bullet once fired. There was no sonar, no self-correcting mechanism to guide the missile after its release from the tube.

Schwieger had to calculate the speed of the ship, the angle, the speed of the torpedo, and then, like someone leading a target with a gun, he would fire and hope his calculations were correct. Many times they weren't and torpedoes powered past their targets either behind or in front. He gave the order to fire at 2:10 p.m. The torpedo blasted into the water and began cruising at 44 mph. This bullet of doom was part of the new mechanized war being waged on the Western Front with tanks, machine guns, and chlorine gas.

A few Europeans had noted the butchery of the American Civil War and recognized the advent of total war with Sherman's "March to the Sea," where he burned the South to the ground to demoralize its citizenry and destroy the Confederacy's ability to wage war. But many had seen the Civil War as an aberration and lacking the civility of European conflicts. It was the barbaric Americans who broke all the rules anyway.

Many still believed in the flying plumes and few understood the mechanized brilliance of death by stealth where machines fired machines at other machines. As Erik Larson wrote in *Dead Wake*, the torpedo was a sophisticated weapon of war.

The torpedo itself was 20 feet long and 20 inches in diameter; its nose, shaped like the top of a corn silo, contained 350 pounds of TNT and an explosive called Hexanite. Through German commanders typically set the depth at 15 feet, this one traveled at 10 feet. It moved at about 35 knots, or 40 miles an hour, powered by compressed air stored in a tank toward its nose, just behind the compartment that contained the explosives. The air rushed against the pistons in its engine, geared to spin two propellers, one clockwise, the other counterclockwise, to keep the torpedo from rolling and veering. The air was then exhausted into the sea, where it bubbled to the surface. These bubbles needed a few seconds to rise, which meant the torpedo itself was always well ahead of the track that appeared above.

The German government had posted warnings in fifty American newspapers not to take the *Lusitania*. The postings served as reminders that a state of war existed between Britain and Germany and that people passing through the war zone did so at their own risk. Still, most people dismissed the warnings with the belief that nothing could sink a fast liner like the *Lusitania*.

The fog had blown off the water and it was a sparkling crisp day on the sea. Passengers strolled leisurely and took in the lazy day. The torpedo approached. Even when passengers noticed a silvery object leaving a long white tail heading toward the ship, they had trouble believing it was a torpedo. Larson writes of an exchange between passengers at the moment they saw the German torpedo approaching.

> Oliver Bernard...saw what seemed to be the tail of a fish, well off the starboard side. Next a "streak of froth" began arcing across the surface, toward the ship. An American woman came up beside him and said, "That isn't a torpedo is it?"
>
> "I was too spellbound to answer," he said. "I felt absolutely sick."
>
> Here it was, this thing that everyone feared. "We had all been thinking, dreaming, eating, sleeping 'submarine' from the hour we left New York, and yet with the dreaded danger upon us, I could hardly believe the evidence of my own eyes."

In the brilliant sunshine the torpedo looked almost beautiful until it slammed into the ship ten feet below the water line. The torpedo punched a hole as the explosives emitted nine thousand degrees of heat with a pressure that blew a hole the size of a small house in the side of the liner. Water rushed into empty coal bunkers at a rate of one hundred tons a second. *Lusitania* listed to starboard and then the stern began to rise.

The damage was fatal, as "Thousands of rivets and the steel plates they anchored came loose over an area about fifteen times greater than the hole itself; the glass in nearby portholes fractured. Bulkheads were damaged and watertight doors dislodged.... Just inside the hull, at the point of impact, stood the starboard end of a major watertight bulkhead that spanned the width of the hull..."

Commander Schwieger watched the carnage though his periscope and later told his friend Max Valentiner:

> The ship was sinking with unbelievable rapidity. There was a terrific panic on her deck. Overcrowded lifeboats, fairly torn from their positions, dropped into the water. Desperate people ran helplessly up and down the decks. Men and women jumped into the water and tried to swim to empty overturned lifeboats. It was the most terrible sight I have ever seen. It was impossible for me to give any help. I could have only saved a handful.... The scene was too horrible to watch, and I gave orders to dive to twenty meters, and away.

The *Lusitania* nosed down and raised up her four monstrous propellers. Passenger Dwight Harris, floating in his life jacket, described the final moments as the ship "plunged forward like a knife blade into the water—funnels, masts, boats, etc., all breaking to pieces and falling about everywhere! A terrible mass of iron, wood, steam, and water! And worst of all, human forms!—A great swirling greenish white bubble formed where the ship went down, which was a mass of struggling humanity and wreckage! The bubble got bigger and bigger..."

Upon hearing the news of the *Lusitania*'s sinking, Colonel House told a dinner party in Britain that night, "We shall be at war with Germany within a month."

# FOURTEEN

# EDITH AND MAJOR CRAUFURD-STUART

1919

IN *THE KING'S SPEECH*, THE PRINCE OF WALES INHERITS THE throne when his older brother, Edward, wants to marry a divorced woman, Wallis Simpson. King Edward has no choice but to abdicate and the stuttering prince of Wales becomes the king on the eve of World War II. But long before this happened, the prince of Wales became only the third person to see the ailing President Wilson outside of the immediate family, doctors, and the king and queen of Belgium. The king and queen had been on the ocean when Wilson's stroke occurred and they waited patiently until they could see him. Edith thought that a royal visit would quiet down the rancor in the Senate over the lack of information.

On the afternoon of November 14, 1919, the king and queen came for tea in the Red Room and Edith asked the king if he wanted to go up to see the president. "Oh, but he must not go yet. We have a present for the President, but in spite of all our care it has never come, and we must wait here until it does so we can present it ourselves," the queen protested.

Finally the gift arrived and the king, carrying a box of Belgian china, headed up with Edith to the president's bedroom. The king entered Wilson's room and saw an old man with a long white beard lying in his bed. His mouth drooped on the left side. They chatted a bit and examined the plates and then the visit was over.

The queen then pressed to see him.

Edith didn't want to put her husband through the stress of seeing more people, but she gave in. When they reached his room she saw the president had changed. "Of course, my husband had put on his dressing gown to receive the King," Edith later wrote. "But a gown was clumsy and uncomfortable when lying in bed and so he had changed it for an old soft woolen grey sweater he had bought years before in Scotland."

Wilson apologized for the sweater but the queen brushed it aside. She was overjoyed to see the president examining the plates in his bed with a large magnifying glass. When the queen descended, she spoke to the press and said the president looked comfortable in his worn Scotch wool sweater. But *worn* became *torn*, and Edith found herself receiving intense criticism for having the president of the United States greet royalty with a "torn sweater." Women from all over the country sent her wool yarn to mend the president's sweater.

The prince of Wales visited a week later and Wilson charmed the younger man. "I am very glad to see you again, Mr. President," he said, referring back to their meeting in London during Wilson's visit for the peace treaty. The prince, the unlikely future king, sat down on the bed and found himself looking for words. He was young and the sight of the sick old man made him nervous. "My, what a magnificent bed this is, Mr. President." The stutter was there. The prince of Wales had a problem getting the words out, literally.

The president smiled, but could only express himself with the right side of his face.

"This is the bed that Abraham Lincoln slept in," Wilson said as the prince fidgeted. The prince would take over the throne from his brother in 1939, the year Hitler invaded Poland, triggering the Second World War. The "speech" in *The King's Speech* is the speech he would have to give over radio announcing the Declaration of War on Germany with all its cataclysmic results. But now he was talking with a man who had ushered the world through the First World War. From a historical perspective it was a poignant meeting, for here are two men whose fates were strangely linked. On the one side, President Wilson is dying from the pressures of the First World War and on the other the prince of Wales, the future king, who would come into his own during the conflict precipitated by the failure of the League of Nations. If it weren't for Wilson's debilitating illness the League of Nations might have been formed and World War II avoided.

This visit also brings into relief the crisis of Sir Edward Grey, a British ambassador who had come out of retirement to get the United States into the League of Nations. But as stated before, Edith wouldn't allow him to see the president; her reasons for refusing him were personal and related to the behavior of Grey's secretary, the British Army officer Major Charles Kennedy Craufurd-Stuart.

The major liked to play the piano and sing witty improvised tunes at parties and didn't care for Americans. At a party in 1918 just before the Wilsons came to Europe, Craufurd-Stuart ripped off a few insinuating lines about Edith and Mary Peck. The rumor that the president had had an affair with Mary Peck had been circulating in Washington society for some time and Stuart surmised Edith saw Mary Peck as a rival and had paid her off to buy her silence.

News of Stuart's transgression traveled to the White House and fell upon the ears of the first lady. As soon as the British Army officer arrived, the State Department requested that he go back to England. Lord Grey inquired why his secretary should have to leave and received no answer. Grey pressed the matter and was told by Dr. Grayson that Craufurd-Stuart had slandered the president's wife. Grey, suspecting Mrs. Wilson was behind this, did nothing.

Edith turned up the heat and sent Dr. Grayson and men from the State Department to see Grey, suggesting Stuart be on the first steamer out. Lord Grey did not put the errant major on the steamer. The State Department then said it would declare the man *persona non grata*, in effect tossing him out of the country. Lord Grey countered by changing Craufurd-Stuart's official status: no longer a British attaché, he was now a member of the ambassador's household.

Edith settled for not allowing Lord Grey anywhere near the White House; and so the prince of Wales saw the president alone. Colonel House would later write in his diary that he thought the campaign against Craufurd-Stuart was the work of the first lady. "If Mrs. Wilson had shown him some attention, even if he had not seen the President, it would have made matters better ... the Craufurd-Stuart incident is the main cause. They [Edith] treated him so discourteously that [Grey] evidently felt free to speak his mind," he wrote, referring to an offensive letter Lord Grey later published in the newspapers.

The tragedy of this episode is that Lord Grey likely would have furthered the cause of the League if he had met with the president. Colonel House summed it up this way in his diary: "If the President had not fallen ill and our relations had continued as of old, the greatest good might have resulted from Grey's visit.... I regard the failure of his mission as one of the great misfortunes that had befallen us." It is worthwhile to note that after being unable to see anyone in the White House, Lord Grey began to meet with congressmen about the League. One of those congressmen was Senator Henry Cabot Lodge.

# FIFTEEN

# THE GARFIELD
# PRECEDENT

## 1881

BEFORE PRESIDENT WOODROW WILSON, THERE HAD BEEN ONLY one instance of a sitting president becoming incapacitated to the point of being unable to perform the duties of his office. It was when President James Garfield, America's twentieth president, was shot by assassin Charles Guiteau. Guiteau believed the nation would be better off with Chester Arthur as president and fully expected he would be freed from prison and become rich through the publication of his books. By killing Garfield, he believed he would be transformed from a lonesome drifter to a man in the public eye forever.

The assassin had visited the White House for months trying to get an appointment from the newly-elected president. In 1881, office seekers could simply walk into the White House and ask the president for a job. Charles Guiteau became a pest and was soon barred from seeing President Garfield. A dream gave him deliverance with a solution: for the good of the country, he must shoot the president.

Guiteau borrowed ten dollars, bought a .44 caliber pistol, and began to follow the president around Washington. His opportunity came when President Garfield went to the Sixth Street train station in Washington on July 2, 1881. Guiteau followed him into the station then pulled the gun from his pocket and fired. The first bullet grazed Garfield's right arm, causing the president to clutch his arm and cry out, "My God! What is this?"

Then Guiteau fired again and shot the president in the back. The bullet entered and hit a rib, then passed through a vertebra in the spinal column and lodged behind his pancreas. The president collapsed and vomited as a bright-red stain spread out on the back of his summer suit. If James Abram Garfield had received no treatment from there on, he would have survived.

The bullet hit no vital organs but Dr. Willard Bliss chose to ignore the work of Joseph Lister, who had recently theorized that infection was killing patients. Dr. Bliss was a longtime friend of Garfield's and took charge after the president was carried to a room above the station. Bliss put his unwashed finger into the bullet hole and immediately inserted a dirty porcelain probe into the president's back. His search for the bullet with the probe would eventually lead to the president's death on September 19, 1881 from physician-induced sepsis.

But on July 2, the president was still very much alive. He was transported to the White House and taken upstairs. Much like the Wilson bedroom vigil, the Garfield vigil began with a crisis of constitutional succession. The parallels between Garfield and Wilson are striking. Control over President Garfield was grabbed by Dr. Bliss, who began issuing bulletins claiming that the president was doing fine.

As Candice Millard writes in *The Destiny of the Republic*, "Taking on the role of chief physician, Bliss's first orders were to isolate the president. In this he had the help of armed military sentinels.... Inside the White House, Garfield was confined not to just one wing, or even one room, but to a small space within that room. At Bliss's direction, his bed was pushed to the center of the room and encircled by screens. Even if a visitor made it past the locked gates and armed guards....and into Garfield's room, he would still be separated from the president."

It is the same fortress mentality that pervaded the Wilson White House. Garfield's personal secretary, Joseph Brown, was the forerunner of Wilson's Joseph Tumulty. Millard writes again in *The Destiny of the Republic*, "Brown personally took charge of the fortification of the White House and the protection of the president. With complete confidence and authority, he ordered the gates closed and sent a telegram to the chief of police, requesting a 'temporary but adequate detail of officers.'"

Dr. Bliss jealously guarded President Garfield against anyone he deemed unworthy of seeing the president. He fought off other physicians and forged a letter by the president saying he was the physician in charge. It wasn't until the first lady arrived and brought in some of her doctors that Bliss was forced to deal with other physicians.

Meanwhile, President Garfield took a turn for the worse as infection set in. He performed a cabinet meeting from his bed with Bliss ordering cabinet members to do nothing that would excite the president. His secretaries performed what duties they could. Only Secretary Brown maintained contact and directed the operation of the White House while the president fought for his life.

The parallels between Garfield's and Wilson's vice presidents also are remarkable. Vice President Chester A. Arthur was an operative for party boss Roscoe Conkling, who was the leader of the Stalwarts of the Republican Party and controlled the New York Customs House. Garfield had defied Conkling and turned down his nominations for patronage jobs. So when President Garfield was struck down, many realized with horror that Conkling's stooge could become president.

Like Vice President Marshall, Arthur had little contact with the White House and wasn't considered a viable candidate for the presidency. Neither Marshall nor Arthur wanted the job. As Millard writes, "The Constitution was of no help. Nothing in it offered any guidance on how to determine when a president was no longer able to perform his duties. Nor was there any precedent.... Finally, [Secretary of State] Blaine sent a cabinet member to New York to discuss the transition with the vice president. Arthur, however, made it clear that he wouldn't even consider taking over the presidency while Garfield still lived."

Like Vice President Marshall, Vice President Arthur didn't want to be the man who usurped the presidency. This left Garfield in his bed in the agony of summer heat with the nation drifting. Only Brown saw him regularly: "the young man divided his days and nights between the sadness of the sickroom and the madness of his own office, where he replied to thousands of letters and telegrams, fielded journalists' questions and greeted dignitaries."

A reporter for the *Evening Critic* summed up Brown's role this way: "During all this terror, hope, despair, and rush at the White House, a reporter for the *Evening Critic* wrote, Brown had been 'the ruling spirit of the Mansion, and his young hand, guided by his wise head and kind heart, has been upon all.'"

So, like Edith in the Wilson White House, Secretary Brown would do the lion's share of the business while Garfield lay upstairs at the White House. In an act that foreshadows the handling of Wilson's stroke, Dr. Bliss continued to issue statements saying President Garfield was improving when in fact he was declining quickly.

First Lady Lucretia Garfield was no Edith Wilson. She had never been involved in the business of the White House and was never part of the power play that occurred while Garfield languished for two months. Dr. Bliss was more Edith-like in that he controlled access to Garfield. Very few people saw the president as a result. As Millard writes, "Bliss permitted no one to see the president but the handful of friends and family members who had become his nurses. His children, whom he ached to see, were allowed only rare visits. Even [Secretary of State] Blaine had not seen Garfield since the day he had knelt over him in the train station.... On a Friday morning in late July, Blaine was ushered into the president's darkened sickroom.... Just six minutes after Blaine had entered the room, Garfield's doctors politely showed him back out."

So the circling of the wagons, the isolation, the lack of information and outright misinformation about the condition of the president, a vice president who didn't want the job, and a fuzzy constitutional gray area on what constitutes a functioning and able president—all of it adds up to a foreshadowing of what would occur fifty years later. In both cases, retaining the president's power necessitated secrecy, obfuscation, and the protection of the status quo at all costs.

The difference of course is that after a little more than two months President Garfield died and Chester Arthur did become president. The charade ended and it would come out later that the president died from infection brought on probably by the man who was trying to save him. Dr. Bliss would be the poster child for ego run amok and give new meaning to the phrase "ignorance is bliss."

Fifty years later, President Wilson would become the new President Garfield: isolated, alone, and cut off from the world and his own advisors with an incurable illness and two years left in his term in office. The same limbo of presidential power would be created by the lack of specificity of what constituted a functioning president. The same reluctance on the part of the vice president to assume command would allow others to step in. The new Secretary Joseph Brown would be Secretary Joseph Tumulty, and the new Dr. Bliss would be Dr. Cary Grayson.

And President Edith Wilson....she would run it all.

# SIXTEEN

# CUPID'S TRIUMPH

## 1915

THE PRESIDENT WAS BUSY WRITING LOVE LETTERS TO EDITH WHILE the 128 Americans traveling on the *Lusitania* thrashed in fifty-five-degree water until they drowned or died of hypothermia. "There are some things I must try to say before the still watches come again in which the things unsaid hurt so and cry out in the heart to be uttered," Wilson wrote in one letter, "if you cannot give me all I want—what my heart finds it hard now to breathe without—it is because I am not worthy. I know instinctively you could give it if I were."

It was later, when Wilson had finished lunch and was getting ready for golf, that he received the telegram informing him that the Germans had just sent the *Lusitania* to the bottom of the sea. He took a drive in his Pierce-Arrow to try to relax. He had dinner and received telegrams confirming that there had been many Americans on board with heavy loss of life. President Wilson then did something very alarming to his Secret Service detail: he left the White House and went for a walk alone in the rain.

The Americans who died might have been the catalyst for America to rally around its president. Certainly Teddy Roosevelt believed so. "Every soft creature, every coward and weakling, every man who can't look more than six inches ahead, every man whose god is money, or pleasure, or ease, and every man who has not got in him the sterner virtues and the power of seeking after an ideal is enthusiastically in favor of Wilson."

But Cupid wouldn't rest even for impending war. "My happiness absolutely depends upon your giving me your entire love," he wrote Edith. He was wound up by Edith's indecision and that night stepped out of the White House as if he was going to walk over to her house.

The full loss of life was soon known and Henry Cabot Lodge recalled, "The country was horrified, and at that moment the popular feeling was such that if the President, after demanding an immediate reparation and apology...had boldly declared that...it was our duty to go to war, he would have had behind the him the enthusiastic support of the whole American people."

President Wilson met in the cabinet room with Secretary Bryan, who pointed out that the Germans had placed advertisements in American newspapers warning Americans that the *Lusitania* was carrying munitions and might be fired upon. It turned out the munitions—4,200 cases of rifle cartridges and 1,250 cases of shrapnel—were within allowable limits. Still, it did complicate the black-and-white world Lodge and Roosevelt were painting.

As citizens wired the White House and urged war on Germany, Colonel House in London encouraged the president to take a tough stance: "the United States must consider the inevitability of going to war.... America 'must determine whether she stands for civilized or uncivilized warfare.'" That night in Philadelphia, Wilson gave a speech he would soon regret.

"The example of America must be a special example…not merely of peace because it will not fight but of peace because peace is the healing and elevating influence of the world and strife is not. There is such a thing as being too proud to fight. There is such a thing as a nation being so right that it does not need to convince others by force that it is right," he declared.

The newspapers had a field day with "too proud to fight," and many questioned the president's will to take on the Germans. "This was probably the most unfortunate phrase he ever coined," Lodge would say later. "I never again recovered confidence in Mr. Wilson's ability to deal with the most perilous situation which had ever confronted the United States in its relations with other nations of the earth."

Theodore Roosevelt went even further and called Wilson "a prime jackass" and said "he would skin him alive if he didn't declare war on Germany." Even Wilson knew it was a political gaffe and wrote Edith, "If I had said what was worth saying to that great audience last night it must have been because love had complete possession of me."

The next day Wilson backpedaled and said he had been thinking out loud, but privately told Tumulty, "I could go to Congress tomorrow and advocate war with Germany and I feel certain that Congress would support me, but what would the country say when war finally came and we were witnessing all its horror and bloody aftermath."

In the end, Wilson called upon Germany to renounce the act and demanded an explanation. The Germans said the *Lusitania* had been constructed as a war ship, had been carrying the munitions of war, and had flown neutral flags before. The Germans said the British were using Americans as human shields, but they promised to avoid attacking ships from neutral countries.

Wilson drafted a note to the Germans arguing that the *Lusitania* was not a military ship and that it was carrying civilians. Secretary

Bryan didn't like the note. He pointed out to Wilson that he shouldn't be shocked at the drowning of people when he supported the starving of an entire nation with sanctions and blockades (Germany). Bryan refused to sign the letter and offered to resign.

The country was ready for war. Woodrow Wilson had seen the ravages of war as a child and didn't have the bloodlust of Roosevelt. He believed mankind should be able to rise above fighting it out in trenches on the Western Front. At least America should. In a cabinet meeting Wilson crossed swords with Bryan when he accused members of not being neutral toward Germany and Britain. "Mr. Bryan," Wilson said, "you are not warranted in making such an assertion. We all doubtless have our opinions in this matter, but there are none of us who can justly be accused of being unfair."

The issue came up again when the president invited Edith on the presidential yacht, the *Mayflower,* while sailing to New York to review the Atlantic fleet. Woodrow had been quiet during dinner and then he and Edith went for a stroll on deck.

"The night was clear and the Potomac River like silver," Edith wrote later. "...I sensed that something was troubling him. He said: 'Let's lean on the rail instead of walking, as I want to talk to you. I am very much distressed over a letter I had late today from the Secretary of State [Bryan] saying he cannot go on in the Department as he is a pacifist and cannot follow me in wishing to warn our own country and Germany that we may be forced to take up arms; therefore he feels it his duty to resign.'"

Edith turned and said: "Good; for I hope you can replace him with someone who is able and who would in himself command respect for the office both at home and abroad." She then described a play for Wilson where a character was given a chance to act. "Take it, sir, and thank God for the chance," she said, playing on a quote from a play they had just seen. The president smiled and mused out loud about appointing Robert Lansing as a replacement.

"But he is only a clerk in the State Department, isn't he?" Edith asked.

"He is a counselor of the department, and he had a good schooling under old Mr. John W. Foster," the president replied.

The president of the United States was now sounding out important matters of state with his girlfriend. Wilson believed in a team approach and Edith Galt would give him a no-nonsense opinion. Later she would tell him again that she was all for sacking Bryan and added, "I might as well frankly say I would like to be appointed in his place for then I would have daily conferences with you."

"Hurrah! Old Bryan is out!" Edith wrote later after Wilson accepted his resignation. "I know it is going to be the biggest possible relief to you to be rid of him. Your letter is *much* too nice, and I see why *I* was not allowed to see it before publication."

Edith would later refer to Bryan as "that awful Deserter."

Wilson wrote back to his wife:

"You are, oh, so fit for a strong man!...What a dear partisan you are! and how you can hate, too. Whew!...In my secret heart (which is never secret from you)...he is a traitor, though I can say so, as yet, only to you."

Woodrow Wilson was realizing that Edith was a formidable person to have on his side. She could hold a grudge better than any man he knew. He gently suggested that Bryan wasn't the traitor Edith made him out to be, but she did not back down, saying, "You are a fencer so worthy of anyone's steel that fencing becomes a delight.... but you have my heart on your side—which is a tremendous handicap to me..."

Edith continued her rant, saying that if "he [Bryan] were left in my hands by an inscrutable Fate, I would put him where the world would never be troubled with him or his 'peace' sheep's clothing again." Edith was broadcasting to Wilson that everyone in his inner circle was expendable—everyone except for her, of course.

The problem for Woodrow and Edith, as for many new lovers, was getting time alone. There was always Secret Service agent Starling in the back seat or the chauffer in the front seat. They took long drives where the curtains were pulled while they hugged, necked, and probably more. Wilson's wife had died less than a year before and they had to be discreet. Woodrow Wilson was a very sensual man and made the best of a bad situation. The letters reveal what went on behind the curtains.

"For God's sake try to find out if you really love me or not," Wilson wrote in exasperation after one such drive. "You owe it yourself and you owe it to the great love I have given you...remember that I need strength and certainty for the daily task and I cannot walk upon quicksand."

Wilson sounds here like a young man pleading with his girl to give a little. Edith was trying, but her marriage to Norman Galt had not been a romantic one, and probably beyond procreation there was little sex. Still, she promised to make it better in the future.

"I know...that I am asking something that is childish and impossible. But, try as hard as I can, now it seems the only way. If this can be changed it will be because you are the master of my heart and life...but you must conquer!"

Wilson replied, "I have been blind as well as you. I have said that love was supreme and have feared that it was not!"

The curtains would continue to be drawn and Edith would continue to work on "this more than painful subject." Then Wilson's old friend from his Bermuda days appeared, Mary Peck. Wilson was aghast. She had come for a loan for her hard-luck son. Like many people who lived the life of a bohemian, Mary had fallen on hard times and hoped her special relationship with the president might have some cachet.

After a quick tour of the White House, Wilson assumed $7,500 on two mortgages for her son, and Mary left soon thereafter. It wasn't hush money; more like expediency money. It was expedient for Mary

Peck to be on her way because the courtship of Edith Galt was at full speed. Wilson's bodyguard Edmund Starling compared the two women when he wrote in his diary that he thought Mary Peck "a drab, faded woman of middle age" and he didn't see "how anyone could have cast her in a romantic role."

Edith was invited to the presidential retreat at Cornish and on the way back was shown around Princeton. Wilson stayed back and sounded out Colonel House. "What do you think about me getting married again?" House approved, but was privately worried about how voters might react.

At Cornish the couple went for long walks and sat on the porches. Even here, Edith's apprenticeship continued. She would later write, "Cornish is a charming spot, a mecca for artists and cultivated people.... whenever my thoughts turn back to that wonderful summer, there seems about it all a halo of gorgeous color...the President was like a boy home from school...with the curtains drawn to shut out the cold night air, we would gather before the fire and together read the latest dispatches sent from Washington, from Europe, from everywhere. The President would clarify each problem for me, and outline the way he planned to meet it."

After Edith and Woodrow "took care of business," they would sit up in front of the fire. Edith later said the days in Cornish "brought the banishment of any doubt of my love for Woodrow Wilson." She sent him a note after one of these long evenings. "I promise with all my heart absolutely to trust and accept my love...and unite my life with yours without doubts or misgiving."

Things culminated on May 10, 1915, when they told each other they were in love. Cupid triumphed and they became secretly engaged. Edith's training continued as she received bundles of state papers that Wilson commented on. This included a draft of the final note to the Germans over the *Lusitania*. The forty-three-year-old Edith read all of it and gave the president her opinion.

On August 13, she wrote Wilson from Geneva, New York, "I felt so queer this afternoon reading all these reports from different theatres of war, sitting here in my quiet room, away from everything, in a tiny little town beside a calm lake...I—an unknown person, one who had lived a shelter inconspicuous existence."

The president responded by saying "whatever is mine is yours, knowledge of affairs of state not excepted." This is an extraordinary statement for a president, but power is an aphrodisiac, and Edith Galt was clearly attracted to the power of the presidency. On August 24 Wilson sent a large envelope and told Edith it contained shocking news from their consul Snodgrass in Moscow. The Russians were abandoning their defenses and the government was on the run. The Russian Revolution had started and Edith Bolling Galt could say she knew first.

Today, we might believe this to be a violation of secrets of state. But Woodrow Wilson wasn't a man who stood on protocol. He routinely used other people as sounding boards. Edith was a lover, confidant, and advisor all in one. Wilson probably thought he was having his cake and eating it too. He would have never imagined that he was grooming Edith Galt for his seat of power.

# SEVENTEEN

# THE PETTICOAT GOVERNMENT

## 1919

SENATOR ALBERT FALL OF NEW MEXICO WAS FURIOUS. THE SMOKY air in the Senate fumed around him. The floor creaked under his cowboy boots as he paced back and forth among the spittoons. The Mexicans had kidnapped an American diplomat and the White House was doing nothing. Nothing! Falls stopped and smashed his fist on the Senate table. He shouted, *"We have a petticoat government! Wood-row Wilson is not the President...Mrs. Wilson is President!"*

President Edith Wilson was busy. On December 18, Secretary Tumulty sent Edith a letter stating the need to address appointments. "Please don't think I am trying to crowd you or to urge immediate action by the President, but I thought it would help you if you could have before you a list...appointments as follows: Secretary of the Treasury, Secretary of the Interior, Assistant Secretary of Agriculture, Action upon Secretary Lansing's recommendation of William Phillips for Holland, Oklahoma appointments, Civil Service Commission, Federal Trade Commission, Interstate Commerce Commission, United

States Shipping Board, United States Tariff Commission, War Finance Corporation Director, Waterways Commission, Rent Commissioners, Vacancies in Diplomatic Corps for Bulgaria, China, Costa Rica, Italy, Netherlands, Salvador, Siam, Switzerland."

The stasis is obvious in the situation of the secretary of the interior, Franklin Lane. He had wanted for some time to resign and accept a position outside of government, but in December 1919, he could find no one to accept his resignation. "Things are going well notwithstanding the President's illness," Lane wrote to a friend in frustration. "No one is satisfied that we know the truth, and every dinner table is filled with speculation. Some say paralysis, and some say insanity. Grayson tells me it is nervous breakdown, whatever that means."

Finally on January 5, Lane asked Grayson to "be perfectly frank" and advise him what to do. It was time for the new president to step in. Edith summoned Secretary of Agriculture David Houston to meet with her. Houston had a bad cold, but Edith said to come anyway. They met in the sitting room and after the servants had cleared the tea, Edith looked at Houston and said: "You are wondering why I wanted to see you and why I sent for you this afternoon...the President asked me to tell you that he is very anxious for you to accept the Secretaryship of the Treasury."

Houston, who had been fiercely loyal to the president, did not flinch. "Please give my greetings to the President and tell him that I am very grateful to him for this further evidence of his confidence. I am in the harness until March 4, 1921, if he wishes it, and as long as I am with him I will dig stumps, or act as Secretary of Treasury or assume any other task he assigns to me."

Edith smiled.

"That is very interesting," she replied. "That is just what the President said you would say."

Houston later wrote where the conversation went after that.

"Mrs. Wilson said that the President would like to know whether I had anybody in mind to suggest for Secretary of Agriculture. I asked if he was thinking of anybody. 'Yes Meredith,' she replied." Houston replied that Meredith came from the right section and was in touch with agricultural problems through his newspaper. "She then asked whether I had anybody in mind whom I could suggest for the position of Secretary of the Interior. She added, 'The President is somewhat embarrassed. Secretary Lane has resigned…in the press. The President has not been officially informed of his going. He would like your judgment.'"

The president might never be informed of Lane's resignation. In one of the more revealing letters of Edith Wilson's new position, she settles the appointment of secretary of interior once and for all on December 28.

> My Dear Mr. Jones,
>
> This afternoon the President asked me to write to you for him and dictated the following—"Will you permit me to nominate you Secretary of the Interior and thus complete my official family and fulfill my dearest birthday wish."

Edith then continues.

> I am sure you have seen from the papers that Mr. Lane wants to resign, and is only waiting until my husband is better before making it definite. I am sure you feel that with you at the head of this Department the President would rest secure knowing your splendid ability and loyalty. Just now he needs this assurance, for he has so many things that necessarily must come direct to him, that he longs to have you, and those like you, to depend on, while he is convalescing.

I am writing you frankly, because I know I can, and will you be good enough to let him hear as soon as you can—for it will greatly relieve his anxiety. Please address the letter to me as otherwise it will be opened in the office. We send you every good wish for 1920...I have written in the midst of interruptions so please pardon repetition.

Faithfully Submitted, Edith Bolling Wilson

Edith dispenses with the charade that the president is in charge and has the letter directed to her because the president is *convalescing*.

The Volstead Act belied the claim Edith made years later, "I, myself, never made a single decision regarding the disposition of public affairs." The Volstead Act was the law enforcing prohibition under the Eighteenth Amendment. President Wilson didn't support the proposed law and had threatened a veto earlier, but now he was barely conscious and couldn't sign the veto. All signs point to Edith's approving it without her husband's knowledge. As John Milton Cooper writes in *Woodrow Wilson*, "Tumulty wrote the message, almost certainly with Edith's consent, and Secretary of Agriculture Houston revised it." This action was consistent with Wilson's opposition to prohibition. Congress would override the veto the next day.

The issue of presidential signatures is a vexing one. Presidents must sign many documents and the operation of government can be held up for want of a signature. But here was a man paralyzed on his left side going in and out of consciousness. Edith "helped" the president by "steadying his right hand and guiding the pen." But there were questions.

It is interesting to note that early on Edith was concerned with Tumulty's ability to replicate the presidential signature "I never liked Tumulty, but got along with him in spite of that. One thing that made me nervous was that he could copy the President's signature so even

I could not tell the difference." Woodrow Wilson's well-known signature had been affixed to important documents, including a declaration of war. But now the signature had dramatically changed.
Senators took this as evidence that the first lady was either signing
documents or that she was guiding the president's hand.

Edith did sign documents, probably many of them. President
Wilson was a paralyzed man who could barely talk, had lost control
of his bodily functions, and lived in post-stroke twilight. There is no
doubt Edith Wilson signed when necessary. As his valet Ike Hoover
observed, "Finally, when it could no longer be delayed some matters
of importance requiring his signature were read to him and with a
pencil, his hand steadied and pointed, he would sign where the hand
had been placed. I saw many of these signatures and they were but
mere scribbles compared to his normal signature."

Edith governed by access, often funneling correspondence away
from the president. When Wilson's advisor Colonel House returned
from Europe, representing the interests of the president with the
various governments involved in the Treaty of Versailles, Edith chose
not to tell the president he was back. This incensed House and was
the first indication that she was running the White House.

House wasn't really a colonel at all. Educated at Cornell, House
was a novelist and political progressive. He had helped elect four Texas
governors before moving to New Jersey and becoming a close friend
and supporter of then-Governor Woodrow Wilson. When Wilson was
elected president, House declined an official position, seeing more
power in the role of "Presidential confidante." He became a key player
in foreign affairs and was the chief broker in the negotiations to end
World War I. After the sinking of the *Lusitania*, he believed war was
inevitable.

House had helped Wilson with the Fourteen Points, the statement
of principles that helped end World War I, as well as in writing the

Treaty of Versailles and the Covenant of the League of Nations. He was Wilson's man on the spot during the negotiations in Paris, but when the president left he bargained away the League of Nations. The two men diverged further as House favored compromise with Henry Cabot Lodge to get the treaty ratified. Things got worse when House's son-in-law Gordon Auchincloss, working on the American peace commission, said derogatory things about Wilson and the president dismissed him.

Edith had long seen House as power crazy and made it a point to keep the colonel away from her husband. The colonel became frustrated and went to the White House, where Edith intercepted him. He offered to do anything he could for the president, to which Edith replied coldly, "Thank you for your offer to be of service. I know of nothing now, for the best cure seems to be rest and freedom from everything."

The colonel didn't buy it and years later wrote, "My separation from Woodrow Wilson was and is to me a tragic mystery..." He blamed the "bedroom circle." House wasn't wrong. Edith had strong likes and dislikes, and to fall into the latter category was to be banished. Even Joseph Tumulty suffered. "Mrs. Wilson is keeping me from the President," he told friends. Even if House and Tumulty had seen the president, it is doubtful it would have made a difference. He was in the depths of a severe stroke and fighting for his cerebral life.

Postmaster General Burleson complained to Tumulty that the president hadn't acted on a series of Post Office appointments. The secretary then sent a letter to Mrs. Wilson requesting action. The letter came back, "The President says he is waiting to discuss the matter with Mr. Burleson. E. B.W." Those initials would become very familiar. If anyone tried to see the president they were met by a tall woman who responded to any request for an interview with her husband by saying once again, "I am not interested in the President of the United States. I am interested in my husband and his health."

*Request Denied E.B.W.*

This was not the age of email. It was not even the age of fax. This was the age of letters and telegrams. It was an epistolary age with voluminous mail flowing into the White House from outside and inside. Letters came from the various departments by messenger and were routed to the president accordingly. The letters now went into a void and many would not be opened until 1952 in the National Archives. It wasn't that Edith was consciously disposing of correspondence, it was just that she had no answers. Answers required troubling the president. Answers endangered his health. So there would be no answers unless Edith could solve the problem. Bills were passed without signatures. Orders were given without signatures. Shortcuts were taken where they could be.

A good example was when the Secretary of the Navy Josephus Daniels had some midshipman who got drunk on a cruise and contacted syphilis or "immoral diseases." To kick the midshipman out of the Naval Academy, the secretary needed the president to endorse his action. He sent the necessary letter. He heard nothing. The secretary sent another letter. He heard nothing. The midshipman stayed in the Navy.

Something as mundane as resignations couldn't be accomplished. Herbert Hoover had a series of wartime posts from which he had to resign. The letters of his resignation were never accepted and technically he was still employed by the government. Little things like these, which make up the everyday functioning of government, were often neglected, but there were big things not being attended to as well.

Lord Grey from Britain had been waiting to present his credentials as ambassador. He remained in limbo. Nor was there anyone to recognize the new government of Costa Rica. Joe Tumulty sent up these requests to the family quarters, but nothing came back. The pleadings from the president's secretary (this position later changed to chief of staff) to Edith Wilson sound almost sophomoric.

*"Dear Mrs. Wilson, I hope you will let the President read the enclosed papers..."*

*"Dear Mrs. Wilson, Will you kindly read the enclosed letter..."*

*"Dear Mrs. Wilson, This matter is vitally important that I send this letter to you..."*

*"Dear. Mrs. Wilson, I know the President will not be pleased with some parts of this editorial, but I hope you will have a chance to read it to him..."*

*"Dear Mrs. Wilson, Will you please have the President mark 'Accepted' on the Fletcher resignation so that we may dispose of this matter..."*

*"Dear Mrs. Wilson, I do not know whom the President intends to appoint to succeed..."*

As Tumulty later wrote, "Dozens of appointment-to-office forms were sent up for signature and, unsigned, they piled up, although the men they concerned would be taken into governmental offices and assigned work." Forty years later the same unsigned forms would resurface in files. The deciding of what was important and what was not was ongoing. We can imagine Edith holding envelopes, muttering to herself: *essential, not essential, essential, not essential.* It was governing by assigning importance, and nothing was more important than the president's health. Tumulty was reduced to asking the president's daughter, Margaret Wilson, to ask the president questions "when you think fit." Lord Grey was still hanging around four months later. After having gone so far as to try and get his aide Craufurd-Stuart tossed out of the country, Edith then simply ignored Grey, and even after Secretary Lansing (another man Edith detested) suggested she meet with him for an informal chat, she still did not reply.

Finally Tumulty sent a note to Edith: "Dear Mrs. Wilson, What shall I say?" The response...nothing. Lord Grey sailed back to England with no goodbye telegram, no letter even recognizing he had come. Edith had used her best weapon of governing: absolute silence. Freeze the dogs until they go away.

But things did get accomplished. As Gene Smith wrote in *When the Cheering Stopped*, "Over the wide left margins of an elegantly typed letter, down to the bottom space under the typing, up the right margin and then across the top, weaving in and out of the title of the writer and his seal of office, there were each day penciled notes by a woman who had a total of just two years formal schooling and whose round and enormous script resembled that of a twelve year old. The reader of these notes, Secretary of War, of Labor, or whatever—would have to rotate his returned letter in his hands and sometimes continue on to the envelope to find out what the message in the childish handwriting was."

Again, each scrawl began, "The president says" or "The president wants" with no one to say what the president did say or did not say. Lansing wrote to secretary Tumulty again on the issue of the recognition of the provisional government of Costa Rica. He felt the president would want to move ahead and Tumulty wrote to Edith with the letter attached:

"When you think an opportune time has arrived, will you not be good enough to present the attached letter to the President from Secretary Lansing?"

Edith responded in a scrawled note on White House stationary: "The President says it is impossible for him to take up such matters until he is stronger and can study them. So if an answer must be made—the Sec of State can say he cannot act without the President's consent and that the P directs the matter be held in abeyance until he can act."

Secretary Lansing grew frustrated with the process and told friends, "The President is in such a condition that he was utterly unable to attend to public business." He then said that he often sent Edith memos reduced to their essentials and received in reply "answers communicated through Mrs. Wilson so confused that no one could interpret them."

Secretary Lansing wrote to Wilson again on November 5 about the friction between the United States and Great Britain over the holding of the Imperator group of ships by the U.S. shipping board. Lansing believed that the seven ships being held should immediately be returned to Great Britain. The three-page letter was forwarded to Tumulty, who forwarded it to the president. Edith responded on the bottom half of the memo in her now trademark scrawl: "The President says he does not know enough about this matter to act upon it and that no action can be taken until he is well enough to act upon it...EBW."

Secretary of State Lansing then wrote to Wilson on the military situation of Syria. "'I venture to suggest should it meet with your approval,' instructing the ambassadors to England and France to inform the Peace Conference and British government that since the United States Mission was not prepared to take part, Washington would have no objections to other powers proceeding with those negotiations."

Tumulty once again wrote to Edith requesting she speak to the president about the memorandum from the secretary of state. Lansing followed this with a memorandum of a list of issues that needed to be dealt with. The reply came on a sheet of undated paper:

"The President says please inform the State Dept. he will not act on these until he is stronger."

Lansing then sent another letter asking what to do about their representatives in Paris since the United States had still not ratified the peace treaty. Tumulty was the messenger boy and wrote to Edith: "Dear

Mrs. Wilson, I leave it to your judgement as to what to do with this letter." Edith responded to Lansing this time, initialing her letter EBW.

"The President says he agrees with the Secretary as regards to withdrawing out representatives in Paris and of retaining our member of the 'Supreme Council.'"

No one knows who was behind these scrawled responses. Edith banished Gilbert Close, Wilson's confidential secretary and one of two stenographers. Close didn't see the president again until he resigned. Close later remarked, "I just had nothing to do and I got awfully tired of doing nothing." The truth was Close had been replaced by Edith, who scribbled presidential directions on anything at hand.

At a point, Edith decided the scrawled instructions weren't working very well and took to receiving cabinet members in her sitting room. She would instruct the secretaries of the various departments in what the president wanted done. Sometimes the cabinet member would ask for clarification and Edith replied that he must make do with her instructions. The fact is that none of the cabinet men saw the president and few saw his writing except for the strange signatures appearing on documents. When Ike Hoover procured a wheelchair from Atlantic City that gave the president the ability to keep from falling out, the cabinet members would spy a slumped figure in the distance on the South Portico, scarcely believing that man was the president of the United States.

The business of the United States piled up at the "Edith Wilson dam" like driftwood after a flood. Secretary Tumulty took it upon himself to send Edith a laundry list of the most pressing issues. He mentioned that the railroads taken over during the war needed to be returned to the owners, that Costa Rica still needed to be recognized, and that a commission should be set up to deal with the miners' strike. Tumulty then added issues concerning the League of Nations.

No one knows what Edith did with Tumulty's letter. But few appointments were made. No commission was set up to settle the strike. Costa Rica was never recognized, the post office appointments were never made, and the midshipman never disciplined. Tumulty handled what he could, but the nation was in transition after the war, and there was nobody home to guide the ship. Unemployment would rise from 3 million to 4.75 million in 1919 and a coal strike threatened the fragile economy.

Tumulty wrote a statement on the coal strike that the president never saw and handled the transition of the railroads back to private ownership. He asked Edith to have Wilson sign a letter written by Walker Hines on the railroads and received a typical EBW response. "The President says he cannot do anything with the RR situation until he can write something himself to send or deliver to Congress." The president was in a dark misty land and Edith was trying her best to keep a finger in the dam.

# EIGHTEEN

# THE OTHER WOMAN

## 1915

**IT'S THE SUMMER OF 1915 AND THE WHITE HOUSE IS ON A SUMMER** schedule with a lot of people on hiatus. Woodrow Wilson prowls the musty halls like a man in a prison. Edith said she would marry him after the election of 1916. She didn't want to be the wife of a sitting president, understanding any chance of privacy or a real personal life would vanish if she became the new first lady. She assumed Wilson would lose the election and they could go on with their lives and enjoy the world as Mr. and Mrs. Woodrow Wilson.

But Germany was still sinking ships and the president had come to realize that war was inevitable. He was depressed in the torrid heat of vacant Washington and wrote Edith no fewer than 250 letters pouring out his feelings for her and detailing his heavy responsibilities. She was "the companion I want (nobody satisfies my mind or my fancy as you do) the counsellor I want (nobody steadies me as you do) the wife I want (nobody can glorify or complete my life or give me happiness as you can)."

Edith was weakening in her determination to wait until after the summer of 1916 to marry. "Though I tried to keep to what I then deemed to be a wise decision, Mr. Wilson's letters told in every line his need of the sustaining power of love..." He was wearing her down, and the truth was that Wilson was being worn down by the dark clouds of World War I now gathering over the United States.

Edith and Wilson began to golf and she continued to dine at the White House, sharing long car rides afterward when Wilson would talk about the coming war. On one of these rides, Woodrow seemed particularly disturbed over America's inevitable entrance into the conflict. After painting a dark picture, he turned and said, "And so, little girl, I have no right to ask you to help me by sharing this load that is almost breaking my back, for I know your nature and you might do it out of sheer pity."

The chauffeur and the Secret Service agent were in the car along with Helen Bones in the back seat. Edith paused and then consented to become the next Mrs. Wilson. As she would later write, "I put my arms around his neck and said, 'Well, if you won't ask me, I will volunteer and be ready to be mustered in as soon as can be.'"

So much for waiting until after the election; they told the president's daughters, Margaret and Nell, of their engagement the next morning. Margaret wrote, "I'm so glad that he has your love to help him and support him in these terrible times." Edith told her mother and her brothers and sisters that she wanted to wait a year for the wedding, but the president couldn't wait that long.

They made their first public appearance at a World Series game in Philadelphia, where Wilson became the first president to throw out the first pitch. Newspapers noted that the president spent more time talking to Edith Galt than watching the game. Still, they had gone public with their relationship and this took a lot of pressure off the new couple. They could now court in the open.

The president had announced that he was going to support women's suffrage in New Jersey and some speculated this position was due to the influence of his young fiancée. The truth was that Edith didn't believe in the suffrage movement and Wilson supported only state suffrage. He didn't believe that the right of women to vote was a federal issue and privately thought the vote would hurt American families.

John Tyler and Grover Cleveland were the only two presidents who had married while in office and there were many who saw the president's quick engagement to be in bad taste. Henry Cabot Lodge took a dim view of the "vulgar marriage," seeing all that he detested in Wilson also in the new first lady-in-waiting. A local columnist in *Town Topics* went after Edith's standing in an October 14 article: "From an obscure position in Washington society—obscure because her husband was in trade—Mrs. Galt becomes Mistress of the White House.... The tradesman's widow is exalted to the first position in the land."

Some felt Edith was a distraction for the president, and there was talk of neglected business and of the president's "obsession" with his girlfriend. And those in the White House inner circle didn't like the politics of the marriage at all. One year after the death of his wife the president was marrying a young shapely woman with no real pedigree except that she came from an old Virginia family.

The grieving widower would no longer be honoring the memory of his dead wife. It was 1915 and mourning still had to be done, traditionally a year. Besides, the election was only twelve months away. Somebody had to put the brakes on the thing and at least get the president to wait until after the election. Enter the other woman, Mary Peck, who had recently asked Wilson for a loan for her son.

Mary and Edith had some similarities. They were both women whom life had dealt hard blows and who had an unusual amount of freedom. One can see Woodrow Wilson on the beach having the same conversation about being president with Edith that he had had with Mary Peck. Wilson seemed to be attracted to a certain bohemian quality in both women. The epistolary relationship between him and Mary Peck had become voluminous during those years. Now she would be used as a chess piece against the president.

There were rumors that Mary had been offering to sell the president's letters to the highest bidder. Not that there was anything overtly scandalous in them, but a long correspondence with another married woman was enough to hurt his reelection prospects. There was no real evidence that Mary Peck was about to unload the president's personal correspondence. But Colonel House had Wilson's son-in-law, William Gibbs McAdoo, do the dirty work. House and others calculated that even the threat of the letters being made public would force the president to slow down the marriage. McAdoo met with the president and told him the letters were about to be sold. Wilson was devastated and knew what this would mean to his fiancée.

He wrote to Edith and said, "there was something, personal to myself, that I must tell you about at once." He asked if he might call on her at home and she said for him to come to her. But the president didn't go and then "went white to his lips" when he tried to write her. He would later write to her about "a passage of folly and gross impertinence…" Finally, he sent Dr. Grayson to tell Edith the whole story and to release her from their engagement.

Grayson did as he was told and Edith was stunned. From her vantage point, it did look sordid. She told Dr. Grayson to let the president know she would think on it and would write him. She wrote in her memoir years later, "When he was gone, I sat for hours thinking, when, as suddenly as the blow had fallen, its weight lifted, and I saw things in their true proportions. It was our lives that mattered, not politics, not scandal. If I did not care enough for the man to share his misfortunes, his sorrows, then it was a futile love!"

Edith sat down and wrote the president a testament of her love for him. "The dawn has come and the hideous dark of the hour before the dawn has been lost in the gracious gift of light. I have been in the big chair by the window where I have fought out so many problems and all the hurt selfish feeling has gone with the darkness and now I see straight, straight into the heart of things and am ready to follow the road where love leads…I am not afraid of any gossip or threat, with your love as my shield and even now this room echoes with your voice as you plead, 'Stand by me…don't desert me!' This is my pledge dearest one, I will stand by you, not for duty, not for honor, but for love…trusting protecting, comprehending love…. "

Edith mailed the letter in the morning and waited. She received no word back. Two days passed and still no word from the president. Then on the third day, Dr. Grayson appeared at her door and, "Without even shaking hands, he said, 'I need you to come with me to the White House. The president is very ill and you are the only person who can help. I can do nothing…he does not sleep, eat, or speak.'"

Edith didn't know what to do. Why had the president not responded? Had her letter been intercepted? She now doubted Wilson's love for her, but "Then I remembered what I had written, 'I will stand by.'" She went with Grayson to the White House and to the president's bedroom.

Edith would write later, "The curtains were drawn and the room dark; on the pillow I saw a white, drawn face with burning eyes dark with hidden pain." She went to the bed and the president held out his hand. "No word was spoken, only an eager hand held out in welcome, which I took to find icy cold. Strangely in these tense moments things are understood with no need of words. I never asked him why he had not answered my letter, only had it reached him. He said, 'Yes.'"

It is amazing: a president who can't get out of bed at the prospect of losing his fiancée. Woodrow Wilson was prone to wild mood swings that at times prevented him from functioning. He seemed to have the heart of a Victorian poet in which the spurned romantic lover sees only darkness. F. Scott Fitzgerald once said, "a sentimentalist is someone who hopes things will last, while the romantic has the desperate conviction they won't." The ardent letter writer did seem to have a bit of the tragic romantic about him.

One night three months later, Wilson said he had a confession to make to Edith. He drew out the letter she had written him from his pocket and she saw the seal on the envelope was unbroken. The president looked at her and as Edith recounted later, said, "I think I am rarely a coward; but when this letter came that Sunday morning after a sleepless night, I could not open it, for I felt the world slipping from under my feet."

Woodrow then opened the letter and they read it together. It was a testament of her love for a man in his darkest moment. The president begged her to make sure the letter was never destroyed. Clearly, Woodrow Wilson couldn't bear the thought of reading a letter where he might lose Edith.

The Mary Peck letters were never sold, and the closest they came to being made public was in 1912 when Teddy Roosevelt declined to publish one of the letters, wanting to maintain the public image of Wilson as a phlegmatic "druggist" (as he called him) and not a lover. Years later, Edith would confront Colonel House about the contrivance to stop their marriage and House would seal his fate by admitting his part.

The letter survives today.

# NINETEEN

# MR. AND MRS. PRESIDENT

## 1915

IT IS DECEMBER AND THE SNOW IN WASHINGTON LINES THE sidewalks and hoods the headlamps of Model Ts and the big Pierce-Arrow that would drop the president at Edith's home. They had announced their engagement and the high drama of the early days was gone. Now they could spend time together as a properly engaged couple.

Many times Wilson would shake off the presidential limousine and walk back to the White House from Edith's house with Agent Starling trailing behind. One can imagine the long-legged strides as this man in love traversed the soft crunching snow. Wilson would hum to himself and whistle, his breath luminous against the arc lights, and then while Starling watched, he would break into song. He had found true love again and this was of more immediate concern than Germany's insistence on sinking just about any ship on the North Atlantic.

Agent Starling was not used to this. The morose man who seemed like a Dickens character was now as light and animated as George Cohan, the man who wrote "Over There" and other patriotic ditties. Many times Starling would watch the president puffing smoke in the Washington night as he walked briskly, breaking into song, "Oh you beautiful doll, you great big beautiful doll!" And then to Starling's utter amazement, the president would jump up and click his heels. But there were people who disapproved of the relationship. They felt the president had moved on too quickly after his wife's death and bawdy jokes about Edith were bandied about. One joke making the circuit went: "When Wilson proposed to the second Mrs. Wilson, she was so surprised she nearly fell out of bed."

On Sundays after church the couple would often seclude themselves in the White House. The Secret Service followed Edith everywhere and among themselves said she was a very attractive woman with a full figure. The fifty-nine-year-old president had done very well for himself. The White House was re-energized. The president began smiling in photos and activity abounded with preparations for the wedding and Mrs. Wilson's arrival.

They would marry in Edith's house. "My house was turned over to the decorators and caterers," she later wrote. "Mr. Hoover had offered to relieve me of all the detail in these matters." And then came the first snafu that would foreshadow an imperial will. Edith was an Episcopalian and the president was Presbyterian. Both faiths would be represented at the wedding and Edith called on an Episcopalian bishop to perform part of the ceremony. All was fine until the bishop showed up with his wife.

As Edith wrote in her memoir, "I could not ask his wife to be present as I was asking no one outside our immediate families, and as she did not live in Washington it would not seem a discourtesy to omit her." The bishop felt otherwise and had brought his wife, writing the future first lady that "they were sailing in a few days for England where it would cause his wife 'much chagrin to acknowledge to her titled friends she had not been asked to the marriage of the President where her husband had officiated.'"

The bishop felt sure his wife would be welcome at the ceremony. Edith wasted no time in her reply. "I walked straight to my desk and wrote the answer. I thanked the Bishop for letting me know of the embarrassing situation his wife found herself in regarding my wedding, but I reminded him that I had explained why I could not include her in the wedding party."

Edith then rang up the president and told him she was firing the bishop. Wilson counseled caution.

"Why not wait and think it over a little?"

In what would become a hallmark of the Edith Wilson presidency, the line between politics and personal was forever obscured.

"No," she replied. "This letter goes to him right now. I will postpone our wedding rather than be bludgeoned into a thing of this kind."

President Wilson was faintly amused and replied, "Yes, I was afraid of that. But after all, the poor fellow has enough to stand with a wife like that."

Edith sent the letter and the bishop was replaced. This is emblematic of the way the president's wife would deal with problems. If people crossed Edith they were removed, banished, isolated, or fired. The bishop never got past the front steps, and we can only imagine his chagrin when he realized his wife had cost him a place in history. Edith omitted his name in her memoir; not worth the ink, really.

December 18 came clear with a dusting of snow the night before, making the streets of Washington cheery and the air cold and bracing; a perfect day to marry a president. "The President reached my house a half hour before the time for the ceremony, coming alone except for the escort of the Secret Service." Wilson went to her sitting room and waited until Hoover his valet knocked on the door. "It's time, Mr. President."

Edith Galt and Woodrow Wilson descended the stairs together to the strings of the Marine Band playing the wedding march. The couple walked down the stairs and giving up their former lives, entered into a new world. They had a buffet supper of "oyster patties, boned capon, Virginia ham, chicken salad, caramel ice cream, and a three-tiered wedding cake." Then they slipped upstairs for some James Bond maneuvers with the press.

No one knew the destination of the honeymoon except Agent Starling and the chauffeur. "We had a lovely drive over in the moonlight with the world lying white with snow around us," Edith would recall. Agent Starling had made sure the train car was ready and the Pierce-Arrow was aboard along with another car for the Secret Service. They shook the press and ended up down at the edge of a freight yard. Starling blinked his flashlight three times and the Wilsons and their entourage entered the train car.

"The railway car was filled with flowers. On a table some dainty sandwiches and fruit were arranged," Edith wrote later, "and so we left about midnight for our two week's holiday." The engineer received his orders and the train left for The Homestead in Hot Springs, Virginia, a resort of natural springs nestled in the mountains. Agent Starling approached Wilson's bedroom in the morning and saw a man in tails and a top hat, singing, dancing a jig, and once again, clicking his heels.

The couple enjoyed the view of the mountains from their room and played golf and enjoyed the warm springs. One day they drove to White Sulphur Springs but found the road blocked by a stream that had overflowed. The chauffeur was afraid the car might get swamped. As Edith wrote, "We decided to get out and let him try it and see if we could make it…we would cross on a tree which had fallen across the stream."

The big Pierce-Arrow plunged though the water and did make it, so the president and first lady had to inch across the fallen tree. Edith would later recall: "The old tree which was to form a bridge for us was slippery and wet and very rotten in places; but by forming a sort of human chain—the five Secret Service men, the two chauffeurs and ourselves—we steadied one another with a real thrill of adventure reached safety."

On December 30, a U-Boat sunk the British cruiser *Persia*, leaving 350 people to die in the icy water. Then two more ships were sunk in the Mediterranean. The Germans were moving toward unrestricted submarine warfare with the calculation that President Wilson would be slow to react and by the time the Americans mobilized it would be too late. The newlyweds would soon face America's First World War and the repercussions would eventually put Edith in the White House. There would be no more helping hands across the treacherous waters waiting for the happy couple. The honeymoon was cut short and from here on, Edith and Woodrow Wilson would have to go it alone.

# TWENTY

# THE LEAGUE FIGHT

## 1919

HENRY CABOT LODGE WORE SPATS AND WAXED THE TIPS OF HIS mustache. His wife had died the year before and he had become cold. The world seemed to be turning away from him, and the pompous man in the White House had been a continual irritant. He detested the Southern academic who fancied himself an oracle of knowledge. He was not, Lodge thought. More like a Southern blowhard who had no idea what he was doing. The League of Nations would never see the light of day. And the woman he married was as common as dirt.

One cannot underestimate the role that the League of Nations played in Edith Wilson's White House. The League had been a cloak and dagger character in the play between Senator Lodge and President Wilson ever since he went to Paris to negotiate the peace treaty. The president had fought World War I using every resource at his disposal. But as Colonel House observed, the president was "not well fitted" to be a war president. "He was too refined, too civilized, too intellectual, too cultivated not to see the incongruity and absurdity of war."

What House gleaned was that Wilson would have to attach World War I to the Fourteen Points as the basis for Germany's surrender and the founding of the League of Nations. The League, unlike its child, the United Nations, relied on a provision called Article X, which said that all nations would be obligated to act together against an aggressor nation. This would keep the peace as no one country would take on the world. This was Woodrow Wilson's answer to the millions of dead soldiers. American mothers had not given their sons in vain, because the world would have an organization ending war.

President Wilson had gone to Europe to negotiate the Treaty of Versailles with the League of Nations at the center. Upon his return, he ran into a brick wall called Henry Cabot Lodge. Lodge, a conservative senator from Massachusetts, had graduated from Harvard and received the first Ph.D. in history from the university. After becoming Massachusetts' representative, he became a close friend of Teddy Roosevelt and joined the Mugwump faction of the Republican Party.

Lodge had a razor-sharp mind that didn't bother with idealistic niceties. He was vain, vindictive, and would do anything to further a cause. When he became senator, he was the unofficial majority leader of the Senate for the Republican Party. Lodge was critical of President Wilson's handling of the war—from the sinking of the *Lusitania* to the perceived loftiness of the Fourteen Points. He lambasted the president about his slow entry into the war and thought Wilson's conduct played to the pacifists and let the United States go unprepared for too long.

In Lodge's view, the president was an idealist in his dealings with Germany. Lodge believed that Germany should be broken economically and militarily. But he reserved his greatest ammunition for the League of Nations and what he saw as a breach of America's sovereignty. He loathed Woodrow Wilson and the League of Nations equally.

"I never expected to hate anyone in politics with the hatred I feel toward Wilson," Lodge would confide to his friend and political ally Teddy Roosevelt. This fight gave the Brahmin pilgrim vision to stop the high-minded Southern preacher. The League, in Lodge's view, violated the Monroe Doctrine as well as George Washington's tenet to avoid foreign entanglements. Only Congress could authorize the use of American troops.

"The United States is the world's best hope, but if you fetter her in the interests and quarrels of other nations, if you tangle her in the intrigues of Europe, you will destroy her power for good, and endanger her very existence. Leave her to march freely through the centuries to come, as in the years that have gone. Strong, generous, and confident, she has nobly served mankind. Beware how you trifle with your marvelous inheritance, this great land of ordered liberty, for if we stumble and fall, freedom and civilization everywhere will go down in ruin."

This was Senator Lodge's problem with Article X. He was dealt a blow when his amendments were defeated, but he began tacking on reservations to water the League down. Lodge was a superb parliamentarian and said to a colleague, "I do not propose to beat it by direct frontal attack, but by the indirect method of reservations." Lodge also had an eye to the 1920 election. Congress split into a patchwork quilt of people: those against the treaty, those for reservations, and those for mild reservations. Lodge and the majority of Republicans would never approve the treaty the way it stood and President Wilson would never accept changes. The problem for Wilson was that the two-thirds majority required for ratification was out of reach and he had come back from Europe severely weakened. He saw only one alternative and that was to take the League to the people.

As Edith wrote, "The increasing demands on my husband's brain and body exacted a toll which pyramided...when there was apparently no more he could do alone to get the treaty ratified by the Senate, he said that...he must go to the country to explain what failure to ratify the Treaty would mean." The president's whistle-stop tour was working when he fell ill and was forced to go back to Washington. Wilson might have been able to negotiate with the strengthened hand of public opinion. As it turned out, he was unable to participate in any League negotiations in October and November. "Picture the situation when my husband was stricken," Edith wrote later. "His tour a success; public sentiment which had been worked upon incessantly by the enemies of the League once more responding to Mr. Wilson's logic; the initiative again in the hands of the friends of the treaty...and then the President laid low, ruled out of the fight, which he would have continued though he knew it would cost him his life."

After President Wilson's stroke, Edith became the general in the war against Lodge. This was terrible timing for there were Republicans (mild reservationists) who could have thrown in with the Democrats upon Wilson's approval. But the Democrats weren't willing to do anything until they heard from the president and nothing was coming from the White House. The problem was that the president depended on Edith and Dr. Grayson for information. As William Allen White writes, "Admiral Grayson had no access to the truth about public opinion, no means of interpreting the facts, no great interest in the clamor outside the sick-room. Tumulty saw his chief rarely, with Mrs. Wilson standing at the head of the bed to shake her head when he broached a subject that might irritate the President. It was easier for those about him to hold to his face the mirror of his own conception of public opinion than to irritate him with the story of a gradual, inevitable change in the American attitude to the League of Nations."

The Republicans were left with the Lodge proposal of fourteen reservations as the basis for bargaining. It all pivoted on Article X and how it could be tweaked to be acceptable to Senator Lodge and the president. This was the circumstance that led to Senator Hitchcock's

Thirteen-year-old Edith Bolling in Wytheville, Virginia. *Courtesy the Library of Congress*

President Woodrow Wilson and First Lady Edith Bolling Wilson participating in Armistice Day activities. *Courtesy the Library of Congress*

Dr. Cary Grayson, who gave updates to the press on the president's condition.
*Courtesy the Library of Congress*

Edith ran Galt Jewelers successfully after her first husband Norman Galt died.
*Courtesy the Library of Congress*

Woodrow Wilson and
Edith Bolling Wilson in
the back seat of a Pierce-
Arrow. *Courtesy the Library
of Congress*

Edith and Woodrow
taking a drive. *Courtesy
the Library of Congress*

Edith Bolling Wilson remained active in public life after Woodrow Wilson's death. *Courtesy the Library of Congress*

Edith Bolling Wilson at an event after the death of Woodrow Wilson. *Courtesy the Library of Congress*

President Woodrow Wilson asking Congress to declare war on Germany, causing the United States to enter World War I. *Courtesy the Library of Congress*

The childish scrawl that ended up on many official documents. *Courtesy the Library of Congress*

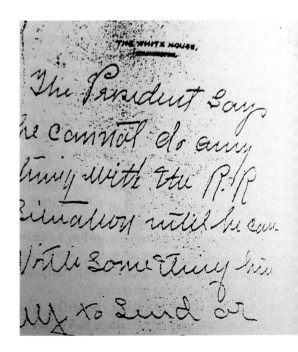

Joseph Patrick Tumulty, private secretary to Woodrow Wilson. *Courtesy the Library of Congress*

Colonel Edward Mandell House, foreign policy advisor to Woodrow Wilson during World War I. *Courtesy the Library of Congress*

Henry Cabot Lodge.
*Courtesy the Library of Congress*

Railroad guard on
duty during the Great
Railroad Strike of 1922.
*Courtesy the Library of
Congress*

Silent Sentinels of Maryland picket the White House for suffrage in early 1917. Suffragettes are shown during the "Maryland Day" picket. *Wikimedia Commons*

Picket line of November 10, 1917. Left to right: Mrs. Catherine Martinette, Eagle Grove, Iowa. Mrs. William Kent, Kentfield, California. Miss Mary Bartlett Dixon, Easton, Maryland. Mrs. C. T. Robertson, Salt Lake City, Utah. Miss Cora Week, New York City. Miss Amy R. Ju[e]ungling, Buffalo, New York. Miss Hattie Kruger, Buffalo, New York. Miss Belle Sheinberg, New York City. Miss Julia Emory, Baltimore, Maryland. *Courtesy the Library of Congress*

becoming the first man to see the president after the royals' visit. Lodge smelled blood with the president sidelined and was going in for the kill.

On November 15, Senator Hitchcock informed Edith about the situation in the Senate. "My Dear Mrs. Wilson, Great progress was made today in consideration of the Lodge reservations, the Senate adopting reservations 4 to 13 inclusive... the time is close at hand when I must learn from the President definitely whether in his judgment the friends of the treaty should vote against the adoption of the resolution of ratification containing these Lodge reservations and thus defeat it."

This letter from Hitchcock was followed by another, from Secretary Tumulty. "Dear Mrs. Wilson, Will you get the following information to the President before he sees Senator Hitchcock this morning. Senator Underwood says the President ought to insist on his friends in the Senate voting to defeat the Lodge resolution of ratification, and that he should insist upon Senator Hitchcock's favoring a vote on unconditional ratification of the Treaty."

Edith had barred Senator Hitchcock from seeing the president in October, but relented later in November. Hitchcock spent a half hour with the president and was shocked. "I beheld an emaciated old man with a thin white beard which he had permitted to grow," he later recalled. Hitchcock had managed to fight the initial Lodge amendments and forced the old senator to come back with the reservations. Hitchcock was the man with his finger in the dam, but he needed help. The president sandwiched his left arm under his covers and gestured with his right. He wanted to know how many senators would vote for the treaty without the Lodge reservations.

"Not forty-five out of ninety-six," Hitchcock replied.

Wilson groaned, "Is it possible?"

"Mr. President it might be wise to compromise—"

"Let Lodge compromise!"

"Well of course, he must compromise also. But we might hold out an olive branch."

"Let Lodge hold out an olive branch!"

Another letter to Edith from Senator Hitchcock suggested the Republicans were open to negotiations. "Dear Mrs. Wilson...the Senate today rejected by large majorities the fourteenth and fifteenth reservations proposed by Senator Lodge. There are additional indications which come to me from hour to hour of uneasiness in the Republican camp."

On November 17 an article in the *New York Times* appeared with the headline, "President will Pocket Treaty if Passed as Modified": "President Wilson told Senator Hitchcock, the Democratic Leader, at a conference at the White House, that he would 'pocket' the treaty if the Lodge resolution of ratification, with the majority of reservations as part of it, were adopted."

Hitchcock went back to the fight. Edith continued to filter the information that reached the president, fearing it might be too much. Secretary Tumulty reported that his mailbox was full of messages but they weren't getting to the president. Secretary Lansing was equally frustrated. As Ray Stannard Baker wrote in his diary, "Mr. Lansing told me pathetically how he put up one problem after another to Mrs. Wilson and never got any answer at all! I can do nothing whatever, he said. 'We are just drifting.'"

Lansing later noted in his diary, "Tumulty phoned that the President told Hitchcock he would withdraw the treaty if Lodge reservations were adopted." Secretary Tumulty sent up notes to the president imploring for him to compromise with Lodge and the reservationists, but Edith responded telling him that no compromise would be accepted.

American democracy is founded on compromise, especially in the Senate where common ground is often found between the two parties. Woodrow Wilson had compromised on many issues before, but here there would be no compromise at all. The problem was the stroke had left Wilson without the larger view. In *The Aftermath of Wilson's Stroke,* Dr. Bert E. Park wrote a damning interpretation of the psychological implications of Wilson's thrombosis:

> The psychologic manifestations of strokes were poorly defined in Wilson's day and have been intensively studied only during the last two decades. It was not until 1975 that the results of these studies were taken into account in the classification of mental disorders. Only then was what is known as 'focal psychosyndrome' induced by brain injury recognized in this country as a basic organic mental disorder of which Wilson's behavior by 1920 appears to have been an archetype. It includes disorders of emotion, impaired impulse control, and defective judgment in the presence of well-preserved intellectual function. In Wilson's case these traits included intransigence, stubbornness, insistence upon having his own way, self-righteousness, a tendency to fall back upon principals as a means of finding some basis for policy making.

To Woodrow Wilson, he was right and Lodge was dead wrong and there would be no shading of the issue. Edith knew the treaty was extremely stressful to her husband and accordingly she blocked the majority of entreaties to compromise. As Ray Stannard Baker wrote in his diary, "That is the trouble. He has been ill since last year and cannot know what is going on. He sees almost nobody and hears no direct news. Was there ever such a situation in our history! Everything must come through one overstrained woman.

Dr. Grayson, of course, is very close to the President, but everything of importance is handled by Mrs. Wilson!"

On November 18, Hitchcock wrote to Edith of an encouraging movement toward compromise. "My dear Mrs. Wilson, The real significant developments consist today of some indication on the Republican side to consider a compromise...it was intimated to me that Senator Lodge would be willing to confer with me on the subject."

Colonel House stepped in and asked Steven Bonsal, an aide during the peace conference, to meet with Lodge to find out exactly what the senator would accept. Then they could hammer out a deal. Bonsal secured a one hundred-word document acceptable to Lodge. The aide had him write the "inserts" on the treaty itself and encouraged the senator to put the congressional authority verbiage there as well.

It came down to this for Lodge: Article X must be subject to congressional approval as to where American troops would be committed. Bonsal knew that if he could get Lodge's writing on the treaty then he would have a basis for negotiation. He gave the document to Colonel House, who turned it over to the White House. The Bonsal document, which would have been ratified in the Senate, was never heard of again. Senator Hitchcock never saw it. Edith's opinion of House was very low and the colonel surmised later that the first lady destroyed it and never passed it on to the president.

In all probability, Edith viewed it as a document that would upset her husband. This is Edith Wilson's governing style at its core. The League of Nations was the heart of Wilson's tenure in office. There was simply nothing more important than getting the United States to join the League. Edith intercepted what might have been the answer to ratification of the League, but it never reached the man for whom it was intended.

President Wilson wouldn't have liked it but it could have been tweaked again. In all negotiations there must be a starting point.

Lodge was softening and here was something that House, Tumulty, Hitchcock, and the president could bend, tweak, and cajole. It was the light in the storm, and the president could have paddled toward it, but he never got the chance.

Senator Lodge took the non-response as another slap in the face by the president. There just weren't enough pro-treaty members in the Senate to give Wilson what he wanted. As Gene Smith surmised in *When the Cheering Stopped*, "There were the 'Irreconcilables' who would not vote for the League under any circumstances, and it was of no use to talk to them. But there were also the 'Mild Reservationists,' who wanted the United States in the League just so long as certain safeguards were taken, safeguards generally described as aimed at preventing too free use of American troops in policing the world. If these men could have their reservations, then the United States would be in the League. But denied their reservations, they would vote nay."

Democracy involves compromise, but Edith inferred that the president wanted no compromise at all. Joe Tumulty kept sending up letters and begging for President Wilson to compromise on his issues. Edith sent the letters back saying there would be no compromise and verbally affirmed this when he approached her. She finally gave in and allowed Secretary Tumulty to see the president to argue for acceptance of the reservations. But she stayed in the room and glared at the Secretary with a threat not to excite the president. Tumulty left empty-handed.

Colonel House sent more letters to the president recommending compromise. He first wrote Edith, "You can never know how long I have hesitated to write the President about anything while he is ill, but it seems to me vital that the Treaty should pass in some form. His place in history is in the balance. If the treaty goes through with objectionable reservations it can later be rectified. The essential thing is to have the president's great work in Paris live."

House also enclosed a letter for the president urging him to compromise and let the treaty be ratified with Lodge's reservations. Basically, House recommended letting Hitchcock negotiate in the Senate and, if the Allies were willing, to go along with the reservations. Then the president could save face and say he was doing the people's will. "Your conscience will be clear," he concluded. House argued that the treaty would still be effective.

By November 27 House had received no reply from Edith and followed up with another letter. "May I trouble you again with another letter to the President? I am afraid that I did not make myself altogether clear in the last one," he implored. House then went over the same ground, assuring Wilson that he could not be held responsible for the reservations. He summed up again: "On the one hand your loyalty to the Allies will be commended and on the other, your willingness to adopt reservations rather than have the treaty killed will be regarded as the act of a great man."

House received no reply at all. He realized then that Edith Wilson had supplanted him and he was now *persona non grata* with the president. House's prescient letters directing Wilson through the shoals of ratification of the treaty were never opened. The colonel had no way of knowing that Woodrow Wilson never saw them and that the letters would not see the light of day until 1952 in the archives of the Library of Congress.

But even Edith began to question not accepting the treaty reservations, which again brings up the effects of the thrombosis on Wilson's ability to make level-headed decisions. "Wilson's emotions were unbalanced, and his judgment was warped. Whereas he had formerly been able to offset his driving determination, combativeness, and overweening self-confidence with detachment, reflection, and self-criticism, those compensations were largely gone."

Truly, he was not himself. And Edith, interpreting the president's desires, had become the gatekeeper of what would reach him. Was any one of the telegrams or the people who wanted to see the president the extra bit of pressure that would have prompted him to relent? Edith shielded Wilson from the psychological pounding someone must go through when considering an opposite course. She did it to help her husband survive. But in doing so, she also deprived him of the necessary input to adjust his position.

Would it have been better for the United States to be in the League of Nations with reservations rather than not at all? Yes. But Wilson's surrogate president was acting with a black and white mandate. Senator Hitchcock saw disaster looming and returned on November 24. He was met outside the president's bedroom door by a stern woman with a stare that could cut through steel.

"You haven't come to talk compromise, have you?" Edith demanded.

Hitchcock pleaded his case right there and said defeat would shake the president, implying it might hurt his health. Edith, who had admitted the League fight was "eating into my soul," told the senator to wait outside. She wrote in her memoir, "In desperation, I went to my husband, 'For my sake,' I said, 'won't you accept these reservations and get this awful thing settled?' The president turned his head on the pillow and stretching out his hand to take mine answered in a voice I shall never forget: 'Little girl, don't you desert me; that I cannot stand. Can't you see that I have no moral right to accept any change in a paper I have signed without giving to every other signatory, even the Germans, the right to do the same thing? It is not that I won't accept it; it is the nation's honor that is at stake.' He went on quietly. 'Better a thousand times to go down fighting than to dip your colors to dishonorable compromise.'"

Edith went back to Senator Hitchcock outside the bedroom and said she had seen the thing clearly, "and I would never ask my husband again to do what was manifestly dishonorable." She then left Hitchcock with his mouth hanging open and returned with a letter that the president had dictated to her.

Dear Senator,

You were good enough to bring me word that the Democratic senators supporting the Treaty expected to hold a conference before the final vote on the Lodge resolution of ratification and that they would be glad to receive a word of counsel from me. I should hesitate to offer it in any detail but I assume that the senators only desire my judgement upon the all-important question of the final vote on the resolution containing the many reservations by Senator Lodge. On that I cannot hesitate, for, in my opinion, the resolution in that form does not provide for ratification but, rather, for the nullification of the Treaty. I sincerely hope that the friends and supporters of the treaty will vote against the Lodge resolutions of ratification.

Hitchcock returned to the Senate, pulled Wilson's letter from his pocket, and read the instructions to the president's loyal supporters. Senator Ashurst wanted to see the letter and noted that it had been "rubber stamped in purple ink." Another account of the letter had the signature in pencil. Whatever the case, clearly Wilson wasn't signing his name to documents. The senators followed his directions in Edith's letter, assuming they were the president's wishes.

But really how much information was Wilson acting on? He had not seen the Bonsal document. He had been shielded from most of the people who wanted compromise. Democracy is swayed by numbers and Wilson had seen maybe three or four people who had been vetted by his wife. When Hitchcock came to give Wilson the bottom line that "half a loaf is better than no loaf at all," Edith wouldn't allow him to enter the presidential sanctum.

It was government by access. Edith, in her bulldog determination to not stress her husband, deprived him of the last bit of reality that might have given him insight to save the League. Clearly, Edith Wilson had all the information at her fingertips. She was the informed president, not the shadow of a man behind the door with half his body paralyzed. When she did go to his room to implore for compromise, it sounded more like a harried wife than an experienced legislator pointing out policy nuances and political realities.

Senator Hitchcock was denied access to his boss—and possibly the opportunity to turn history around—by Edith Wilson, who was the final arbiter of power. Add together the censoring of the Bonsal document, not opening Colonel House's letters, the blocking of correspondence and access, and the final blocking of Senator Hitchcock on the very day of the vote, and you have a woman with presidential power at the center of possibly the biggest decision of the twentieth century.

Surely a United States-led League of Nations would have been better in checking a rising Germany than the isolationist cocoon the country found itself in. Would the United States have stopped Hitler's rearmament and the Anschluss of Austria? Would Germany before a world court have been able to hide the intent to regain her status as a world power? Half a loaf was better than no loaf at all, but it was all too late.

The treaty and the League of Nations were voted down by Lodge and his followers. Edith delivered the news to her husband. He paused, she wrote later, and then said, "All the more reason I must get well and try again to bring this country to a sense of its great opportunity and greater responsibility."

But Dr. Grayson wrote later that the president had said, "I feel like going to bed and staying there." He would call for Edith and Grayson later and have them read him Bible verses. Grayson read, "We are troubled on every side, yet not distressed, we are perplexed but not in despair.... "

Then the president turned to his closest friend and his wife and said, "If I were not a Christian I should go mad. But my faith in God holds me to the belief that He is in some way working out His own plans through human perversities and mistakes." The words are from a man who cannot deal with reality anymore; a man behind a door with a centurion at the gate, if not a president.

# TWENTY-ONE

# MRS. EDITH GOES TO WASHINGTON

## 1916

EDITH MATCHED THE LETTERS IN THE CODEBOOK. SHE STAYED BENT over her desk with the clock ticking out the hour. She could hear the president's fountain pen scratching paper. Model Ts rumbled down Pennsylvania Avenue trailing blue smoke. She wanted to get the latest message decoded before he walked to the Oval Office. Edith finished decoding the message and heard the president stand up. They walked to the Oval Office together.

There haven't been any presidential couples quite like Woodrow and Edith Wilson. As Alden Hatch wrote in *Edith Bolling Wilson*, "Very few husbands and wives have ever been as close as the Wilsons. The president's need for companionship; his complete devotion to his wife; his trust in her judgment; and, paradoxically, his lone wolf method of conducting the government which required a confidant rather than advisers, had led him to expose her and her alone to his most intimate thoughts and to make her a party to his every decision."

Historically, first ladies had stayed in the shadows of their husbands and hadn't been involved in the day-to-day work of the nation. But Edith and Woodrow spent more time together than any presidential couple before, and there was an expectation, at least on Edith's part, that their time in the White House would be short. Nineteen sixteen was an election year and the president had been under attack for some time over the war. It is surprising how quickly Edith became part of the day-to-day work of the White House.

A. Scott Berg writes of their routine this way in *Wilson:* "The president now took to rising at six o'clock in the morning, at which time he would have a small sandwich and a cup of coffee from a plate and thermos that had been set on a small table outside his bedroom. Then he and Edith (and a Secret Service agent) would go to a course for at least an hour of golf. They would be home in time to breakfast together at eight o'clock sharp and then go to his study together to check 'the Drawer,' the bin in his desk in which all documents demanding immediate attention had been placed. Edith would sort the papers, placing those requiring his signature before him and blotting each as she set down the next item. Time permitting, he discussed each document with her. By nine o'clock, stenographer Charles Swem would arrive; and Edith would sit close by, listening to Woodrow dictate replies to his mail… "

Then Edith and her secretary would tend to her mail while the president finished up. Edith picks it up here in her memoir: "From my vantage point in the big window-seat I could always see the President when he left his study to go to the Executive Offices. He would signal to me and I would leave all the puzzling questions and walk over with him. If the day were fine we would walk through the garden; if not, under the sheltered arcade, and there have a brief moment together."

Edith would see him again at lunch, where they never discussed business. "We talked of books and permanent things that the present unrest could not disturb.... Before dinner we sometimes could go in the motor for a little breath of air; after dinner, occasionally, to the theatre. More often there would be work to do and I would take my book, or unanswered letters, or other work, and sit in the study while the President studied or used his typewriter.... Often it was long after midnight before he finished."

Wilson wasn't a great golfer but Edith continued to improve. One entry in her diary reads, "Played golf with W and Grayson—beat them both." Many times Wilson would ask Edith to decode top-secret memoranda and read them back to him. Much of the business of state was conducted this way and the amount of coded messages had become voluminous. The president was appreciative of Edith's help. "You don't know how much easier it makes all this to have you here by me," he told her.

Among the codes Edith deciphered was one concerning the fifteen hundred Mexican banditos under Pancho Villa who had crossed into New Mexico and killed seventeen Americans and burned buildings before escaping across the border. The country demanded war against Villa. The president did send troops, but he took a beating in the press. "There won't be any war with Mexico if I can prevent it," he told his cabinet. "I came from the South and I know what war is."

General Pershing invaded Mexico and General Patton returned with Villa's second in command dead across the hood of his jeep. What Wilson didn't tell anyone was what he had learned in the decoded messages: Germany was deliberately trying to stir up Mexico to keep the Americans occupied while it conducted unrestricted submarine warfare.

Edith probably received the codes letting the president know that on March 24, 1916, the Germans sent the *Sussex* to the bottom of the sea. Eighty passengers died and former President Theodore Roosevelt attacked the president for wavering on his own policies and not holding the Germans accountable. The president issued an ultimatum.

" . . . unless the Imperial Government should now immediately declare and effect an abandonment of its present methods of [submarine] warfare against passenger and freight-carrying vessels this government of the United States can have no choice but to sever diplomatic relations with the government of the German Empire altogether."

The Germans promised to stop their attacks on neutral ships, but war was now on everyone's lips. One incident reveals how the fear of Germans affected everyday citizens. The president and Edith took cruises on the presidential yacht, the *Mayflower,* on the weekends. Once they picked Tangier Island as an interesting place to visit.

The water around the island wasn't deep enough for the yacht, so they took a rowboat. "Accompanied by two of the officers and the Secret Service staff," Edith wrote later, "we transshipped to the tiny boat, landed on a wooden 'dock' and made our precarious way over a single plank which led to dry land at one end of the small street that composed this quaint little town. On either side were neat little one-story houses, each with a tiny front garden, surrounded by a picket fence. . . . we saw only closed doors and drawn blinds; not a person in sight. It truly seemed a city of the dead."

The president and Edith returned to the dock. Wilson then looked back and said, "Let's go back again and see if we can find out what this means." When they returned they found the townspeople outside, but upon seeing the president and first lady they scurried back to their houses. Edith recalled later, "Only one old man stood his ground, peering at us through his glasses. My husband lifted his cap."

"Good morning sir," he said, "I hope we are not disturbing your quiet homes here."

"The old fellow stood agape and, slowly removing his own hat, said, 'Isn't that the president?'"

"Yes, I have that honor, sir," Wilson replied.

"The old man broke into a hearty laugh and said, 'Well, sir, I want to shake your hand, for we all think a lot of you down here.'"

"After a hearty handshake he continued to laugh and then told us that early that morning they had seen a big ship anchor outside in the river, then some men in uniform put out in small boats for their island. This gave them a great alarm for they decided that the officers were Germans coming to blow up the island."

In an age when radio was just on the horizon, people considered a German invasion a real threat. As President Wilson told a crowd in St. Louis, "One reckless commander of a submarine...might set the world on fire." This was true; every U-boat commander who had his finger on the trigger might draw America into the war. And if that was not enough, Wilson had to run for reelection.

# TWENTY-TWO

# CITIZEN KANE

## 1919

THE WORLD WAS SIDEWAYS NOW. WILSON COULDN'T STRAIGHTEN up, with his left side paralyzed. A wheelchair or an "invalid rolling chair" was tried, but the president didn't have the muscular control to support his own body. Ike Hoover suggested using one of the chairs from Atlantic City that people used to roll up and down the boardwalk. The White House hired a chair for five dollars a week. Hoover modified the chair when it arrived. "Upon arrival we changed the foot rest part of it, making it stand out straight on a line with the seat thereby avoiding the bending of the legs when he was placed in it.... this chair was used every time the president got out of bed for the remaining days of the White House.... "

An article in the *New York Times* dated November 17 commemorated Wilson's first trip to the South Lawn. "For the first time since his return to Washington from his Western tour President Wilson today went outside of the White House. He was rolled in a wheel chair on to the lawn near the South Portico and for more than an hour enjoyed the fresh air and sunshine."

Secretary Lansing had been holding regular cabinet meetings, but without the president there was little business to transact. The various secretaries sat around a table and discussed the state of the president. "The question as to whether the president is actually and generally performing his official duties and whether he is mentally and physically capable of doing so is growing more and more insistent," Lansing wrote later.

In the White House, Secretary Tumulty guarded the West Gate and Edith continued her vigilant watch over the sickroom. The first lady banned the public from the White House to maintain silence for the president, and the staff tiptoed around and spoke in whispers. On gray, misty days the government of the United States had the air of an abandoned house with its locked gates, drawn curtains, and darkened windows.

But this was the prescribed treatment for someone who had suffered a stroke or a heart attack or any malady medical science had no easy answer for. All over the country people were sequestered in their homes to live doctor-ordered lives of rest and silence. It would be much later that doctors realized this imposed isolation actually hampered the recovery of damaged brains and that it was stimulus that allowed neurons and ganglia to reconnect and rebuild.

Edith and Grayson and the president's staff were following the logic of the day. *Rest. Rest. Rest.* But this didn't stop the talk or the rumors. The persistent story that the president was mad and muttering limericks continued to surface, even though the bars on the windows had been explained away as installed by the Roosevelts so their children wouldn't fall out. President Wilson had gotten better, but "better" was relative to where he had been. As Hoover later stated, "If there ever was a man in bad shape he was. He could not talk plainly, mumbled more than he

articulated, was helpless and looked like a man fatally ill. Everybody
tried to help him, but he was so dependent for everything."

"So dependent for everything." This sounds like a man on his
deathbed or a man who has had a catastrophic stroke. A man who
was dependent on everyone would live a challenged life. But a man
"dependent for everything" who also happened to be *the president
of the United States* wouldn't nearly be able to fulfill all his duties. Is
it any wonder that Edith Wilson assumed the duties of the president?
It was not a matter of want, but of necessity.

Senator Lodge never let up. He perpetuated the rumor that not
only was the president crazy but that the Wilsons had received millions of dollars' worth of gifts while in Europe. But as Edith pointed
out, "Even newspapers ardently opposed to Mr. Wilson declined to
take stock in such cock-and-bull stories, but the sinister rumor of Mr.
Wilson's impairment persisted."

The anniversary of the armistice was approaching and the public
expected a statement from the president. Secretary Tumulty wrote
the armistice document. The State of the Union was also coming up
on December 2. Tumulty wrote that as well. A rather serendipitous
collaborative process then followed, with cabinet members contributing lines and parts from Wilson's Western Tour speeches hammered
in. An early draft was sent to Edith on November 24.

"Dear Mrs. Wilson, I am sending you a draft of a proposed message to Congress by the president. You will notice that I followed the
spirit at least of the western speeches in many of the things I say....
Joseph Tumulty." The president's secretary didn't bother sending it
to Wilson directly. It went to Edith, the real holder of power, who
suggested some changes. On November 25, Tumulty sent her another
draft.

"Dear Mrs. Wilson, I have completed the memorandum you
desire to lay before the president. I have added a paragraph with

reference to the work of the farmers during the war." The State of the Union was delivered to Congress as written by Tumulty, with Edith's tweaks.

As John Milton Cooper wrote, the message was grossly out of step with the times. "This message's references to domestic problems glaringly understated the troubles that plagued the country at the end of 1919. Inflation, or HCL, still ran rampant, unemployment was soaring as veterans returned to the workforce, and strikes were disrupting major industries, including coal and steel. A radical-led general strike earlier in the year in Seattle, explosions of bombs in May at the homes of public officials, including one on the doorstep of the home of Attorney General Palmer himself, and the police strike in Boston in September—these events had made many people shudder at the specter of revolution."

The world careened on while the White House went silent. The reception of the president's State of the Union was lukewarm at best. The president's foes pointed to the generic quality of the statement, and many openly said the president hadn't written it. Party lines dictated the reaction, with Democrats lining up behind it and Republicans questioning its authorship.

In an interview with the *New York Times*, Secretary Tumulty tried to stem the tide of questions and circulating rumors. The paper ran a front-page story about how much the president had improved and even detailed improvement in his handwriting.

The Senate was not mollified. Politico Albert Burleson called Tumulty's work "a fine piece of political work," and Secretary Lansing mused privately, "There has been a great deal of speculation as to the authorship of the president's messages.... there are portions which seem to be written by another's hand...if it ever gets out it will make a fine scandal..." Lansing went on to say that Senator Spencer of Missouri pointed out that, "in the signature of the president's which he had seen, the 'Woodrow' could not have been read if one covered up the 'Wilson' and that it all looked like the writing of a child."

The writing of a child bespeaks of Edith, whose handwriting was like a childlike scrawl. But of course Tumulty, House, Grayson, and Edith had no choice. The White House was grinding to a halt as a functioning organ of state. We can almost see Edith counting the days like someone in a lifeboat who knows she will eventually see land if she can just hold out. The land Edith wanted was the end of President Wilson's term, which was still a year away.

Her boat began to take on water when in Mexico an American consular official, William Jenkins, was arrested and accused of staging his own kidnapping to further implicate the regime of Carranza. The corrupt and violent government hadn't been above suspicion in the Pancho Villa attacks in New Mexico, and now came confirmation that the Mexicans were bent on a confrontation with the United States.

New Mexico Senator Albert Fall, who despised the Carranza government, and had been leading the call to get rid of President Wilson on the grounds that he couldn't govern, demanded military action. In a debate about the president he slammed his fist on the Senate table and declared: "Wilson is not acting! Mrs. Wilson is president!"

The Mexican crisis gave him a perfect pretext to call the issue into question. The Senate Foreign Relations Committee (which Senator Lodge headed up) was on the hunt for war with Mexico and to show the president was no longer capable of leading. Fall demanded the president send troops and that he meet with him and Senator Hitchcock.

Senator Fall was an extreme isolationist and in league with Lodge during the war. He wore a drooping mustache with rancher clothing and a ten-gallon hat. He would later become secretary of the interior and the only cabinet member to go to prison for taking a bribe from an oil company to drill in the protected Naval Reserves. Fall was in so deep with the oil companies that others in the Senate called him "Petroleum Falls."

People in the senator's state blamed Mexico for everything from high unemployment to strikers and racial tensions. A war would solve a lot of problems, and when counselor agent Jenkins was kidnapped at Puebla, Mexico, Senator Fall and his cronies saw a pretext for a war with Mexico. The Senate Foreign Relations Committee, headed by Lodge, formed a subcommittee to investigate the Mexican kidnapping.

Secretary Lansing was interviewed and asked if the president had been consulted on the kidnapping. Lansing, who had wanted the president to step down before, said *no one* had talked to the president. Senator Lodge saw another way to show Wilson was incapable of performing his job. Fall introduced legislation calling for a meeting with the president. Lodge thought Wilson would refuse to meet with Fall, which would allow them to start proceedings to get him removed from the White House.

Senator Putman wrote Dr. Grayson on December 5, the day Hitchcock and Fall were to see the president, "Dear Admiral, I beg you not to interfere any more than you have to with the opportunity that the president is offered to kick Senator Fall in the slats." Many, including Edith, knew what the senator was up to. She wrote later in her memoir, "Albert B. Fall engineered a maneuver in the Committee by which a subcommittee was named ostensibly to confer with the President on the Mexican situation. The real object was to see whether the president was mentally capable of administering his office.... Senator Hitchcock had opposed the whole business, but he consented to accompany Mr. Fall to the White House."

Now Senator Fall would confirm his suspicion that Edith had become the president. Edith couldn't stop the senator at the door of the sickroom and tell him the president was fine. The temperature in the Senate had risen to a point that the White House had to put out the fire or impeachment would occur. Fall would have a gang of reporters waiting for him when he emerged and it would come to him to declare the president fit or not. The country had been leaderless for months and people wanted to know if President Wilson had gone mad or was insane or was just a hopeless drooling invalid locked away in the recesses of the White House.

And if Woodrow Wilson wasn't fit to be president, was it true that Edith Wilson was running the country? Was it a petticoat government? Was Edith Wilson the first woman president? Suffragettes who had been picketing outside the White House ever since the Wilsons returned from the Western Tour would have loved to know that one. The world would soon find out the answer.

# TWENTY-THREE

# THE SNOWS OF SIERRA NEVADA

## 1916

**THE PRESIDENT LAY WITH A WASHRAG OVER HIS EYES IN THE** darkened bedroom. It was the only thing that gave him relief. High blood pressure pounded in his temples and made light painful to his eyes. He lay in the heat of summer and could hear distant airy traffic. The electric fan pulsed by the window. These mini retreats lasted only a day, but lying quietly temporarily relieved the pressure of narrowed arteries. But then he was up and back at it. There was an election to be won and maybe a war to be fought.

The president started to blend the war and his reelection with "America First" and with the slogan *"He kept us out of the war."* By "America First," Wilson meant to put the country first in deed and thought. The president wanted people to "think first, not of them-selves…but of the country which we serve."

The president went into campaign mode as a railroad strike threatened the country. "That summer of 1916 was crowded with every sort of thing," Edith wrote later. "First on the list was the ever-encroaching menace of the War in Europe. Then came the presidential campaign.... Now not a day passed without consultations with the men in charge of Democratic headquarters, and with the party leaders from far and near."

Wilson was fighting a two-front war and it began to take a toll. "The days were never long enough, so we decided to start them at 5 AM and try, as my husband said... 'steal up on them in the dark,'" Edith recalled. "I told the cook and butler to fix things for us, and leave them in the icebox in the pantry, and I would cook some eggs and make coffee on the electric burner. Never once did they allow me to do it..."

The war was on the lips of Americans. Patriotism was sweeping the country and Chicago had a parade of 130,000 flag-carrying people who marched down Michigan Avenue. Long Island had a similar celebration with twenty-five hundred pilgrims marching through Oyster Bay to the Roosevelt home at Sagamore Hill. Patriotism demanded a leader, and many saw the Rough Rider as the man of the hour. A developing modern media made sure everyone knew about people dying in the icy Atlantic at the hands of the "Huns."

But even though people marched in time to the Roosevelt drumbeat, the Republican National Committee remembered he had split the party and cost them the election in 1912. They nominated an associate justice of the Supreme Court, Charles Evans Hughes. Teddy would not have his day after all. No matter; he would lead a division of soldiers once war was declared. If only the president would declare it!

The Democrats renominated Woodrow Wilson in St. Louis along with Vice President Marshall, who didn't bother showing up. The president complained of severe headaches and was run down from the constant stress of the looming war, the election, and now the railroad strike. It wasn't until mid-September that Edith and

Woodrow were able to depart to a large summer estate called "Shadow Lawn."

Edith at first didn't care for the summer retreat. "The first impression was awful. We entered a room which looked more like a lounge in a summer hotel—very large, with a staircase wide enough for an army abreast, opposite the front door.... The worst thing in the house was a white marble statue in the center of the 'lobby.' It must have weighed tons, or we would have had it removed. So we draped it as much as possible."

A notification committee arrived and informed the president he had been nominated. Wilson gave an acceptance speech and then headed to dedicate a marble shrine at Lincoln's birthplace in Kentucky. Then he went back to Washington to take care of business. Dr. Grayson told Edith that the president must "slow up" because he could not keep going. A stop at Atlantic City gave Wilson no relief, with meetings with suffragettes and charity concerts. The next morning a pounding headache kept him in bed.

For most people with hypertension, stress is one of the triggers, and the headaches showed Wilson's blood pressure was soaring. To pile misery upon misery a telegram came saying the president's sister, who had been ill, had taken a turn for the worse. "We were three days at a hotel and then the *Mayflower* was ordered up from New York," Edith would write later. A Dr. Davis boarded the presidential yacht and took the first lady aside. "The president is under terrific strain and there is nothing he can do. His sister may live for weeks, and she may go any minute.... I will stay and do what I can, but I do not answer for the consequences if he does not get away and have some let-up."

Here we have the very same scenario that would play out three years later between Edith and the doctors. *She must do something. She must control the president.* The doctors can better persuade the wife of a president to administer their prescription for health. Back at Shadow Lawn "stacks of work" awaited the president. Wilson's stenographer, Charles Swem, met Wilson there and they began the work. Edith would later write, "As Mr. Wilson spoke and Swem wrote, a panorama of world affairs passed before me.... In the briefest time the letters, typed and ready for signatures, were back on the desk, with the ones that were pressing signified by a square of red cardboard clipped to the top. I always watched for these, and, when a free moment came, put them before my husband and blotted the signature..."

Two days later the president's sister died and the Wilsons made the journey to Columbia, South Carolina. Woodrow showed Edith where he had grown up and then they returned and huddled with advisors. The president met with Walter Hines Page, the ambassador to England, then Colonel House; then the Wilsons left for Baltimore to address a meeting of grain dealers and then to Sea Girt, New Jersey, so the president could mount a horse and trot up and down a line of New Jersey National Guardsmen.

After the review, the president and Edith returned to Shadow Lawn to be greeted by the Young Men's Democratic Club of New Jersey, "fifteen hundred strong marching through our gates with bands playing. My husband made his first 'political' speech of the campaign to them," Edith wrote in her memoir.

When Wilson returned, the study was piled high with Army commissions. Edith assisted the president in signing the papers. "We had a large table especially for them, with blotters and everything ready," she later wrote. Edith put the documents in front of Wilson, who signed, and then she would blot and move onto the next one. "We tried to do at least one hundred a day, but even then the stacks never seemed to grow less, for new ones came each day."

The president was being buried in these commissions as the country geared up for war. Thankfully, a change was later enacted that made the president's signature necessary only for the rank of captain and above. Wilson was exhausted and Edith made sure they took a drive or played golf every chance they got. Edith struggled hard to find "a private life" with the president among the meetings for campaigns and the constant war news. "I write to refresh my spirit," she wrote, "with the memory of the few comparatively serene days we were able to spend in the quiet of the shaded, cool lawn or in the big house." But the campaign loomed large and they left on October 3 for Omaha for another speech.

After Theodore Roosevelt realized he couldn't be the presidential nominee, he settled for being presidential pit bull. "Instead of speaking softly and carrying a big stick," he said, "President Wilson spoke bombastically and carried a dish rag!" The Republican approach was one of constant attack using the president's campaign slogan of "He kept us out of the war" against him. Roosevelt called Wilson an "evolutionary ostrich" and said his war slogan was "ignoble shirking of responsibility…clothed in an utterly misleading phrase, the phrase of a coward."

Woodrow Wilson understood the meaning of total war better than Roosevelt did. The president had seen the ravages of the Civil War as a child and while Roosevelt had fought in the Spanish American War, he had not seen modern warfare. War had changed due to the machine gun, chlorine, mustard gas, and the awesome ferocity of high explosive shells. Theodore Roosevelt had plans to lead a brigade of rough riders and cowboys into battle once war was declared. He didn't understand that the dash he made at Kettle Hill didn't exist anymore. He and his men would be cut to pieces the second they rose from the trenches.

The static lines of the trenches allowed just a few yards at the sacrifice of hundreds of thousands of men. America had not been bled dry of her young men the way France and England had. Verdun and the

Battle of the Somme left more dead than both sides of the Civil War combined. President Wilson believed men would seek peace over war, but each side had given too much to compromise now. Like tired wrestlers, the Allies and the Germans circled each other for a knockout punch, conscious of the millions of dead young men behind their backs.

This misunderstanding also extended to the use of submarine warfare. The German High Military Command would never give up unrestricted submarine warfare. Even when the order was given to sink only enemy ships, the U-boats would have to make a judgment call through a dim periscope as to who was a neutral and who was an enemy. Many times the U-boats fired knowing that any ship sent to the bottom contributed to the gruesome statistics that are modern warfare. The Germans believed the quickest way to bring the Allies to their knees was to sink anything on the high seas.

Meanwhile, President Wilson spoke to the "Commercial Club" in Omaha, then reviewed a pageant in an open car for "sixty blocks." He and Edith returned to Shadow Lawn briefly before leaving for Indianapolis, where Wilson addressed a luncheon and gave a speech at the county fair. Two days later the presidential couple went to Chicago, then Cincinnati, then Buffalo, passing through New York City for a final speech. "There we spent a very busy day, ending with a tremendous meeting at Madison Square Garden," Edith wrote later. "The crowds were so dense it was impossible, even with the help of hundreds of police, to get near the entrance of the building."

When Wilson rose to speak, the cheering went on for a half hour. After the presidential couple left the building they went to Cooper Union, where the president addressed thirty thousand people. They returned to Shadow Lawn, where one final speech was given. Edith had been first lady for less than eleven months at this point. She later recalled: "I tried to picture to myself how in this brief time since we were married…my whole life had changed; and how much happiness had been crowded into those busy months."

On Sunday, November 5, with the election the following Tuesday, Edith wrote, "I had never felt that we could win the majority of electoral votes, for while the masses seemed for my husband, there was so much money in the hands of the Republicans." Edith also had taken to heart the brutal verbal assaults of Roosevelt and others. President Wilson had kept the country out of the war, but war was imminent. Walter Lippmann, who founded *The New Republic*, put it this way: "What we are electing is a war president…not the man who kept us out of the war. And we've got to make up our minds if we want to go to war with Hughes or Wilson."

The president was convinced that the United States was facing the worst crisis since the Civil War. He drew up a plan in which the vice president and secretary of state would resign and he could appoint Hughes secretary of state and then he could immediately take office. Wilson believed he "would have no right to risk the peace of the nation by remaining in office after I lost my authority."

But the president also didn't believe he would lose. He had spoken to hundreds of thousands of screaming supporters and carried their enthusiasm with him. But Edith was already thinking ahead. "I began to speculate on what we would do when we should leave the White House, which I calculated would be in just four months." While she reveled in the attention, Edith still harbored the fantasy of a private life with Woodrow.

The president stopped into her room the night before the election and Edith told him of her plans for the future. The president looked down at her. "What a delightful pessimist you are! One must never court defeat. If it comes, accept it like a soldier; but don't anticipate it, for that destroys your fighting spirit."

On Election Day, Edith and her husband had an early breakfast and drove to Princeton to vote. The president went in to vote at the Engine House. Edith couldn't vote, as New Jersey hadn't granted women the right to vote. They then returned to Shadow Lawn to wait for the results of the election that would determine their collective destiny. They played a game of Twenty Questions when the phone rang. Wilson's daughter Margaret jumped up to get it. It was a friend from New York sympathizing with her over her father's defeat. "Why, he is not defeated. What are you talking about?" she cried out. The friend replied that the *New York Times* had already called the election for Hughes.

"Impossible," Margaret replied. "They cannot know yet. In the West they are still at the polls." But after a quick call to the White House with a confirmation from Secretary Tumulty, President Wilson replied, "Well Tumulty, it begins to look as if we have been badly licked."

Edith accepted their defeat. "I found real consolation in the thought that, at last, we should be alone together." The president decided not to send Hughes a telegram of congratulations until the morning. Theodore Roosevelt couldn't contain himself. "I am doubly thankful as an American for the election of Mr. Hughes. It is a vindication of our national honor." The president had a sandwich and a glass of milk and went up to bed. Edith followed him minutes later. Wilson was in bed and looked up.

"Well, little girl, you were right in expecting we should lose the election. Frankly I did not, but we can now do some of the things we want to do."

Edith sat on the bed and held her husband's hand. She thought he might want to talk, but soon she heard his restive breathing. At 4:00 a.m. Edith heard a knock at her door. It was Margaret. "... she said she had just talked to Mr. Vance McCormick at Democratic headquarters in New York," Edith later wrote, "and he told her better news was coming in, and he had not given up hope."

"Shall we wake Father and tell him?" Margaret asked.

"Oh no, do let him sleep," Edith replied, not sure if the news was real or not.

When the day came the results were uncertain. The big Western states, California in particular, had not come in with their electoral votes. A reporter called for a comment from Hughes and was told that the president couldn't be disturbed as he was sleeping. "Well," the reporter replied, "tell him when he wakes up he is no longer president."

The real president received two embarrassed Princeton friends who had come to congratulate him on his reelection. By evening the election was still too close to call. On Thursday, November 9, the Wilsons' last day at Shadow Lawn, Edith wrote in her diary: "Thursday…Got up about 8; found no one knew a thing more than the night before. Margaret had to go to New York and we spent the evening receiving telegrams and winding up things at Shadow Lawn. Played golf at Spring Lake, and when we were on the 8th tee Dr. Grayson arrived with news…they thought California was safe and if so that meant Democratic victory."

They boarded the *Mayflower* and stayed up on deck until 9:00 p.m., and had to put off the shipboard cook who had fallen ill. The strain tore at Edith as she later wrote: "I suppose the suspense and strain were making my nerves queer, for I felt so weepy over the old Chinaman [cook]…" An orderly came in with wireless messages and they gathered in the smoking room to hear them. "They all told of new gains in the West, but the issue was still uncertain."

In 1916 people counted votes by hand. There were ballot boxes from far-flung towns that had to be brought in. The country was not yet congregated around the big cities that would sway elections. One big reason for the delay in 1916 was snow. The early snow had buried the roads, and Sierra County, high in the Sierra Nevada mountain range, had not been heard from. A horse-drawn wagon with a ballot box making its way along snow-covered roads would hold the answer to whether President Woodrow Wilson would have a second term.

# TWENTY-FOUR

# A SMELLING
# COMMITTEE

## 1919

UNCLE SAM WAS NOW IN THE PRESIDENT'S BED. WILSON HADN'T shaved since he had the stroke, and the thin white beard looked like the old man on the poster beckoning men to war. Dr. Grayson stood uneasily waiting for an answer at the foot of the bed. He knew Senator Fall was ready to go to the press if he weren't allowed to see the president. The room was stuffy and warm with the medicinal odor of the shut-in. Wilson picked at his beard, then looked up with a crooked smile. "A smelling committee," the president remarked, "The sooner the better."

Grayson nodded and left, setting the meeting up for 2:30 in the afternoon on December 5. Ike Hoover recorded the preparations. "When the Senate Committee came the great camouflage took place. He had been sitting up in his rolling chair, but when the time came for the committee to arrive he was put to bed. The room was darkened, only one light on the bedside table left burning. He was propped up with pillows and covered over entirely, except his head and his right arm. It was quite impossible for one coming from a well-lighted part of the house to see anything to satisfaction. Mrs. Wilson stood at the foot of the bed, the nurse on the side of the bed, Dr. Grayson in the doorway."

Wilson carefully tucked his left hand under the covers, and Edith put the Senate report on Mexico on the nightstand so the president could pick it up. All they had to do was wait for Senator Fall. This was high-stakes poker for the presidency and it could have gone either way. Senator Lodge had called Secretary Tumulty and inquired about a meeting with the president beforehand. Tumulty consulted with the first lady and she talked with the president before Dr. Grayson's visit. Robert Woolley, head of the Democratic Party publicity, had told Tumulty that the president would have to see Fall and Hitchcock or there would be impeachment proceedings.

The president, Tumulty, Grayson, and Edith were all conspiring to present a normally functioning president to the Senate. The Senate, at least the Republican side, had become the enemy circling the castle and looking for a way in. The drawbridge was being let down to admit two and then would be drawn up. The two would report what they had seen to the world.

Secretary Tumulty asked Robert Woolley if he might help them with a "dress rehearsal" in staging the visit. It was Woolley who suggested placing a copy of the Senate report by the table. Wilson often drifted off in midsentence or lost his thought completely. Edith usually nudged him back to the subject; now she might not be able to help her husband if he got in trouble. But she, Grayson, and Hitchcock would be present to try to help.

So the stage was set. The play called for the projection of a recovering president who still had firm control of the levers of power. Newspapers around the country picked up the story. The *New York World* proclaimed that the actual purpose was "disclosure of the president's condition." More than one hundred reporters were positioned outside the White House to catch Fall and Hitchcock when they emerged. If the president stumbled, there would be no second act.

The two senators appeared in the afternoon and were met outside the president's bedroom by Admiral Grayson.

Fall asked if there would be a time limit and Grayson said, "No, not within reason, Senator."

They went in and saw the president, who had positioned himself with pillows. He was sitting up just enough to use the covers to keep his paralyzed left side hidden. Wilson used all his strength and extended his hand for a firm handshake.

"Well senator, how are your Mexican investments getting along?" the president asked, motioning to a chair. Edith was in the room with a pen and a paper. She wrote later, "Senator Fall entered the room looking like a regular Uriah Heap, 'washing his hands with invisible soap in imperceptible water'.... I had taken the precaution to carry a pad and pencil so I would not have to shake hands with him. I sat on the other side of the bed and carefully wrote down every word that passed between them."

Fall was certain the strange presidential signatures were forged and he stared at Wilson's right hand. He had assumed that the president would not have the ability to shake hands, much less sign a document.

"If agreeable, I wish Mrs. Wilson to remain," said the president, motioning to the first lady.

Fall nodded and Edith immediately began taking notes. The senator in the large cowboy hat looked at her and said, "You seem very much engaged, madam."

The first lady looked up.

"I thought it wise to record this interview so there wouldn't be misunderstandings or misstatements made," she replied icily.

Senator Fall looked away and turned back to the president. He asked if the president had seen the Senate report on Mexico.

"I have a copy right here." Wilson reached over and picked up the report and waved it in the air. "You see, despite the stories going the rounds, I can still use my right hand."

The president mentioned the medical opinions spread by Senator Hawk Moses, who said the president was, among other things, insane. Wilson looked at Fall.

"I hope the Senator will now be reassured, but he may be disappointed."

Fall then went into a speech about Mexico and the kidnapped counselor agent. He was just building up when Dr. Grayson was called away and returned a few minutes later to announce that the counselor agent had been released. The doctor later said "that he felt like an actor making a sensational entrance."

The president, playing the wise statesman, counseled against too much haste with Mexico. Senator Fall had stumbled, for now it seemed his mission for coming had just vanished over the next hill. Edith had run out of paper and had begun writing on a large brown envelope Senator Fall had brought in. She took down the final words between the president and the humbled senator.

"I have been praying for you," Fall finished up.

"Which way, senator?" the president replied.

Grayson took Senator Fall downstairs where he asked about his health. The senator said he had been working too hard lately. Dr. Grayson raised his eyebrows.

"You have just left a man suffering a breakdown due to overwork and concentration. You had better be more careful," he admonished. Grayson would later say that Fall and Hitchcock were "amazed at his wonderful grasp of the entire Mexican problem." He left the senator to the gathered reporters. Senator Hitchcock led off. "The president looks much better than when I last saw him. He was sitting up in bed wearing a dark brown sweater. His color was good...He was mentally most alert...." Senator Fall agreed and added that the president was certainly capable of handling the Mexican situation and "seemed to me to be in excellent trim, both mentally and physically...."

In her memoir, Edith noted with triumph that Fall "assured the reporters that the president was mentally fit and that he had the use of his left side and his right which of course was an overstatement for Mr. Wilson's left side was practically useless." The *New York Times* covered the meeting with the headline, "Senators See President; Fall and Hitchcock Report that his Condition is Excellent." It didn't get much better than that for Edith and company.

Secretary Lansing wasn't buying it. In a memorandum he wrote, "Well, the president received Senator Fall and Hitchcock as I thought he would. Senator Fall did most of the talking but the president took a keen interest in what was said...Fall says that the president received him and Hitchcock lying flat on his back in bed and moved none of his arms except his right arm...I think that the American people are entitled to know and the cabinet ought to know the truth. It is not a matter of invading the privacy of the individual. It is not Woodrow Wilson but the president of the United States who is ill. His family and physician have no right to shroud the whole affair in mystery as they have done. I would not blame Congress if they instituted an investigation to ascertain the facts. It would not be an unreasonable thing for them to do."

President Edith Wilson had pulled it off for now, and this took the air out of the factions calling for Woodrow Wilson's resignation. Everyone settled in for the long haul and accepted that this was the new White House...and the new president.

# TWENTY-FIVE

# THE SHADOW OF WAR

## 1916–1917

**THE *NEW YORK TIMES* PRINTED AN EXTRA EDITION THAT SAID THE**
election seemed to be going to Woodrow Wilson. When his daughter
told him, Wilson smiled while he was shaving and said, "Tell that to
the marines." So it went to November 10 and Edith's diary again
records the moment. "Up at 7:30. Brooks brought a wireless that
seemed to make victory certain." When they left the *Mayflower* and
boarded the train, crowds already began congratulating the president.

On November 10, California went for Wilson officially. The
electoral count was 277 to 254 with the popular vote at 9,126,868
for Wilson and 8,548,728 for Hughes. The Republican candidate held
out for a recount, but on November 22, he sent a telegram conceding
the election. Wilson later remarked that the wire from Hughes, "was
a little moth-eaten when it got here, but quite legible."

Edith Wilson would have to wait for her life "alone" with the
president. Writing later she said, "This was really the first time I had
felt certain that, in spite of all the reports to the contrary, the people

had stood by my husband." Victory had come at a high price for Wilson. "My husband, too, was weary and unwell—reaction from the strain of the campaign," she wrote later. "But a graver problem was the European situation. Germany's disregard for its pledge not to sink vessels without warning." The Germans were going for a knockout punch.

Meanwhile, a girl with a pony stared out from the shores of the Outer Banks of North Carolina. The ship crossing the sky-blue horizon seemed not to be moving at all. An explosion ripped up from the water in a plume of white and black smoke and the girl fell down. The ship had stopped and was nosing down into the water. A second flat boat appeared on the horizon and the girl jumped up and galloped toward her family's cottage. The Germans were coming.

Germans U-boats were now off the coast of the United States. The Germans had continued with their strategy of bringing Britain and France to their knees by strangling their lifeline. They sank four more merchant ships, killing seventeen Americans. The Germans had become better at obfuscation as the military realized they had a reluctant warrior in President Wilson.

"Foreseeing an inevitable crisis with Germany over the frequent sinking of our ships," Secretary Tumulty later wrote. "The president would not draw the country into war until he had tried every means for peace." The meat grinder that was World War I continued with 800,000 casualties in the Battle of Verdun. The world had never seen carnage on this scale, and Wilson thought of proposing a peace initiative to both sides with the League of Nations as part of it.

The Wilsons came back from a wedding on August 28 to find members of the Women's Party at the White House gates commemorating the fall of the Bastille. Three groups of suffragettes held signs up, *Liberty, Equality, Fraternity.* This began an almost two-year siege of the White House by the suffragettes. "Detestable suffragettes" and "disgusting creatures" were some of Edith's choice words. She would encounter the suffragettes again in a surprising way.

Then the president's health gave out again. "My dear one felt so wretched he went back to bed soon after breakfast and I sent for the doctor," Edith wrote. Indigestion and the excruciating headaches had come back. Grayson arrived and ordered rest. Wilson played the electric piano that night and then sat by the fire and listened to operas. On November 25, 1917, Edith wrote in her diary: "Woodrow still not well; helped him in his study until 12; he is writing what he says 'may prove the greatest piece of work of my life.'"

It was the peace proposal. Colonel House had pulled in scholars and people in government in a meeting he called the Inquiry. From this meeting he and Wilson culled out fourteen points for a peace proposal. The fourteenth point was the League of Nations. The earliest critics of Wilson's League of Nations were in his own administration. They were two men whom Edith Wilson didn't like. The first was Colonel House, who feared his position with the president was being usurped by the new first lady. House listened to the president, read the document, and said it was wonderful, but found Wilson's statement about the "causes and objects of the war" being "obscure" to be inflammatory to the Allies.

The colonel didn't believe President Wilson would be a good war president. "I am convinced the president's place in history is dependent to a large degree upon luck. If we should get into a serious war and it should turn out disastrously, he would be one of the most discredited presidents we have had." Like a lot of men seated next to power, House believed he could do better. "...as an administrator he [the president] is a failure, and it is only because of a generally efficient Cabinet that things go as well as they do."

Secretary Lansing didn't like Wilson's proposed peace initiative either. In evaluating the plan's implementation Lansing said, "I am not sure that it would be a good thing for the world if it could be [realized]...*we must* go in on the side of the Allies, for we are a democracy." Lansing feared what might happen if the Allies rejected Wilson's plan and the Germans accepted it. He recommended dropping the League of Nations altogether.

Then Secretary Lansing told reporters that the United States was very close to entering the war. As Edith wrote in her memoir, "Two days later...in discussing the President's [peace] note with newspaper men, [he] mentioned 'the possibility of our being forced into the War.' The headlines were enormous. 'Woodrow dreadfully worried,' my diary says. 'He asked Secretary Lansing to make a second statement to correct the wrong impression, which he did, but it was a blunder in the face of all Woodrow had done to present his note to prevent friction.'"

The president was close to asking for Lansing's resignation. When the dust settled, neither the Allies nor the Germans were willing to enter into any discussions. War was quickly becoming a reality. The Germans blundered again when, on January 16, German Foreign Secretary Arthur Zimmerman cabled the German embassy in Mexico with orders to set up a military alliance with Ruler Carranza, offering recovery of Texas, New Mexico, and Arizona as incentives. This telegram pushed the United States further toward war with Germany; the West had just been settled and it was unacceptable to have another country fomenting war on the nation's borders. The Zimmerman telegram made war a foregone conclusion.

Wilson's second inauguration took place on March 5.

There had been rumors of an assassination plot, and armed soldiers surrounded the president and Edith as they proceeded from the inauguration. A machine gun was aimed at the crowd from a pediment on Wilson's right. Edith wrote of the tension of that day. "The heavy escort of Regular troops and Secret Service men which attended us during the procession to the Capitol had a look of grim preparation—as indeed was the fact, for letters had been received threatening the President's life.... One warning letter contained the details of a supposed plot by which a bomb was to be thrown from the roof of a house overlooking the route. Consequently soldiers and Secret Service men had been detailed to all the roofs. Just beyond the Peace Monument there was an unaccountable halt in the procession and suddenly *plump*! something fell in my lap. *The bomb*! I thought. Happily, only a clump of flowers had been thrown from a window."

The president's speech spoke of the new world they were entering. "We are provincials no longer. The tragic events of the thirty months of vital turmoil which we have just passed have made us citizens of the world. We cannot turn back…" Still, the president didn't give up on peace and unveiled his League for Peace to Congress. Wilson said he wanted a treaty that would "create a peace that is worth guaranteeing and preserving, a peace that will win the approval of mankind…a peace without victory. Victory would mean peace forced upon the loser, a victor's terms impressed upon the vanquished. It would be accepted in humiliation, under duress, at an intolerable sacrifice, and would leave a sting."

On December 12, Germany agreed to discuss peace and proposed a settlement, but it was a double-edged sword. As Edith would write later, "my husband considered a message from our Embassy in Berlin hinting that should the Germans' peace offer fail they would declare a ruthless submarine campaign."

The president tried to bring the two sides together, but the Germans had come to the conclusion that unrestricted submarine warfare was their best way to bring the war to a close. This was not unlike the belief in a later war when Hitler thought bombing would bring Great Britain to her knees. The new policy directed any ship in the war zones around Britain, France, or Italy, to be sunk. The generals were betting that they could choke off the supply line to the Allies before the Americans could get an army across the sea.

On January 31, 1916, Edith was waiting for the president in the Oval Office. He came in late, pale as a ghost.

"What's wrong, Woodrow?"

He handed her a yellow sheet of paper.

"Read that."

It was an Associated Press dispatch from Berlin.

"The German government has announced that unrestricted submarine warfare will begin around the British Isles tomorrow, February 1, 1917."

Edith looked up.

"What does it mean?"

"It means war," the president said grimly.

Edith would write of this moment twenty-one years later, "I felt a sense of impending climax to the series of crises to which I had been exposed..." On February 3, the president spoke to Congress and announced a severing of diplomatic relations with Germany. "Within an hour after the President had ceased speaking, Count Von Bernstorff was given his passport." He accepted it, saying he was not surprised: "...he had done all he could 'to prevent this.'"

The following day Wilson ordered merchant ships to be armed. A nationwide railroad strike broke out and the czar was overthrown in Russia in a bloodless revolution. Edith's diary catalogs the speed of these events.

> March 13, 1917: We did not get up until lunch-time; he [the president] still feels wretched. There is a streetcar strike in the city and a national railroad strike threatened to begin on Saturday. W. saw several people and telephoned others to see if it could be averted.

March 14... Still raining. W. in bed until one, but seemed better.

March 15... Thrilling news from Russia regarding an almost bloodless Revolution. Overthrow of the Government and taking control by the people.

No one understood what Vladimir Lenin, the founder of the Communist Party, had in mind, and many interpreted the Russian Revolution as a triumph of democracy. No one understood communism and saw only that the Russians would now have a say in their government. The Germans got to work and sunk the British liner *Anaconia* with the loss of two American lives and followed up with the sinking of the American ship *Algonquin*. Then on March 19 and 20, three American ships were sent to the bottom of the Atlantic. Fifteen Americans perished. Teddy Roosevelt declared again, "If he [Wilson] does not go to war with Germany, I shall skin him alive."

"The shadow of war," Edith's diary reads, "is stretching its dark length over our own dear country." The president called for a special session of Congress on April 2 to consider "grave questions of national policy." Alden Hatch in *Edith Bolling Wilson* describes the writing of the president's war message this way. "The night of March 31st was warm and muggy. Woodrow Wilson carried his battered old typewriter downstairs and out to the South Portico. In the light of an electric lantern hanging between the tall fluted columns he sat down to write alone. That fact was symbolic—this was a cross that only he could shoulder. Even his beloved wife could not help him tonight."

"She [Edith] sat upstairs in the Oval Room, listening through the open windows to the hesitant click of Wilson's machine, writing history by the hunt-and-peck system. The Secret Service men guarding the park-like grounds heard it too, and were careful to keep out of sight." They all sensed that the president must feel himself alone. The words that would send thousands of men to their deaths were the staccato pecks of one man looking for letters in the night.

President Wilson was interrupted only when Edith brought down some milk and crackers. "She took it and went silently out onto the portico. The air was wonderfully alive with all the sweet smells of a sudden spring. Without speaking she put the tray on a little table at her husband's side...never changing the broken rhythm of his typing."

The president continued work on his war message the next day while Edith attended to other business for him. "On this day while he worked I decoded some cipher messages that had come for him." On the morning of April 2, 1917, Edith and the president went golfing. She thought it important that he get some exercise on the day the United States was going to war.

A misty summer rain began to fall as the Wilsons were driven to the Capitol around 8:00 p.m. They could see the Capitol lit up when they reached Pennsylvania Avenue for the extraordinary night session. Two troops of Cavalry in dress uniforms met the president at the House of Representatives. Edith left her husband on the steps and took her seat in the House gallery facing the speaker's rostrum.

Edith wrote about that night twenty years later. "Troops were standing on guard round the entire building which stood out white and majestic in the indirect lighting...when I reached the gallery after leaving my husband I found every seat taken and people standing in every available place both on the floor and in the galleries.... When my husband came in and all rose to their feet, my heart seemed to stop its beating..."

The president waited for the cheering to stop and looked up at Edith and smiled. He began speaking at 8:30 and quickly reached the climax of his speech. "There is one choice we cannot make, we are incapable of making, we will not choose the path of submission..."

Chief Justice White leaped to his feet and gave the rebel yell. Then Wilson added the words that elevated World War I for all time and would lead to the League of Nations. America would fight, he continued, for "the ultimate peace of the world and for the liberation of its people, the German peoples included; for the rights of nations great and small and the privilege of men everywhere to choose their way of life and obedience."

President Wilson promised that by going to war the United States would "vindicate the principles of peace and justice in the life of the world...*to make the world safe for democracy.*"

By tying the United States' involvement in the European war to making the world safe for democracy, Wilson had now taken hold of a grail he could not release. The sacrifice of American lives must stand for more than the settling of land squabbles or aggression. It must change the world. Senator Lodge approached the president as he was leaving. "Mr. President, you have expressed in the loftiest manner possible, the sentiments of the American people." Some would say it was the greatest speech since Lincoln's Gettysburg address.

On Good Friday, Wilson was told that the war resolution was on its way from Congress for his signature. The president rushed through his dinner as the messenger arrived with the document. The president was in the State Dining Room where Edith handed him a gold pen he had given her.

"Stand by me, Edith," he whispered as he signed the war resolution with the gift to his wife. He signed the resolution and handed the pen back to her. Later that day the president drafted his last will and testament, leaving all his property to Edith Bolling Wilson.

# TWENTY-SIX

# THE COAL STRIKE AND PALMER RAIDS

## 1919

ON JUNE 2, ATTORNEY GENERAL A. MITCHELL PALMER WAS ASLEEP in his home with his wife and daughter. Crickets pulsed outside the windows with light brimming in the east. Palmer woke when he heard a car pull up outside. He glanced at the dresser, where he kept his service revolver. A man got out of the car with a suitcase and crossed the lawn, then tripped in the Palmers' garden and the suitcase exploded in his face.

Palmer's neighbor Franklin D. Roosevelt ran over at the sound of the explosion from next door. The would-be bomber was dead, but Palmer's family was shaken and their house was largely destroyed. Bombs exploded that morning at the homes of eight judges and senators who were deemed anti-radical. Labor strikes and riots were breaking out all over. The mayor of Seattle called on government troops to stop a workers' shutdown in his city and several plots to assassinate President Wilson had been stopped by the Secret Service.

A mail bomb blew up when a housemaid opened it at the home of Georgia Senator Thomas Hardwick. Then five more bombs were mailed to senators and cabinet members, as well as industry titans J. P. Morgan and John D. Rockefeller. Anarchist Eugene Debs had just been sentenced to ten years in prison and would be the last man Woodrow Wilson would consider pardoning before he left office. The Russian communist threat became clear on May Day when demonstrations broke out all around the country.

The upheaval that followed World War I, with men returning home to find no jobs, had taken an ominous turn on the night of June 2, 1919. Palmer saw red all over. Russia had become the poster child for what could happen to the Western world if communism was not checked. Palmer got a young lawyer, J. Edgar Hoover, to help him destroy the "Red Menace." He wanted Hoover to head a new department, the General Intelligence Division of the Justice Department's Bureau of Investigation. His charge was simple: to collect information on radicals and deport them.

On November 1, the United Mine Workers under John Lewis went on strike. They had taken wage cuts during the war and now wanted to claw back some of their lost money. Palmer invoked the wartime Lever Act, which defined critical industries to the war and made it a crime to interfere with production. Palmer had obtained an injunction the day before, but four hundred thousand miners walked out anyway. He claimed to have had the president's backing and in a cabinet meeting Josephus Daniels recorded that "Palmer said Judge Anderson had taken case in his hands—had summoned Grand Jury—and it looked like he was going to imprison many miners for contempt because they had not gone back to work."

The *New York Times* ran an article on December 7 with the headline, "President Makes Proposal to Coal Miners, Leaders Accept, Strike Likely to End." Joseph Tumulty was running between the

Union and the miners and the sick room. Edith sent him a letter on the same day, "Dear Mr. Tumulty, the president says will you see the Secretary of Labor and ask to let him know if the Federal Govt is still carrying on the investigation in the Mooney case [case of an anarchist accused of throwing bombs] in California...Edith Wilson."

Then Tumulty tipped his hand as to the author of the settlement of the coal mining crisis. "Dear Mrs. Wilson, I have re-read the statement the president signed Saturday night with reference to the coal mining situation. Frankly I do not find any limitation in it embodying the paragraph in Mr. Garfield's letter...at his leisure the president might peruse the statement again."

Tumulty obviously wrote the statement and had Edith sign it, or she directed the president's hand. Woodrow Wilson was only marginally involved in the negotiations.

World War I sedition laws were still on the books, and Palmer had authorized raids on perceived enemies across the country. Not until the McCarthy Hearings would "communist hysteria" grip the country again with the subsequent trampling of personal liberties. As early as November 6, Hoover had launched attacks all over the country with agents and deputized police forces. It was the second anniversary of the Bolshevik Revolution and the symbolism was not lost on Palmer, who saw a bomb-throwing "red" lurking in every bush and every tree.

Doors were knocked down in middle-of-the-night raids that resulted in the arrest of six hundred radicals. In the hysteria, two hundred and fifty citizens were deported to Russia with activist Emma Goldman following soon after. The press saw this as fighting the scourge of anarchy and "red infiltration." Palmer unleashed police forces and his newly minted federal agents under J. Edgar Hoover concentrated on "Centers of Red Activity" all over the United States. Warrants were issued for immigrants who were accused of conspiring to overthrow the United States. The attorney general had little control over the conduct of the police forces used to knock down doors and drag out suspected radicals in the middle of the night. The end justified the means. Local police caught red fever all over the country and started arresting more people. Hundreds more were deported.

When the hysteria started to die down and the raids stopped, people began to wonder about whether these actions were violations of the constitutional rights of freedom of speech, liberty, trial by jury, and civil rights. The worst part of the Palmer Raids was that they established a pattern for J. Edgar Hoover.

President Wilson knew nothing of the raids and the only mention he makes of them is to tell Palmer in a cabinet meeting, "not to let the country see red." Edith didn't tell the president about the arrests and Grayson agreed with keeping him in the dark. So while vigilantes were unleashed all over the country against ordinary citizens, the designated president slept on.

# TWENTY-SEVEN

# THE WAR TO END
# ALL WARS

## 1918

PEOPLE IN FARMHOUSES ALL OVER AMERICA STARED OUT THEIR windows. It was still light out at 8:00 in the evening. The calendar on the wall said March 31, 1918. The president had just changed the hours of the day. Daylight Savings Time gave everyone an extra hour of work and the kerosene lanterns didn't have to be lit or those new electric lights switched on. The president's challenge was to take a nation of rugged individuals and make them act as one. He started with a speech to Congress asking for the declaration of war against Germany. The vote for war in the House of Representatives was 373 to 50 with the first woman in Congress, Jeannette Rankin, voting against the war. In the end she said, "I want to stand by my country, but I cannot vote for war."

Edith wrote later of the wartime routines of the White House. "There the day began at five. Before six the President was at his desk, and often he was there at midnight. People descended upon the White House until their coming and going was like the rise and fall of the tides. To achieve anything amid such distractions called for the most rigid rationing of time. Otherwise the result would have been chaos…"

The Navy put every government ship under its command and seized ninety-one German vessels and interred their crews on Ellis Island for deportation. This didn't stop German crews from scuttling their ships by sawing off bolt heads. The president turned toward food. Students were sent home and promised diplomas if they would work on family farms. "Victory Gardens" popped up everywhere. The United States offered unoccupied land to anyone who would farm it.

Edith wrote later of this practice, "Edith Benham, my secretary, took over one of these tracts, and, in addition to her secretarial work, tended it early and late with wonderful results. The Government ploughed the land, and staked it off, but the individual did the rest…it will be hard to visualize the Potomac Drive from where the road goes under the railroad trestle, all the way to Hains Point, as one vast truck garden."

In the beginning of the war the United State had disjointed rail systems. The Anti-Trust Act of 1890 had kept the competing railroads from joining up and making the nation's transportation system cost effective. Wilson seized the railroads and put them under his son-in-law with the mandate to improve efficiency by unification. Two million men were under Secretary McAdoo at the stroke of the president's pen. McAdoo quickly eliminated one-sixth of the lines considered redundant, and saved $100 million while increasing pay and efficiency. The president justified his action under the Army Appropriations Act, saying, "Only under government administration can an absolutely unrestricted and unembarrassed common use be made of all tracks, terminals, terminal facilities and equipment of every kind."

Herbert Clark Hoover was asked by the president to organize food production and get the nation's crop yields up. The nation produced more wheat, corn, barley, rice, and oats, and "meatless" Mondays began and then "wheatless" days followed. Everyone got into the act, including Edith. As she later wrote, "the Cabinet ladies and I had subscribed to a pledge to reduce living to its simplest form and to deny ourselves luxuries in order to free those who produce them for the cultivation of necessities.... We make an appeal to all women of America to do everything in their power along these lines not only as individuals but organizations to hasten the end of the struggle and win the War."

There were "heatless" Mondays with citizens bundling up so oil could go overseas or be used in factories producing war materiel. This was followed by "gasless" Sundays in which cars were parked and horses brought out from stables and carriages were dusted off. Edith wrote of going to church on one of these gasless Sundays. "We set forth to church in an ancient Victoria found in one of the White House stables. But the Secret Service Men were put to it to discover anything to carry them. Finally an old time surrey with a fringe around the top was procured."

Power was dimmed in cities and advertisements were turned off as the country fell dark on "lightless" nights. Even Broadway turned off her lights. The president gave the country an extra hour of daylight for farm work and the reduction of electric light usage, which saved oil and coal; Daylight Savings Time became a permanent part of American life. Wilson then created the conscription army of the United States with mandatory service; the draft had arrived.

All of this took a toll on Wilson, and Edith found herself too exhausted at times to carry on. "I know that the emotional drain and the work combined were too much for me," she wrote in her memoir, "and after we had been in the war just eight days I had to take a day off in bed." Admiral Grayson suggested some new form of presidential exercise besides just golf. Edith looked at the doctor.

"What do you suggest?"

"Horseback riding," said Grayson. "And you have got to make him think it was your idea." Edith positioned it this way to the president: she had always wanted more than anything to go horseback riding with him. "I'll get Grayson to go over to Fort Myer and pick out a couple of mounts for us," the president responded.

The next afternoon, Edith met Army grooms with the horses on the lawn. "The president came out in a makeshift outfit, Grayson in the immaculate perfection of London's finest tailors and boot makers," as Alden Hatch would write in *Edith Bolling Wilson*. "Secret Service men unhappily clambered aboard unwilling nags in their regular dark business suits. And off went the whole cavalcade with a merry jingle of accoutrements."

On the way back, Edith's horse stumbled and she was pitched over its head and landed in a muddy path. "I was not hurt to speak of and got on him again. But I did feel nervous and shaky...thereafter our rides became a regular thing...of course the Secret Service went too, and although we might not have made very promising candidates we had lots of fun."

When the British came over with the first Allied Mission, Wilson and Edith learned something that shocked them. The president saw America's fight as eventually ushering in a new age of peace, but what the British told him was that if America didn't get over there quickly the Western Front would collapse. The president immediately ordered destroyers to help with the British antisubmarine patrols. The U-boats were sinking nine hundred thousand tons of shipping per month, and no country could bear that for long.

Edith set up a sewing machine and a Red Cross workshop in one of the guest rooms. She also joined Red Cross canteens and served troops at train depots. She wore the same blue and white dress as the rest of the Red Cross ladies. Many times troops didn't know who she was. On one warm night, Edith had a basket of cigarettes and chewing gum around her neck. She moved through the smoke-filled station with her hair damp from humidity and coal dust griming her cheeks.

She wrote later, "A tall western boy in the high-collared blouse, spiral puttees and Rough Rider hat, then the unrealistic uniform of the American troops, hailed me. 'Beg pardon Ma'm, but the boys are saying you're the first lady. Is that a fact?'"

Edith smiled at the young soldier.

"Yes, I'm Mrs. Woodrow Wilson."

The soldier studied her for a moment.

"Well, Ma'am, you sure don't look it!"

During the first months of the war, Edith came down with the grippe. She was in her room for two weeks and the president visited in the evenings and read to her. Edith looked out from her room at night and saw the State, War, and Navy buildings. Washington had been transformed, and Edith saw a light on in every window. She would turn off the lights in her bedroom and "Always there were figures moving back and forth, as busy men went from office to office; and in the telegraph and decoding rooms there was never an end to work."

Usually news from abroad arrived late at night, and the president would sit up with the secretary of war reading the decoded messages. Edith later wrote in her memoir, "they would both look so grave and so tired. My own heart was heavy with theirs, but the lights across the way always cheered me, and after watching them I would go to bed more hopeful."

But it wasn't always all work and no play. Sometimes late at night Mr. and Mrs. Wilson would go to the Oval Office and put a record on the Victrola. "Now, I'll show you how to do a jig step," he once announced. Edith thought Woodrow light on his feet and said he envied Primrose the minstrel dancer. The president loved vaudeville and became a regular at Keith's Theatre. Edith would later say, "No matter how foolish the skit, he said it rested him because it took his mind off responsibilities and refreshed his spirit..." Returning to the White House, they would go to "The Drawer" and find it filled. The president would work under his green lampshade while Edith handed him one paper after another.

The United States had been a country in which more people lived on farms than in cities. This changed with a migration to the cities after the Civil War. The White House purchased a flock of Hampshire sheep to keep the lawn trimmed and do their part for the war. It was a curious sight, and shows the crossroads of the times where a mighty rural country would become an industrial behemoth like the world had never seen.

The sheep were largely symbolic, but Edith was committed to the cause. She wrote years later, "When shearing time came and the sheep furnished ninety-eight pounds of wool, the question arose how best to dispose of it, so that it might yield the best for the cause. We decided to send the wool to the Red Cross [for auction].... The total sum...from...'White House wool'...was nearly a hundred thousand dollars."

One morning Edith came out and found one of the baby sheep sick and near death. She took it into the White House kitchen and sent for Admiral Grayson.

"Do you think it's dying?" she asked

"I'm afraid so," he said kneeling down and examining it.

"Do something," Edith commanded.

"Whiskey," said the doctor.

Some bourbon was found and poured down the sheep's throat. The baby sheep opened its eyes and then stood up, clicking around the kitchen.

Meanwhile, the Allies were watching as the Bolsheviks and the Whites fought it out for control. Edith received war news daily from encoded messages. "Ordinarily the President's foreign communications were handled by the code room in the State Department, but [the president] and Colonel House had a private code known, so far as I am aware, only to them and to me," she wrote two decades after the war. "It was used in matters requiring the greatest secrecy, Colonel House himself coding and decoding messages and I performing that service for my husband."

Edith Wilson's knowledge of the war and of the United States' participation in it came from primary sources. She was getting information only a president would be privy to. These coded messages flowed as the blood between the Allies and the United States. Edith learned first of the Italian defeat at Caporetto and of the Bolsheviks' occupation of Petrograd and the Kerensky Government's flight. She understood how dire the situation was for the Allies now. A few days later, on March 3, 1918, the Russians sued for an armistice and were out of the war. As she wrote in her memoir, "The situation was graver than it had been since 1914."

The president was due to give a speech to the American Federation of Labor at Buffalo. Just before the speech, another long coded message came from House that Edith decoded for the president. The message stated there was uncertainty in the parliaments of England and France. The war was wearing down both countries. The next day the president gave his speech and then he and the first lady rushed back for news. "Next day came a cable which took me three hours to decode," Edith wrote. Colonel House said that the president's speech had helped with its talk of victory. England and France could hang on until the Americans arrived.

During this time Edith was opening some of the White House mail. Many of the senders promised to kill the president. Edith later wrote that she would be reading the letters when the president would say, "Don't bother over that. No one who is going to commit such an act is going to write about it beforehand; and I firmly believe that as long as a man is useful in the world he will survive. So dismiss this as one person at least we do not have to concern ourselves with."

Edith and the president worked on his annual message to Congress. Edith knew the speech by heart: "we had gone over every word together so that I could repeat them almost line by line..." The president wound up his address with a call to ultimate victory while the Allies waited. "With victory an accomplished fact peace will be evolved, based upon mercy and justice—to friend and foe."

In his address, Wilson outlined the Fourteen Points that would be the eventual blueprint for peace. Even the *New-York Tribune*, Wilson's longtime foe, asserted, "The President's words are the words of a hundred million. Today, as never before, the whole nation marches with the President..."

The fourteenth point was the one Wilson would hang his hat on. *"A general association of nations must be formed under specific covenants for the purpose of affording mutual guarantees of political independence and territorial integrity to great and small states alike."*

The League of Nations was the flame that must burn to justify the millions who would die in World War I. Already Woodrow Wilson was looking ahead to a framework for world peace. But for now it was up to the Americans to save the Allies, and maybe the world.

# TWENTY-EIGHT

# SUNSET BOULEVARD

## 1919

THE COWBOYS GALLOPED ACROSS THE LINCOLN BEDSHEET HUNG
in the Red Room of the White House. Edith and her husband watched
with the projector clattering in time with the pounding of the horses.
The president didn't want the piano accompaniment that occurred in
cigar-choked theaters across the country. The president wanted to
watch westerns of men who galloped in silence, saved the girl, then
rode off into the sunset.

A strange Howard Hughes-type existence had descended upon
the inhabitants of the White House. Wilson was awakened at eight
by Ike Hoover and propped up in his Atlantic City chair. Then he was
wheeled out for breakfast with Edith while she read him headlines
from various newspapers. After that he had a nap while she went to
attend to the business of the White House.

When Edith returned they discussed the issues of the day, with
Wilson saying little. When he did speak it was in a thin, raspy voice
she had to strain to hear. Sometimes the president would stop in

midsentence and lose his train of thought completely. Edith would then gently nudge him back to reality by reminding him of what he had just said. Many times, the president sat silent with his head cocked to one side as if listening for the return of the bustling White House that vanished when the gates were locked and the shades drawn.

At times, the White House had the air of a hospice in Victorian gloom, with few people in the large empty state rooms and even fewer admitted from the outside. Below in the Red Room, the State Dining Room, and the East Room, servants' footsteps echoed, as the rugs had been rolled up to make it easier for the rolling chair. The reporters smoked and played cards in the pressroom with little to report on.

Ike Hoover's White House diary used to record ten visitors in a few hours; now he had just a single entry. "Dr. Grayson spent the night." Later he would write, "On sunshine days he [the president] would be wheeled out into the south grounds for an hour or so. If there were some papers or matters pending these would be read to him. But only those that Mrs. Wilson thought should be read to him."

Sometimes Wilson's daughters or Dr. Grayson would come speak to him. Edith often pushed the wheelchair past windows along the veranda and stopped outside Joe Tumulty's window. The secretary would then come out and speak to the president. Afterwards, Edith would push her husband inside, where they would take lunch in the study. The president then went back to bed while Edith took care of piles of correspondence. The problem was the piles had been growing with no hope of ever catching up. Many times the first lady would walk the White House grounds alone, a captive as much as the president. Around four in the afternoon, the president was in bed and they talked about the cabinet vacancies that remained open. After dinner the president went to sleep for a while and then Edith read to him from mystery novels. Often right in the middle of a page, Wilson started crying. Edith took the president in her arms, whispering "darling, darling," until the mood passed.

On December 20, snow was on the ground now and the president was wheeled outside for some air. The *New York Times* reported "Mr. Wilson will eat Christmas dinner in his room and there will be no Christmas tree at the White House this year." When Christmas came the president watched a movie in the East Room. Robert Long, a local theater manager, brought the movie and played it on a projector given to the White House by Douglas Fairbanks. Long was shocked when the president was wheeled in the first time. He had seen Wilson before as a vigorous man at his theater. As Gene Smith wrote in *When The Cheering Stopped*, now he saw a man, "in his wheel chair, his head bent forward and down...Long and his assistant looked at each other in horror. They could hardly believe this bent figure unable to sit up straight was the same man."

The movie gleamed in the crystal chandeliers of the East Room and reflected in the giant mirrors. The president enjoyed the western projected onto an enormous sheet from the Lincoln Bed. One cannot help but think of a retirement home where people are wheeled in to watch television. Sometimes the movie became too exciting for the president and it had to be stopped.

The movies became a ritual for Wilson; for really what else did he have to do? Edith was running the White House assisted by Grayson and Tumulty. So around 10:30 a.m. the president would come down the elevator and be wheeled through the empty rooms, smiling at the servants and announcing, "My tour of inspection." The maids didn't let on that their hearts were breaking at the site of the broken president.

At 11:00 a.m. the film began, and many times the president saw early releases the country wouldn't see for months. Wilson preferred big outdoor movies, including any kind of western. The president watched the films in silence with the projector clickety-clacking away in the flickering darkness.

Edith kept her eyes on the president most of the time, but once the first lady was busy talking to someone and the president slumped in his chair. Long noticed Wilson's head had fallen forward and he became alarmed because the president looked dead. Edith saw what had happened and went and pulled Wilson's head over to rest on her. The next day Long appeared with another film.

In a scene from the movie *Sunset Boulevard*, Norma Desmond sits in her mansion watching silent movies of herself from the 1920s. She had grown old while the world had moved on to talkies, and she was reduced to watching her faded glory with her butler Max and a young writer she had picked up. The president had his own Norma Desmond moment when he had Long put on reels from Paris.

It was the greatest hit of the Wilson presidency. The president had gone to Europe as a savior after World War I. He had gone to restructure the world and make war impossible with the League of Nations. Wilson stood with Edith and waved from a balcony. Millions cheered as the president doffed his hat, not seeing the broken man watching in the darkness.

# TWENTY-NINE

# ALL QUIET ON THE WESTERN FRONT

## 1918

SNOW FELL OUTSIDE THE WHITE HOUSE WINDOW. THE WOMAN working over the cable from Europe felt her heart. Four years before she had been concerned with her next vacation and taking her electric for a spin. Now she was decoding a message that would tell the world that the great catastrophe of World War I had ended. She mouthed the words as she matched the letters in the codebook. The snow fell harder.

After the British Conference with the Americans, Wilson upped the number of troops from six hundred thousand to four million. He would win the war the way General Grant had beaten Robert E. Lee in the Civil War—by massive attrition and the ability to replace every soldier lost with three more. This strategy, coupled with a massive outpouring of materiel, would become the American boilerplate for war that would be copied a quarter century later in World War II.

The president proved an able warrior. After a review of several new ships, he spoke on the deck of the *Pennsylvania* to assembled officers. Wilson said he was tired of hearing the British speak of prudence. "Please leave out of your vocabulary the word 'prudent'...do the thing that is audacious to the utmost point of risk and daring...and you will win by the audacity of method...." The British had yet to come up with a system to keep their fleet safe from submarines. The Americans would develop the convoy approach for getting their troops across the Atlantic.

The U-boats had come to America with submarines reported off the East coast. The president and first lady wanted to the take the presidential yacht *Mayflower* out for one last cruise and were met by three destroyers. An officer boarded and let them know a U-boat had been cited off Nantucket Island and it wasn't safe to proceed. The president countermanded the order and said they would be fine.

The destroyers escorted the *Mayflower* with gun crews manning the antisubmarine guns recently installed onboard. They arrived safely and crossed the island in a surrey. Woodrow and Edith had a great day on the beach, then returned in the surrey driven by an islander in dense fog. The old man dropped his whip every now and then and licked the end. "Taking soundings, Captain?" Wilson asked. "Yes, Mr. President," he replied. "I know the taste of every foot of ground on this island." Once they reached the *Mayflower*, the fog kept the ship in until the next day. The lurking U-boats moved along the coast looking for anything they could find, but they missed the president's yacht that night.

The summer of 1918 had troops streaming into transports to go overseas. The railroads had their hands full moving men across the country to points of debarkation. Having Secretary McAdoo run the rail system seemed to have been the right move. One consequence of that decision was that Colonel House's power in the White House waned. House took a step forever backward with Edith on the issue of the government paying the railroads.

The president wrote a message to Congress asking for legislation to compensate railroad workers. A rough draft of the request was sent to House for his suggestions. He came to the White House about five in the afternoon, but Wilson was with the war cabinet. Edith picks it up here in her memoir. "I asked him to come in and ordered tea sent up. We sat before the fire, and taking the paper from his pocket, he literally waxed eloquent over a thorough disagreement with the entire policy outlined, bringing up some very good reasons for his side."

Edith said then, "Well, we will have an interesting session after dinner, when you take this up with Woodrow."

"'Suppose you tell him about it first and let him think it over,' he suggested."

"'Very well, I will,' I said."

Clearly House wanted Edith to soften the president up. He went to dress for dinner and Edith heard the president. She told him about their conversation and said House disapproved of his letter. "He doesn't like it at all," she finished up, and said she was inclined to agree. After dinner they went to his study, where the president led off.

"Well, Edith tells me you don't agree with me on this, which is a disappointment, for I have weighed every word of it and put a lot of hard work on it. But let's have it. I want your reactions."

The colonel shook his head.

"Yes, I did tell Mrs. Wilson that, but she fought so well for your side of the question that I sat down and reread the entire paper before dinner and agreed with every word of it."

Edith was floored. She had been converted by House's arguments and now was being left high and dry.

"Why, Colonel, you said you couldn't! You said—"

"Yes, I know I did, but I changed my mind," he snapped.

What had happened was that House saw the president had dug in after Edith raised the issue. Edith had never forgiven House for his scheme to stop their marriage with the Mary Peck letters. But after this she didn't trust him again, leaving House to wonder later why she blocked him from seeing the president.

In spite of daily threats of assassination coming to the White House, the Wilsons went for walks around Washington and Edith still took her electric out with people cheering as she passed through the gates. By the summer of 1918, two million American soldiers had hit the front lines and the Germans were in retreat. The Wilsons listened to George Cohan's "Over There" and the president teared up whenever he heard the song.

On October 6, the White House received a cable from the Minister of Switzerland that the Germans wanted an armistice based on the Fourteen Points. Wilson handed the cable to Edith and exclaimed: "Here is glorious news!" The notes went back and forth for a month with Wilson sending Colonel House to represent him with the Allies. It was during this time that the president made one of the worst political blunders of his career.

The midterm elections in Congress were coming and Wilson wanted the Senate to back him in the final phases of the war. He wanted to ask the American people to give him a Democratic majority in both houses. Wilson showed the letter he had written to Edith. The letter said that the president wanted undisputed mastery in postwar negotiations and that if Republicans were elected it would divide the leadership. The letter went on to say that the Republicans had been *anti-administration*. He then wrapped it up with a big war bow: "In ordinary times divided counsels can be endured without permanent hurt to the country. But these are not ordinary times…"

Edith told him at once her thoughts.

"I would not send it," she told him. "It's not a dignified thing to do."

Edith pointed out that the letter would antagonize the Republicans who had worked with him during the war. Wilson didn't listen and when the letter was published the outrage was voiced by his twin nemeses, Teddy Roosevelt and Henry Cabot Lodge, who accused the president of claiming that the Republicans were less patriotic than the Democrats.

"That message was one of the greatest mistakes Woodrow ever made," said Edith later. She wasn't surprised when the Democrats lost majorities in the House and Senate. The war Democratic machine was now gone; worse than that, Henry Cabot Lodge was in power in the Senate. He would make the president pay for his folly.

The war still had to be wrapped up. Edith wrote in her memoir, "All the negotiations on the Allies' side were conducted by the President.... Cables flew between them constantly and I worked early and late coding and decoding." The president considered going to Europe to ensure that the Fourteen Points would be the framework for peace. Edith decoded a cable from Colonel House saying neither the British nor French approved. When Wilson read the cable, he turned to Edith and said, "We'll go."

But the war hadn't ended yet. There was a false armistice proclaimed by the newspapers on November 7. People gathered outside the White House and Edith asked the president to step outside and wave. Wilson refused, citing no armistice had been signed. The Germans had merely specified the time and date for the signing at that point.

On Sunday, November 10, Edith and the president went to church and returned, waiting for news that the armistice had actually been signed. Edith's mother, sister, and brother Randolph came to dinner. When they saw them to the elevator, Edith's mother told the president to get some sleep.

"I wish I could, but I fear The Drawer; it always circumvents me; wait just a moment until I look."

Wilson came back with five long coded cablegrams, which he handed to Edith. "This is your task," he told her, "and I have many others; so there is no rest in sight for either of us yet." Randolph said, "Let me stay and help you, Edith." The president replied, "Indeed you can help her and I would be very grateful."

Edith and her brother then went and worked at a big table decoding the messages. By 1:00 a.m. they were finished and went to the president's study. Edith would later write: "My recollection is that these principally concerned the expressed desire of M. Clemenceau to work in harmony with the United States during the peace negotiations..."

Two hours later another encoded cable arrived. At 3:00 a.m. Monday, November 11, 1918, the armistice ending World War I was signed. Edith and the president stared at each other and didn't speak. Less than three years before, Edith Galt had been a widow living in Washington. Now she was one of two people in America who had received the news that World War I had finally ended. All was finally quiet on the Western Front.

# THIRTY

# JUDAS

## 1920

THE 1920S CAME QUIETLY TO THE WHITE HOUSE. THE JAZZ AGE
had arrived and F. Scott Fitzgerald was feverishly rewriting *This Side
of Paradise,* in which he would famously say in 1923, "We awoke to
find all wars fought and all Gods dead," while bathtub gin was being
brewed in speakeasies across the country. The Big Party was about to
begin, but the White House was dark, save for the flickering images
on the Lincoln bedsheet in the Red Room.

Christmas brought cards to the White House that Edith read to
her husband. One of the cards came from a little girl, Fairlie of Alabama, who said she was sorry the president was sick, but that if he
would come to Alabama he could have "milk and butter and sausages
and spareribs and a good time." Edith wrote back thanking Fairlie.

The country still didn't know the extent of the president's illness,
but newspapers speculated that Edith Wilson was running the show.
The strain of nursing her husband back to health, keeping his true
condition a guarded secret, and running the country was taking its

toll. Even her personal secretary felt the pressure. "On March 4th my secretary, Edith Benham, fell suddenly ill," Edith wrote later, "and her physician brought me word that she had suffered a complete nervous breakdown and must take an indefinite leave."

Edith took on her work too. "At first I hardly knew how to do without her, but in those days I had to act and not think too long about anything." Edith often worked long into the night on White House communications. "Having tackled the first day's consignment of mail myself I summoned Mr. McGee, Miss Benham's typist and had him copy a series of form replies I had written, numbered 1, 2, 3, 4, and so on. To communications which could not be answered in this way I would scribble replies in longhand which Mr. McGee copied. It often happened that I did not get to the mail until everyone else except the night nurse was in bed and I almost too weary to hold a pencil."

The president knew he was barely hanging on. In Grayson's memoir, the president is quoted as saying, "I am seriously thinking what is my duty to my country on account of my physical condition. My personal pride must not be allowed to stand in the way of my duty to the country." Wilson then asked if he should resign, but Edith and Grayson said the country still needed him. Edith believed leaving the White House would destroy her husband's reason for living.

Dr. Grayson, hoping to make the president feel more involved, suggested he call a cabinet meeting. Edith had recently allowed a physical therapist to begin working with her husband. Wilson was still using bedpans and couldn't leave his bed unassisted. But he made progress with the therapy and was able to partially walk. The cabinet meeting would still be a big risk.

They called the meeting for the next day at 10:00 a.m. Edith and Admiral Grayson got the president dressed and Wilson entered the room on a cane, but they quickly saw through the façade. Secretary of Agriculture David Houston described the meeting this way: "The president looked old, worn, and haggard—it was enough to make one weep to look at him. One of his arms was useless. In repose his face looked very much as usual. When he tried to speak there was marked evidence of trouble. His jaw tended to droop to one side, or seemed to do so. His voice was very weak."

The president managed to shake hands with a few cabinet members and crack a few jokes. The business of the cabinet was transacted, but it consisted of little since Wilson hadn't been involved. After an hour, Grayson appeared to end the meeting. The president shook him off and the meeting continued for another twenty minutes. Edith appeared and suggested the cabinet members had better go and the cabinet meeting ended.

Irwin Hoover's view of these cabinet meetings gives insight into the president's true condition. "He permitted himself to be camouflaged like on occasions of so called cabinet meetings...at all of the Cabinet meetings held he would be rolled into the Cabinet room in his old chair and fixed up prior to the coming of the Cabinet members. He sat there in all the meetings as one in a trance, the Cabinet members doing all the talking. He would have agreed to about anything they said...."

One concrete thing did come out of the meeting and that was the president's resolve to rid himself of Secretary of State Robert Lansing. As Edith put it later, "Mr. Lansing should have retired long before." In her view he had sabotaged Wilson's work with the League of Nations in Paris and was a traitor. "As soon as the President became ill, Mr. Lansing started agitation to put his Chief out of office."

The president was furious when he found out Lansing had been calling cabinet meetings. This smacked of a mutiny to him. Even while Wilson was on his tour of the West to push for the League, William Bullitt testified before a Senate Committee that the secretary of state had said to him, "the League Covenant was thoroughly bad and in his belief, if the Senate thoroughly understood, it would reject it."

Secretary Lansing hadn't been happy for some time. "I don't know how I am going to stand the present state of affairs much longer...I must continue though the irascibility and tyranny of the president, whose worse qualities have come to the surface during his sickness, cannot be borne much longer."

The secretary was most upset with his inability to see Wilson. Colonel House voiced what everyone knew, that Edith Wilson hated Lansing. "Lansing is insulted daily by the White House...his attitude is he will not resign until the president has sufficiently recovered and to indicate whether he wishes him to or not.... Lansing went to the White House the other day to tell Mrs. Wilson how necessary it was to take some action on a pressing matter which he had already brought to the attention of the president...Mrs. Wilson replied to him curtly, 'the president does not like to be told a thing twice.'"

Lansing wrote in a memorandum, "I don't know how I am going to stand the present state of affairs much longer. It has become almost intolerable. Even if he cannot run things himself, the president is well enough to choose my successor." Lansing complained that nobody was allowed to disagree on foreign affairs or otherwise. But what really irritated him was that Edith was instructing him on appointments to be made.

"Dear Mr. Secretary, The president wishes me to say to you that time is of the essence in getting the appointments for the Diplomatic Service confirmed...so he will be obliged if you will let him have the nominations of the recent appointments at your earliest convenience.... Faithfully Edith Bolling Wilson."

In reply, Lansing challenged Edith's authority. "My Dear Mrs. Wilson, I am in receipt of your letter stating the decision of the president as to certain diplomatic appointments. Although I, of course, understand that these appointments are practically settled, I think that I should lay before him the names of those who have been urged for these posts with more or less insistence. I do this with no purpose of changing his declared wishes, but in order that I may be able to say to the supporters of the various candidates that I submitted the names before any appointments were made…If I am not able to say this, I will be placed in a most embarrassing situation…"

Lansing wanted to see the president to confirm the appointments. Instead, Wilson dictated a letter to Edith, which she sent to the secretary of state. "Is it true as I have been told, that you have frequently called the heads of executive departments of the government into conference?…under our constitutional law and practice…no one but the president has the right to summon heads of executive departments into conference."

Lansing shot back.

"It is true…shortly after you were taken ill in October, certain members of the cabinet, of which I was one, felt that, in view of the fact we were denied communication with you, it was wise for us to confer informally together on interdepartmental matters and matters as to which action could not be postponed until your medical advisers permitted you to pass upon them…"

The president sent back that it would relieve him of embarrassment if the secretary would give up his office. Lansing was only too glad, writing, "The most charitable opinion of the president's mental state is that on account of paralysis…his mind is not normal…he is affected by a species of mania which seems to approach irrationality…Woodrow Wilson is a tyrant who even goes so far as to demand that all men shall think as he does or else be branded as traitors…Thank God I shall be a free man!"

Lansing wanted to smear the president and threw in with the people saying that he had lost his mind. In his diary he wrote,

" ...Sen McCumber said that the senators were in unanimous opinion that 'president is crazy,' that they were with me and that the Democrats felt they must go on with the treaty without his leadership."

Edith advised Wilson to relate Lansing's many betrayals, including non-support of the League of Nations. The public wouldn't understand the president firing the secretary of state over some meetings. Secretary Tumulty didn't believe he should do it, saying, "It was the wrong time to do the right thing." The president responded it was never the wrong time to get rid of someone who is disloyal.

On February 9, the same day Secretary Lansing offered his resignation, Edith directed him to coordinate with the secretary of war. "The President as you see submitted your letter of Feb 6th to the Secretary of War and he asks that you now read his enclosed reply and that you cooperate with the Secretary of War in the way he suggests...EBW."

Even at the end, Edith was still instructing Lansing. Wilson accepted his resignation on February 13 and the secretary's justification for his actions; Lansing summed up, saying, "I cannot permit to pass unchallenged the imputation that in calling into informal conference the heads of the executive departments I sought to usurp your presidential authority. I had no such intention, no such thought." He copied the letter and distributed it to the press. He then smugly noted, "The President delivered himself into my hands and of course I took advantage of his stupidity... "

Lansing felt this political stumble would prove how erratic the president's actions had become. Edith was proved right. People did see the worst in the firing of Secretary Lansing. She later wrote, "I begged Mr. Wilson to state both reasons for his acceptance of the proferred resignation, protesting that the letter as written made him look small... "

Every major newspaper in the country took issue with the firing of the secretary of state. To make matters worse, a noted Johns Hopkins urologist released a report on Wilson's cerebral thrombosis. The urologist listed the severity of his condition and said the damage was permanent. Dr. Dean Beven, ex-president of the American Medical Association, weighed in with a dark prognosis printed in the papers. "…the diseased arteries which were responsible for the stroke and the damaged brain, remain and will not be recovered from…a patient who is suffering as the president is…should under no circumstances be permitted to resume the work of such a strenuous position as president of the United States."

The firestorm erupted with the *New York Evening Post* leading off. "We have been repeatedly assured by those surrounding the president during his illness that Mr. Wilson at all times has been in perfect mental condition and in touch with what is going on.… is it at all conceivable that Mr. Wilson never stopped to inquire how the business of the country was being carried on during his illness?"

Other newspapers said the country had been lied to about the condition of the president and questioned those around him. "It is unthinkable that a sane man would offer any objection to the department heads getting together," fumed the *Worcester Evening Gazette*. The *New-York Tribune* said the president was "Like a sleeping princess, alive but in suspended animation…" The *Los Angeles Times* summed up Lansing's firing with a simple headline, "WILSON'S LAST MAD ACT."

Then *The Baltimore Sun* took it a step further and surmised who was really running the government. "They ask in stage whispers at the Capitol whether this is the work of the enigmatical villain of the play, the dark and mysterious Mr. Tumulty or more sinister still, must we look for the woman in the case?" The Canton, Ohio, *Daily News* on March 12 wrote, "One of the foremost statesmen in Washington is a woman." The Maryland *Star* amplified this and surmised that the business of government was being handled by Edith and it had "nothing but the greatest deference and admiration [for] 'Mrs. Wilson, the acting president.'" Edith read all the newspapers and remarked to Navy Secretary Josephus Daniels, "I hate Lansing."

Capitol Hill added fuel to the fire. Senator George Norris of Nebraska interpreted the situation this way to reporters: "First, the President was incapacitated and it was necessary for someone to look after the Government...the mental expert [Dercum] that has been employed at the White House has been discharged too soon." The prevailing opinion among the media and on Capitol Hill was that the president was crazy.

A story circulated that when Secretary Tumulty brought headlines of the firing to the president on the South Portico, Wilson reached out his cane and hooked an iron railing, then swung his wheelchair in circles, shouting, "See how strong I am!" Through all this Edith continued to stay up late deciphering code and responding to the mail. If she listened while she wrote, she could hear the suffragettes who had been camping outside the White House gates. Inside the White House sat the first woman president of the United States, working far into the night.

# THIRTY-ONE

# THE SUFFRAGETTES

1918

**THEY REMINDED EDITH OF BLACK CROWS IN THEIR DARK DRESSES** in the way they clung to the White House gates. The chanting would reach her while she was bent over her desk; a faint voice in the cold winter wind that sounded like a song. When she looked up from her writing, she saw women with signs outside the front gates. The first woman president stared at the women and shook her head. She saw no connection between their right to vote and her running the United States government.

While Edith was running the White House and President Wilson was watching movies and sitting on the South Portico, the Nineteenth Amendment was passed on August 4, 1920, giving women the right to vote. It was somehow appropriate: women had secured the vote in the United States while a woman was president.

But Edith didn't care for the suffragettes. She thought them crude, vulgar, and pushy. That doesn't mean she didn't have a role in getting women the right to vote. Anna Howard Shaw, a doctor, and Carrie

Chapman Catt, a school teacher, had been heading up the National American Woman Suffrage Association. They had been working within the confines of the system, but a more extreme element headed by Alice Paul, an activist from Pennsylvania, believed in a more radical approach.

Alice Paul took what then was the Congressional Union for Women's Suffrage and changed it to the National Women's Party in 1916. As a progressive Democrat, President Wilson had endorsed getting women the vote for years as a state issue. When the president voted in New Jersey in the 1916 election, Edith could not. As she later said, "While my husband was in the old engine house voting, I sat in the car...That was as near as I ever came to voting at the polls for a Presidential candidate. New Jersey had not then granted the suffrage to women."

The president didn't want the federal government involved. "I...am tied to a conviction, which I have had all my life, that changes of this sort ought to be brought about state by state." President Wilson was accused of hiding behind states' rights, and even his daughter, Margaret, encouraged him to push for a federal amendment to grant women the vote.

But the vote was stuck in the backwater of the war. Many people saw the vote as an assault on "family values," and Teddy Roosevelt sided with the times, saying, "Women do not really need the suffrage." Wilson told a family friend, "Suffrage for women will make absolutely no change in politics—it is the home that will be disastrously affected. Somebody has to make the home and who is going to do it if the women don't?"

But Alice Paul didn't believe change came unless you made people uncomfortable. All protests operate with the goal of creating dis-ease. Beginning in 1917, women started protesting outside the White House. The protestors stood outside the gates holding banners;

"Mr. President, how long must women wait for liberty?" One that was sure to rankle Wilson was simply, "Kaiser Wilson."

The protesters arrived at the White House at ten in the morning and stayed there until dark. They began chaining themselves to the fence, and the president gave the order that they weren't to be touched. Wilson knew what Alice Paul wanted. "Miss Paul, an ethereal-looking Quaker with hazel eyes and a melodic voice, combined fragility with the iron will of Mrs. Emmeline Pankhurst, the English suffragette whose tactics she had learned at first hand in England." She was a worthy opponent and used the same tactics of nonviolence employed by Martin Luther King, Jr. fifty years later.

This was the background of a progressive woman coming to the White House. Almost every day the suffragettes were outside the White House gates; a woman with the power of the presidency drove by. Edith recalled one day when the president invited the suffragettes in to warm themselves. "One bitterly cold day while they were there, we were going to lunch when Mr. Wilson's eye caught the yellow gleam of the Suffragette banner. He shivered at the thought of women standing in the icy wind for hours and said to the head usher: 'Hoover, go out there and ask those ladies if they won't come in and get warm, will you? And if they come, see that they have some hot tea or coffee.' Hoover returned very quickly, saying, 'Excuse me, Mr. President, but they indignantly refused.'"

Things came to a head when the Russians visited the White House and Alice Paul's suffragettes unfurled a ten foot banner: "We, the women of America, tell you that America is not a democracy. Twenty million American women are denied the right to vote. President Wilson is the chief opponent of their national enfranchisement." Counter-demonstrators yelled "Treason!" and tore up their banner.

Alice Paul released a statement: "We have ordered another banner with the same wording and we intend to show it in the same place."

The president was outraged and wrote his daughter Jessie, "They certainly seem bent upon making their cause as obnoxious as possible." Edith wrote later, "I was indignant, but apparently no less so than a crowd of onlookers who tore the picketers' banner down." Edith was horrified when Alice Paul's protestors then burned her husband in effigy.

Edith had run into the suffragettes when she toured Europe with her friend Altrude. The women activists in England were kicking policemen, burning letterboxes, and throwing themselves under the royal coach. When Edith and her friend visited the House of Parliament and Westminster Abbey, they came under suspicion of being suffragettes themselves.

Things escalated at the Tower of London. Edith sat outside when she learned her purse would be searched before she entered. She sat down on a bench and began writing as Altrude went inside. One of the scarlet-clothed Beefeaters walked up and stood in front of her. Edith asked what he was doing and he replied, "I am here to watch you; we don't trust women these days." He was joined by two other guards and one had a gun in his hand. Edith's fountain pen and hat-pins were examined and found harmless.

When she was engaged to Woodrow, and the president said he supported the right to vote for women in New Jersey, it was assumed this young progressive woman who drove a car had bewitched the president. But as Ishbel Ross wrote in *Power with Grace*, "For years there was uncertainty as to President Wilson's belief in woman suffrage, but there was never any doubt about his wife's dislike for aggressive, noisy tactics by members of her own sex, a feeling strengthened by every fresh outbreak in public.... It was ironic she had functioned as a successful business woman...and that by chance when Woodrow Wilson collapsed she should become internationally known as the Presidentress, running the country by regency."

In the 1916 election, the suffrage states had gone for Wilson over Hughes, betting he was more sympathetic to their cause. How much of this was the "Edith effect" is not known, but it didn't hurt to have a "modern woman" in the White House. When Wilson declared war on Germany, the president's conversion was complete. He linked the women's movement to the international quest for liberty and infused the suffrage quest with a "moral" push.

The National Woman's Party began picketing the White House on January 1, 1917, and never let up. "Hundreds of women took turns at the vigil and when Edith looked from her windows, or came and went on her busy round of war duties, they were invariably there."

On Bastille Day, Alice Paul brought sixteen women to the White House gates and had them stand there with banners, LIBERTY, EQUAL- ITY, FRATERNITY. The police moved in. The officers politely approached each lady, took off their hats, bowed, and explained they were being arrested. A judge fined each woman twenty-five dollars or sixty days in the District of Columbia workhouse in Occoquan, Virginia. The ladies chose jail and Alice Paul scored mightily against the president. He called in the district commander and Commissioner Louis Brown- low later recalled, "He [the president] told me that we had made a fearful blunder, that we never ought to have indulged these women in their desire for arrest and martyrdom..."

The president pardoned the women, but they refused to leave and the newspapers carried the story of women being forced to rise at dawn and wear bedraggled gray dresses while eating cabbage and vegetable soup. The *New York Times* added insult to injury by stat- ing that the women were forced to live with black women.

Then Dudley Field Malone, an old Wilson supporter and friend, decided to represent the women. His wife was in Alice Paul's party and the collector of the Port of New York insisted to Wilson that he could push through national suffrage. Edith was furious. "I was blazing with anger at Malone's conduct [representing the women] and my husband was deeply hurt."

Women's suffrage was becoming fashionable, and wealthy women descended on the picket lines outside the White House. Mrs. Norman de Rapelye Whitehouse headed the delegation of ladies that included Mrs. J. Borden Harriman, Mrs. Henry Morgenthau, Miss Anne Morgan, Mrs. Frank A. Vanderlip, and Mrs. James Leeds Laidlaw. Mrs. Harriman's devotion to the president overtook her when she saw another woman with "KAISER WILSON" on her sign. She grabbed the sign from the woman and destroyed it. Even rich dowagers have a limit.

Alice Paul still had the women outside the White House and they grew more aggressive. Often they hid signs under their skirts and flashed the president and Edith when they drove by. Fights would break out when people opposed to the suffragettes tried to take their signs. Alice Paul and others were arrested and sent to Occoquan, where they started a hunger strike. The women were force-fed on Wilson's authorization and the press buzzed with horror tales.

In the first week of 1918, the House voted 274 to 136 in favor of the Nineteenth Amendment. The Senate was still two votes short. The president's son-in-law William Gibbs McAdoo approached him and asked if he would speak to the Senate. He would later write, "I felt that since no president of the United States had ever spoken in favor of women's suffrage, and that since we were fighting a war for democracy, it seemed to me that we could not consistently persist in refusing to admit women to the benefits of democracy."

The president said he didn't discuss public questions on the Sabbath and no precedent existed for a president to address legislation in Congress. He added that speaking to the Senate would bring more controversy.

Here is where it gets interesting. McAdoo left the White House with the president's disappointing answer ringing in his ears. There was no way he would speak to the Senate on the issue of suffrage. At five o'clock Edith called and said the president was working on the speech. What happened? We know that Edith wasn't behind the suffrage movement. She didn't approve of pushy women; though many would say she herself was a pushy woman. We know Woodrow Wilson consulted with his wife on just about everything. We know that on the issue of women's rights he would have turned to the woman in his life and asked, "What do you think?"

Edith never held back. We can almost hear her listening to the president's reasons for not speaking to the Senate and telling him not to worry about precedent and that God will understand. This is conjecture, but Edith called McAdoo and told him that the president had changed his mind. Is there any doubt who really changed his mind for him? The president went before the Senate and made his case. He attached the women's movement to the war and their service in support of it. "It is high time that some part of our debt of gratitude to them should be acknowledged and paid, and the only acknowledgement they ask is their admission to suffrage...can we justly refuse them?"

The Senate did refuse them with a vote of fifty-three to thirty-one. When the president returned from Europe, the suffragettes kept up the pressure. Alice Paul was clubbed by the police and jailed for disorderly conduct. But the war had tipped the scales in their favor, breaking long held taboos. The fight over the League of Nations was in full swing, and in June 1919, the suffrage amendment finally passed Congress.

As Edith took over the White House, the amendment for the right of women to vote went to the states for ratification. On April 6, 1920, Mrs. Catt's committee sent President Wilson a book of letters from the presidents of suffrage organizations thanking him for his support. An article in *Collier's* magazine posed the question: who was the real president of the United States during the suffrage movement?

Robert Bender, a well-known journalist, made a list: Tumulty, Grayson, Bernard Baruch (advisor to Wilson during the Paris peace conference). Then he added one more. "...if anyone had even a remote right to claim his title temporarily, it was not one of the four names but Edith Bolling Wilson...never an ardent suffragist herself, Mrs. Wilson is likely to be the person when the full story of the first months is known...[she] proved by herself the finest argument for suffrage that any woman by her work has yet offered to the cause."

Certainly Edith Wilson proved the old maxim that the best way to prove your case is by leading by example. On August 18, 1920, the Nineteenth Amendment to the United States Constitution was ratified by the final state. President Edith Wilson had six months left in her term.

# THIRTY-TWO

# OUR OWN COUNTRY

## 1918

**ON A BRILLIANT DECEMBER 4, 1918, EDITH AND THE PRESIDENT**
set sail on the *George Washington*. It seemed like all of New York
had come out to send them off among a cacophony of bands, fog-
horns, fireworks, and thousands of cheering people. Edith leaned on
the banister and looked out at the people. The president waved as the
steamer churned out of the harbor, past the Statue of Liberty and
thrummed toward France.

Edith hoped the president would leave the sleeplessness, the headaches, and the indigestion behind. They settled into their quarters and
after lunch the president took a nap. "In a minute he was asleep. I was
so happy," Edith wrote later. "The long strain of war was lifting."
Nobody wanted the president to go to Europe except Edith. Colonel
House and Secretary of State Lansing thought Wilson would be
bested by the wily European statesmen schooled in the diplomacy of
Metternich and Talleyrand.

A voyage across the Atlantic Ocean in 1918 still took weeks. Essentially when the president left for Europe he would be absent for months. Secretary Lansing and Colonel House thought Wilson's presence would put the United States at a disadvantage. The president suspected jealousy and said to House, "Your [message] upsets every plan we have made," with the "we" being Edith and the president.

House wasn't wrong. The best analogy is that of having an agent. An agent can give the client room to maneuver. Lansing and House thought Wilson would be in over his head. But the president was going there as a Calvinist reformer and felt he was going to Paris on the mission of God. The president's answer to the criticism that Clemenceau and Lloyd George would dictate terms was that "It is not too much to say that at Chateau Thierry we saved the world...they were beaten." The French and the British owed America. President Wilson wouldn't let others make the peace. He had almost one hundred and sixteen thousand dead Americans on his hands. Someone had to create a world where this wouldn't happen again.

On the *George Washington*, lifeboat drills still occurred with wartime precision as there was a danger of floating mines. People became seasick, including members of the Secret Service. For ten days the Wilsons enjoyed a mini vacation with few official duties. Wilson worked in the morning, then walked the deck with Edith, played shuffleboard, and breathed deeply of the clean salt air. On Friday, December 13, the Wilsons' ship was escorted by French destroyers. The French were the president's biggest adversary in the negotiations. They wanted the Germans to pay for the war and be crippled so they could never wage war again. The League of Nations to them was a necessary chip to give Wilson to get their terms. The French wanted revenge for the 1.3 million men who died in the war.

Woodrow Wilson was coming as president of a country that had emerged as the most powerful nation on earth. As the young economist

John Maynard Keynes, who was advising the British delegation, would later note, "The American armies were at the height of their numbers, discipline, and equipment. Europe was in complete dependence on the food supplies of the United States; and financially she was even more absolutely at their mercy. Europe...owed the United States more than she could pay...Never had a philosopher held such weapons wherewith to bind the princes of this world."

Edith was accustomed to cheering crowds, but nothing prepared her for the outpouring in the streets of Paris. The French saw President Wilson as someone who had done the impossible. The Wilsons went on a whirlwind of meetings with royalty. Edith met the king and queen of Belgium and the king and queen of England. When Edith met Queen Mary she didn't curtsey and caused a minor scandal. President Wilson for his part called the king "sir" and not "your majesty." The United States wouldn't bow to anyone when it had more power than the world had ever seen. King George didn't mince words later to his private secretary. "I could not bear him. An entirely cold academical professor—an odious man."

The president and Edith went to see General Pershing and visit the troops. They stopped at farms and talked to soldiers along the way with Edith climbing a ladder to visit soldiers in a hayloft. One can only imagine her relief to be among the soldiers after the pomp and circumstance of the last four days. The soldiers cheered the president and his vivacious wife as the snow fell right before Christmas.

The Seventy-Seventh Division of New York made Edith an honorary member and gave her a blue and gold insignia, The Goddess of Liberty. The Wilsons and the troops then shared in a Christmas dinner of turkey, cranberry, and pumpkin pie. They boarded a train for England and went on to Rome where they saw the pope with the largest crowds yet.

Finally they returned to Murat Palace to get down to business. Edith was recognized as "a valuable channel for communication." The president's wife never said anything publicly about politics, but as her secretary Edith Benham put it, "All noticed that [Mrs. Wilson] was constantly at [the president's] side, and that a look exchanged between them could sometimes change the tone of the conference."

The armistice was only two months old and the effect of the war was everywhere. The French wanted the president to see the battlefields, but Wilson demurred. "I don't want to get mad over here because I think there ought to be *one* person at that peace table who isn't mad." The French and the British wanted to make the Germans pay. It would be the thorn in the side that festered all through the conference.

The long daily meetings quickly became a burden. As Edith wrote later, "The grinding work of the Conference went on day after day, and late into every night, the only rest for my husband being Sunday, when he dismissed every care, slept late, and often went in the motor for a long drive with me."

The president read the Constitution of the League of Nations to the Peace Conference in January. The French lost no time in attacking Wilson for his impractical ideals. They lobbied to separate the League from the treaty. Even Secretary of State Lansing saw the treaty as most important and the League as secondary. Colonel House thought the League could be sacrificed for the treaty and privately maneuvered behind the president's back. Wilson was the only one who saw the two as inseparable.

In the old school of Metternich, where power is held loosely and seldom revealed, House resembled an American corporate resident who wanted to make sure he was the real point man. The president had lost valuable time with celebrations and ceremonies. In February 1918 he was going back to America for the closing of Congress and to shore up support for the treaty and the League.

Edith saw the issue clearly. "When we first reached Paris his hope had been to get the major terms of the Peace completed so that when we came home for the closing of Congress... it would not be necessary for him to return to Paris." The president was working eighteen-hour days and as Edith said later, "His one hope was to get the Conference to agree on the inclusion of the Covenants of the League of Nations as part of the Treaty." In this way the League would become reality as the treaty would be ratified by all countries— but to separate the two would be the death of the League.

The president desperately wanted to put a copy of the treaty before the Senate Foreign Relations Committee and launch his public relations campaign. Lodge headed the committee and Wilson could bring any changes back to Paris and seal the deal. The day he was to leave for America, Wilson was to read the Covenant of the League of Nations before the full Peace Conference.

Edith wanted to hear her husband read in the House of Clocks but the meeting was for members only. Grayson offered to ask M. Clemenceau (president of the conference) for Edith to attend. But first she asked the president. Wilson paused and then said: "In the circumstances it is hardly a request, it is more a command, for he could not very well refuse you."

"That being the case, then I shall make it," Edith replied.

Edith and Grayson were allowed to watch from a coat room just off the grand hall. "We had been told that we must be in our places before any of the delegates came, to keep quiet, and to stay until all had gone before we came out of hiding," Edith later wrote. She poked her head out of the curtains of the little room. "He was exactly opposite us and as every eye was centered upon him we ventured to part our curtains enough to see the whole scene," she later wrote. "It was a great moment in history and as he stood there—slender, calm, and powerful in his argument—I seemed to see the people of all depressed countries—men, women, and little children—crowding round and waiting upon his words."

The ballots were taken and the Peace Conference voted in favor of the League of Nations. The president and Edith left for America that night. The crossing was fogbound with influenza reported on board. The ship was also bringing back many wounded soldiers. "Every day we would go up on the top deck of the *George Washington* where the sick bay was located to see the patients," Edith wrote later.

The ship had a near disaster near Cape Ann, nearly running aground. Edith asked a soldier if he was frightened as they sat in the thick fog. "No ma'am," the soldier replied. "'Cause I knew if we hit anything and drifted into shore it would be our own country."

Their own country was waiting for the president and Edith to arrive. So was Henry Cabot Lodge. The president quickly set up a meeting with the Foreign Relations Committee headed by Lodge. He then hosted a large dinner at the White House and Edith sat next to him. The president gave them the rough draft of the treaty and asked for their opinions. Several points were raised, but the president and Edith felt none of them were deal breakers. Wilson put the question to the test, as Edith wrote later:

> The president turned to Lodge and said, "Of course you understand, Senator, I will have to go back to Paris and resubmit this to the Conference, for while it is not essentially changed, it is not what they accepted the day I left; and I have some pretty stubborn men to deal with. However, I am going to do my best, and if this draft stands as it is accepted, do you think it will go through the Senate?"

Lodge then replied: "If the Foreign Relations Committee approves it I feel there is no doubt of ratification."

"Very well then," Wilson replied, "I consider that, armed with your approval, I can go back and work feeling you and your associates are behind me."

Lodge bowed his head in assent. Two days later, Lodge went after the treaty and said the League was a violation of the Monroe Doctrine and invoked George Washington, saying the United States should avoid any foreign entanglements. A cadre of senators agreed and the Irreconcilables in Congress against the League formed up.

Wilson was crushed by Lodge's words, and Edith fumed at the senator's betrayal. "Certainly the facts justify the impression that he already intended to block ratification," she wrote later. Edith put it this way in a more candid moment, "I went out to the dining room with that stinking Senator Lodge and sat next to him at dinner. He pretended to me that he approved of everything Woodrow had done." Lodge, the fastidious Brahmin from Boston, remarked to a friend that when Edith put her hand on the table, "her fingernails were black with dirt."

Edith and Woodrow boarded the *George Washington* and sailed back to France. After a week on the high seas they reached Brest and Colonel House came aboard on a tender and conferred with the president. When Wilson emerged he was in shock. Edith wrote later:

> I opened the door connecting our rooms. Woodrow was standing. The change in his appearance shocked me. He seemed to have aged ten years, and his jaw was set in that way he had when making superhuman effort to control himself.
>
> "What is the matter? What has happened?" I asked.
>
> He smiled bitterly. "House has given away everything I had won before we left Paris. He has compromised on every side, and so I have to start all over again and this

time it will be harder, as he has given the impression my delegates are not in sympathy with me."

Colonel House had given Wilson his worst nightmare. He had let the League of Nations be stricken from the treaty. He justified his caving as a result of the negative press coming from the United States. He assumed the treaty with the League would never pass and gave it up for other concessions. The colonel really felt he knew better and like any executive had taken the best deal.

While they were gone, the French leader M. Clemenceau was shot by an assassin and now seemed more determined to punish the Germans for the chaos in the world. The Wilsonian principles based on the Fourteen Points lost steam while those in favor of a severe treaty moved into the ascendency. Lord Balfour tried to trump Wilson with a resolution dealing with the peace and not mentioning the League. Some declared the League a dead issue. The president fired back with a statement saying that the decision of the plenary session on January 25 for the inclusion of the League Covenant in the treaty was final. The press attacked but Wilson stood firm. There would be no treaty without the League.

The president spent long days, often going until after midnight, and others noticed the strain. Journalist Ray Baker said he was grayer and thinner and his face now twitched. Edith did everything she could to lessen the burden. Her husband wasn't sleeping well and his chronic indigestion had flared up. He had no time for exercise. Grayson and Edith became concerned for his health.

The collapse came on April 3, 1919, when a mild stroke occurred. Neuropsychiatrist Wilcox Thewlis saw Wilson and wrote, "on the sad day he wakened with a little stroke so destructive that it had made of him a changeling with a very different personality and a markedly lessened ability." Wilson told Thewlis that his hands were so shaky he couldn't shave.

The world was told he had the flu while Edith stood guard. It was a dry run for the way they would handle the final debilitating stroke. Grayson forbade further work. "We went about on tiptoe as our patient lay utterly spent, fitfully asleep," Edith later wrote. One interesting point here is that Edith wrote in her memoir that the president had "grippe." It was later that historians and medical professionals connected the dots. Wilson's valet, Ike Hoover, said the president didn't know where he was. A combination of high blood pressure, hardening of the arteries, and high fever had caused Woodrow Wilson to become delirious. "The president was sicker than the world knew," he wrote later in his memoir.

The delirium passed and the Council of Four met in the room outside the president's bedroom. Ray Baker thought Wilson's eyes were of extraordinary size and luminosity, a condition of his high blood pressure. The president became paranoid, thinking the French were spying on him, and losing his temper over the use of official cars. He then became obsessed with the arrangement of furniture in his room and couldn't rest until he had changed it. Years later, Grayson would admit to author Gene Smith that the president had suffered a series of mini strokes in Paris.

The members deadlocked over a myriad of issues and Wilson ordered up the presidential ship. If the delegates didn't come to an agreement, he was going back to America. This rash act might have been a function of the stroke or masterful gamesmanship. In any case it worked and the issues of the treaty were settled.

It is here that Edith had it out with Colonel House. She read an article in the newspaper that described House as the "brains of the commission" and that while the president was away House was in charge. The article suggested Wilson should have stayed in America and let Colonel House handle all the negotiations. Edith quickly called the colonel on the carpet.

"Colonel," she began when he came looking for the president "have you been reading these awful attacks on Woodrow?"

Edith pulled the article out of a drawer and read it. "The Colonel's face turned crimson." House hurriedly left, not waiting for the president. Edith had Admiral Grayson read the article. Grayson said the man who had written the article spent time in the colonel's room. House made a point of avoiding the first lady after that, and for Edith the colonel was *persona non grata* in the White House from there on.

The treaty was signed at Versailles by the Germans on June 28, 1919. The Germans had been betrayed on their assumption that the Treaty of Versailles would be based on Wilson's Fourteen Points. The only point that survived was the League of Nations. The rest had been given away, but they had no choice but to sign.

The president and Edith returned to the United States and realized the fight they were in for in trying to ratify the League of Nations. Lodge started amending the treaty to destroy Article X, which bound all countries to act in unison. The president saw that his only chance was to go to the American people and plead his case. He still believed the people were with him and not Lodge, who believed the League would forever bind the United States to foreign entanglements. Wilson would take his case to the people and cross the country by train.

Dr. Grayson bluntly told the president, "The trip may kill you." Wilson looked at his wife and the doctor. "Yes, all that is true, but I feel it is my duty. If the treaty is not ratified by the Senate, the war will have been fought in vain and the world thrown into chaos. I promised our soldiers when I asked them to take up arms that it was a war to end wars and if I do not do all in my power to put the treaty into effect I will be a slacker and never able to look those boys in the eyes."

The train for Wilson's Western Tour pulled out on September 3, 1919, the fifth anniversary of the night Edith promised to marry the president of the United States. It was a ten thousand mile trip across the country. The steam locomotive chugged west, lugging the presidential car toward a rendezvous with destiny outside Pueblo, Colorado.

# THIRTY-THREE

# As Dead as Marley's Ghost

## 1920

HIS HEART BEAT RAPIDLY AND SWEAT PEARLED HIS FOREHEAD. THE night terror was there again. The flashlight clicked on in the eerie quiet of the White House at 3:00 a.m. The president shined his flashlight on First Lady Ellen Wilson's painted face. She glowed in the darkness of the bedroom like a Madonna and his heart began to slow. She was there soothing him now. As long as he kept the light on the painting of his dead wife's face, then he would be alright.

The president of the United States now had such terrifying night terror that Dr. Grayson gave him a flashlight to shine on his first wife. It was the only thing that soothed Wilson in the twisted wreckage of his stroke. On February 15, 1920, an article appeared in the Chicago press: "President Will Never Recover." A Dr. Bevan, ex-president of the American Medical Association, took the known facts and said, "The president's stroke, with the resulting paralysis of one side of his body, is due to a disease of the arteries of the brain, with a plugging up of the arteries which supply that part of the right side of the brain which controls his left arm and leg. The disease of the arteries is permanent and not a temporary condition. In other words the president has permanent brain damage..."

Bevan went on to recommend that the president resign.

"Technically we are still at war...if he were called before a nonpartisan medical board he would be at once retired as physically incapacitated to perform the duties of the position. The proper and normal course would be for the president to retire."

Sigmund Freud and William Bullitt presented a psychological autopsy on President Wilson. They ascertained that the death of Thomas Woodrow Wilson occurred outside Colorado. From then on he was "no longer an independent human being but a carefully coddled invalid." Freud and Bullitt concluded that "The Woodrow Wilson who lived on was a pathetic invalid, a querulous old man full of rage and tears, hatred and self-pity."

This "querulous old man" and Edith had unfinished business with the League of Nations. Edith was the president and everyone knew it. Senator Hitchcock requested her assistance in securing leadership in the Democratic caucus: "My dear Mrs. Wilson, Day after tomorrow at 10:30 AM the Democratic caucus meets to elect a leader. The contest is rather close between Mr. Underwood and myself. Because I have stood firmly by the League of Nations I am opposed by Gore, Reed, Shields, Walsh of Mass. and perhaps Hoke Smith. I lay this matter before you with the suggestion that if something could be done today or tomorrow to influence Senator Harris of Georgia to support me I shall feel quite sure of the support."

Edith begged off saying the president never exceeded the "bounds of executive authority." The point was that Hitchcock was asking the help of *President Edith Wilson*. He knew by now with whom the power rested and who was able to act upon it. But first a presidential letter was expected at a Jackson Day dinner. Secretary Tumulty gave the letter to Secretary of Agriculture Houston for his opinion. The letter rehashed the Senate's failure to ratify the treaty and went on to reiterate the president's uncompromising position on ratification of the League. The president's allies wanted to get the United States into the League, and here was Wilson slamming the door again.

"Personally I do not accept the action of the United States Senate as the decision of the Nation...We cannot rewrite this treaty. We must take it without changes which alter its meaning, or leave it." Then the letter proposed that the president would run for a third term. "If there is any doubt as to what the people of the country think on this vital matter the clear and single way is to submit it for determination at the next election to the voters of the nation, to give the next election the form of a great and solemn referendum."

The White House was bombarded with appeals to compromise on Lodge's reservations so the United States could enter the League. Ray Stannard Baker wrote Edith on January 25, 1920. "I have the feeling that all the president went to France to fight for—for which he fought so nobly—is being swept away.... And I feel so strongly that if the president were not ill—if he were himself—he could and would save the situation."

Baker met with Edith and wrote in his diary later, "I had a long talk with Mrs. Wilson who impressed me again with her sound good sense, her real understanding of the difficulties of the present situation and her eagerness to help. I told her just what I thought people felt...they were profoundly disturbed by the differences over minor matters and they were inclined to blame Mr. Wilson as much as Mr. Lodge.... she came out bluntly, 'They think him stubborn,' she said. 'So much hangs in the balance,' I replied. 'Possibly the existence of the league.' Edith paused. '...the president still has in mind the reception he got in the West. And he believes the people are with him,' she declared."

Baker left without having seen the president and wrote Edith later, "People in the future will forget the minor disagreements if the thing comes into being." He was right, but Edith wasn't budging. Then Wilson had Edith send the postmaster general, Albert Burleson, a list of thirty-five senators asking if these were the ones most against ratification. Burleson tweaked the list and sent it back.

Secretary Lansing had written a letter before his resignation: "Should the American government be unable to take the course [ratify the treaty] the Allied governments see no other way open to them than the immediate opening of peace negotiations with Turkey..."

In short, the stasis in the White House was costing the United States a role in finishing the peace process of World War I. It is during this time that Wilson caught the flu that had recently killed millions. A *New York Times* news report dated February 3, 1920 said: "President Wilson contracted a cold several days ago and had a narrow escape from influenza, his physician, Rear Admiral Grayson said today. Every precaution is now being taken to protect him, Dr. Grayson said, and no person with even the suspicion of a cold is permitted to enter his room."

Woodrow Wilson was now even more isolated during the final effort to get the treaty ratified. Ray Stannard Baker recorded in his diary, "The poor President! So nearly a friendless man. Yet beyond all of this yelping pack he is the only one who has truly constructive ideas...it is to him and to him alone that the world will owe the League of Nations if it ever gets it. There is something indescribably tragic in the sight of this sick man, now willing to kill his own child rather than have it misborn in the world!"

The president wanted to put the League out for a national referendum. It was the Western Tour strategy without the train, but Wilson's scheme touched the edge of madness. He took the list of thirty-five senators and issued a statement, "I challenge the following named gentlemen, members of the Senate of the United States, to resign their seats in that body and take immediate steps to seek re-election to it on the basis of their several records with regards to the ratification of the treaty. For myself, I promise and engage if all of them or a majority of them are re-elected, I will resign the Presidency."

Wilson had been reduced to fantastic schemes to produce impossible results. The president was now his own worst enemy. The man in the Atlantic City wheel chair in the flickering darkness had become increasingly erratic, intransigent, extreme; a hardening of the arteries of his ability to compromise.

In Europe, people started to realize that the United States might not enter the League. Lord Grey wrote a letter to the *London Times* saying that the important thing was for the United States to join, and Lodge's reservations didn't really matter one way or the other. Edith was furious and still harbored ill will over Grey's aide. She went into the president's room and came out with her childlike scrawl on blue-lined notebook paper, "Had Lord Grey ventured upon any such utterance when he was still at Washington as ambassador, his government would have been promptly asked to withdraw." Old grudges died hard with Edith Wilson.

Secretary Tumulty predicted that the League would die if the president didn't accept the reservations. This was the last time. Ray Baker returned and this time managed to get by Edith and see the president. Wilson was buried in blankets with a fur muff wrapped around his feet. He listened quietly to Baker's argument to accept the reservations and then said:

"If I accept them, these Senators will merely offer new ones, even more humiliating...These evil men intend to destroy the League."

Baker stared at him and realized how alone and embattled the president had become. He saw the world painted by the few who could get through Edith. Then William McAdoo, the president's son-in-law, requested that his father-in-law compromise, but Wilson dismissed him, saying, "I am willing to compromise on anything but the Ten Commandments."

Senator Carter Glass wrote to Edith that ex-President Taft had come up with reservations different from Lodge's and implored the president to consider them. "...if we must go to the American people on the issue, it seems to me of supreme importance to the party and of the gravest concern for the treaty also that we should enter the fight fortified not alone by the righteousness of the cause, but able to convince the average citizen that we had exhausted every possible effort to conciliate the adversaries of the administration...."

Edith questioned Taft's good faith by saying the president felt inaction was better than mistaken initiative. Edith fended off critics who were coming daily now. She had effectively isolated the president from his advisors; Tumulty no longer saw Woodrow Wilson. As Ike Hoover later wrote, "Tumulty tried so hard to get to the president but he was kept away as if he was a leper...Grayson would have let him in but Mrs. Wilson would not do so." Colonel House hadn't seen the president since before the Great Western Tour. Secretary Lansing dared not try to get by Edith and Secretary Daniels, along with Vice President Marshall, never saw the president again. And other business was pulling Edith away from the treaty negotiations.

Secretary Tumulty sent her a letter on the railroad strike.

"Dear Mrs. Wilson, Director of Railroads Hines advised me that he has been in consultation concerning the threatened strike of the employees listed in the attached memorandum and tells me that he should see the president..."

He never would. Edith put the letter aside as one crisis unfolded after another. Tumulty followed up with another letter on February 10. "Dear Mrs. Wilson, I went over the railroad situation last night with Mr. Hines. He says that it is most critical and involves a general railroad strike. And he says that the men believe that the president is not consulted about these matters and if the president for five minutes could see a committee of three..." Then from Tumulty, "Dear Mrs. Wilson, Will you please have the president mark accepted on the Fletcher resignation so that we might dispose of this matter."

Edith Wilson barely had time to think as Postmaster General Burleson came and counseled tactics. He met with the president, who cut him off as well, saying, "I will not play for position. This is not a time for tactics. It is a time to stand square. I can stand defeat; I cannot stand retreat from conscientious duty." Like a card player holding his cards close to his vest, the president dared Lodge and his supporters to kill the League.

Woodrow Wilson couldn't bring himself to believe the United States wouldn't enter into the League. He couldn't believe the United States would doom the world to the next disaster. On February 24, Senator Hitchcock gave Wilson the news that Democratic senators might defect. "There is a strong disposition on the party of many Democratic senators to abandon the fight against the Lodge reservations and vote for a resolution of ratification containing them...on the theory that you will accept them ultimately. Perhaps a definite and positive public statement from you or a message to the Senate might bring about a change."

Even his own party wanted compromise, but Wilson wrote the letter that would seal the doom of the League of Nations.

"Any reservation seeking to deprive the League of Nations of the force of Article X cuts at the heart of the covenant itself. Any league of nations which does not guarantee as a matter of incontestable right the political independence and integrity of each of its members would be a futile scrap of paper...either we should enter the league fearlessly, accepting the responsibility and in the role of leader, which we now enjoy, contributing our efforts toward establishing a just and permanent peace; or we should retire as gracefully as possible to our geographical isolation and trust to providence and old world diplomats to work out a peace that will remain a peace."

Wilson laid down the gauntlet for an all-or-none proposition. No compromise at all with Senator Lodge. The senators should vote against anything except the original League of Nations. The impact of the stroke, and the lack of information combined with the delusion that the American people wanted him to stand firm, doomed the League of Nations. The Titanic had set sail and Edith and others knew what was coming. She knew what this would do to her fragile husband. "I never leave except for an hour in the afternoon and at mealtimes. For he gets nervous if alone and allowed to think," she later wrote.

On March 19, 1920, the ship that Wilson had set sail years before struck impenetrable ice and went down once and for all. The Senate voted down entrance of the United States into the League of Nations by refusing to ratify the Treaty of Versailles. Connecticut's Republican senator, Frank Brandegee, observed that the president "has strangled his own child." Henry Cabot Lodge put the finishing touches on the tombstone, saying the League was "As dead as Marley's ghost."

Dr. Grayson stayed with the president that night in the White House. He checked on him every hour. At 3:00 a.m. Wilson looked at the doctor and said, "Doctor, the devil is a busy man.... it would have been better if I had died last fall." A few days later, George Creel, head of the wartime Committee on Public Information, came to see him. "I sat with him miserably, fumbling for words... Only as I was leaving did he look at me seeingly... "

"If only I were not helpless," he whispered.

Edith summed it up this way years later in her memoir:

"My conviction is that Mr. Lodge put the world back fifty years, and that at his door lies the wreckage of human hopes and the peril to human lives that afflict mankind today."

At the time Edith Wilson wrote her memoir in 1939, Hitler had invaded Poland and World War II had just begun. In less than two years, the United States would be attacked by the Japanese at Pearl Harbor and America would once again be at war.

# THIRTY-FOUR

# ON THE ROAD

## 1920

IT WAS A BRISK MARCH DAY IN WASHINGTON AND PEOPLE WERE
strolling along Pennsylvania Avenue. The long funereal car looked like
something out of the 1960s show *The Addams Family*. It was a shiny
high-topped black Pierce-Arrow with a man in the back slumped
down behind the side lanterns. The car passed in a cloud of oily blue
smoke and the old man stared queerly from the back. They couldn't
be sure it was the president, for nobody had seen Woodrow Wilson
for five months.

But then the next day they knew. The *New York Times* reported
in March of 1920, "President Wilson went motor riding today for the
first time in five months. It was his first appearance outside the White
House grounds since a few days after his return to Washington, a sick
man, at the end of September."

There is no precedent for a president disappearing for five months.
In the age of mass communication this would be impossible. But radio
was in its infancy and people still got their news through print. For the

country, this was an election year. For Woodrow Wilson, it would be the year that would free him from the convalescent home of the White House. For Edith, it would mark the end of her presidency.

Wilson now managed to get to his study with assistance. There he worked for an hour before an attendant wheeled him to the elevator, where he went outside to the South Portico. Sometimes he would watch a movie in the East Room. Then he and Edith started going for drives. A platform was built on the south entrance of the White House so that Wilson could be lifted by four Secret Service men into the car. He was positioned on the right side with the paralyzed left side of his face not visible to the public. The Secret Service men then propped him up and positioned his hat.

The very fact that he had appeared in public was news. The *New York Times* reported on March 14, 1920, "President Wilson took his fourth automobile ride since his illness today, braving a typical March wind in an open machine. Accompanied by Mrs. Wilson and Rear Admiral Grayson, the president spent two hours on the park roads."

As Gene Smith wrote in *When the Cheering Stopped*, "And so he was driven through Washington, his face devoid of all color, grayish white, thin, waxlike, a bright-eyed old man trying to smile, the lips revealing the teeth only on the right side, the eyes protuberant, a thin face on a thin neck ducked down so as to hide the paralyzed side."

There was something disturbing in the way people stared at him; here was this man rumored to be insane, just a white face in a dark limousine rushing by. There was a haunted quality and the Norma Desmond comparison comes to mind again. In the movie *Sunset Boulevard*, Norma would take out her old car that looked like something from a horror movie. When Wilson returned to the White House from his ride, a small group of people cheered upon his return. These were workers whom the president wouldn't recognize and relatives of Secret Service men that Grayson had rounded up to welcome the president back. "You see Edith, they still love me," the president would say, waving, tears rolling down his face.

No neurological illness is static and dementia was a factor now. Woodrow Wilson had become paranoid. The president demanded that cars that passed his be pursued by his Secret Service. The Secret Service agents took off but returned, saying the speeders had gotten away. Wilson wanted to try the speeders on the roadside and checked with the attorney general to see if he had the authority.

Time had passed the president up to the point that he didn't recognize the evolving modern world. When his own Pierce-Arrow was in for repairs he demanded to be taken around again in a horse drawn carriage. The sight of the paralyzed, reclusive president under blankets in an open Victoria must have stopped people on the streets of Washington.

There were no cabinet meetings. There wasn't even a secretary of state after Wilson had fired Lansing, until Secretary Tumulty called up a New York lawyer, Bainbridge Colby, and asked him to come to the White House. He was taken to the president and shocked by the deathlike skull under the blankets. Colby had no experience in foreign affairs, but the president offered him the job of secretary of state. He accepted on March 23.

Edith continued working long hours, trying to run the White House while meeting with various cabinet members. The war still had to be ended officially for one thing, since the Treaty of Versailles was not ratified. Tumulty wrote to Edith, "Dear Mrs. Wilson...what should the postmaster general say to the Democratic Congressmen on the Hill who were telephoning him as to what the president's attitude would be toward any resolution proposed by the Republicans to end the war."

Another message Tumulty was writing to Congress had to do with a third term for President Wilson. "Dear Mrs. Wilson," Tumulty wrote her on March 23, "I do not know how the President feels about making an announcement with reference to his attitude toward a third term…" Wilson had hatched a scheme to run and get the League of Nations ratified. Edith and Grayson were horrified but could say nothing. Joe Tumulty even began strategizing.

"I am wondering if, in view of the Treaty situation and the proximity of the convention, that it is not the time to consider making a final statement with reference to his attitude toward this important matter."

Washington still teemed with rumors about the president's condition. For his part, Woodrow Wilson was a depressed man. Grayson later recorded in a memorandum dated March 31 that after saying good morning to the president and remarking that it was a warm day, he replied, "I don't know whether it is warm or cold. I feel so weak and useless. I feel that I would like to go back to bed and stay there until I get well or die."

A nationwide railroad strike was looming. Tumulty sounded the alarm in a letter to Edith. "Dear Mrs. Wilson, Acting Attorney General Ames has just telephoned me that the railroad strike situation is growing more and more serious. He urges early appointment of the Railroad Labor Board." And during all this, Edith had to keep her husband's spirits up as well.

In a letter dated May 24, she tries to buck up the president. "I believe you know—and, because you know, you will struggle on and on until this valley of sorrow is over and together we will stand on the height and look back upon it. Both stronger for the lesson it has taught—and surer of our great love. Remember I want to share everything with you…keep a stout heart under your jacket little Boy Lover and we will win!"

Democrats started coming to see President Wilson about the upcoming election. They were amazed to find him talking about running himself. Democrat Homer Cummings visited Wilson and found him vacant, picking at his left hand with his right. When Cummings said he was giving the keynote address at the Democratic Convention, he said he might mention that Wilson had been close to death and had come back.

The president looked up and said that that wasn't true. Edith, who was standing behind him, mouthed the words, "He doesn't know." The president simply wasn't aware of his surroundings much of the time. But other Democrats came and found out what Dr. Grayson, Edith, and Secretary Tumulty already knew: President Wilson wanted to be president again.

Secretary Tumulty wrote Edith and said she should tell Wilson to announce that he wouldn't seek the nomination. Edith ignored his letter. Then Tumulty enlisted newspaper editor Louis Seibold and they came up with a scheme for an interview where they would draw Wilson into saying he wouldn't run. Edith got wind of their plan and sent Tumulty a letter stating no one was to raise the issue of running for president.

Tumulty put her letter in his files but not before he scribbled across the front, "The first lady could go straight to Hell." When Seibold came for the interview, the plan backfired when Wilson said he was seeking renomination. Cabinet members and other Democrats tried to dissuade the president. Grayson even talked to him, but Wilson said he was going to run and get the League passed.

It was pathetic and alarming. If the president got the nomination and his condition was revealed, then the Republicans would walk into the White House. Charles Swem, his stenographer, recorded in his diary on June 26, "His mind is not like of old. This morning while waiting for a small volume to arrive from downstairs...instead of continuing with the letters as his wont when he is ill, he lapsed into sort of a coma and only when Mrs. Wilson suggested he continue with what was left did he pick up the mail and go on."

If Wilson had run for another term it would have revealed that an invalid had inhabited the White House for the last year and a half. Robert Lansing recorded in his diary on May 29, "Lunched with Polk…he told me he took a foreign minister to see the president the other day, that his impression was of a very sick man, greatly emaciated, with a droop to his jaw and staring, almost unseeing, eyes. He even doubted if the president knew him."

In desperation, Admiral Grayson went to see Robert Woolley the Democratic strategist. He led off by saying he had been with three different presidents and nobody wanted to give up the job.

"Mr. Wilson desires a third term?"

"Correct," Grayson replied. "He fervently believes it is still possible to have the United States join the League of Nations. But it is out of the question—he just must not be nominated. No matter what others may tell you, no matter what you may read about the president being on the road to recovery, I tell you that he is permanently ill physically, is gradually weakening mentally, and can't recover…I repeat he is definitely becoming feeble…we must not take any chances."

Woolley told him not to worry.

"…his ambition to succeed himself is definitely hopeless."

Woolley was right. Governor Cox, the compromise candidate, was nominated with a young man from New York, Franklin Delano Roosevelt. Cox came to the White House and promised to fight for the League.

"I have always admired you for the fight you made for the League," he said, adding, "That fight can still be won."

"I am very grateful," the president said just above a whisper.

They left and the president was assisted to the library where he and Edith dined alone. Wilson used his right hand and didn't speak in the sultry summer air flowing in from the open windows. They waited for the end. Republican Warren G. Harding was elected in a landslide on November 7, 1920. Edith would have to find them somewhere else to live.

There wasn't much for President Wilson to do but count down the days. "I hobble from one part of the house to the other and go through the motions of working every morning," he wrote to his daughter Jessie, "though I am afraid it is work that doesn't count very much." Dr. Grayson noted some improvement in his health but that "He more easily loses control of himself and when he talks is likely to break down and weep." At times Wilson would yell at the attending nurses and threaten to fire them all. Only the movies seemed to soothe him.

When two senators and three representatives came to notify him formally that Congress had reconvened, Wilson saw Henry Cabot Lodge and used his cane as a crutch to avoid shaking hands. "Gentlemen, I hope you will excuse me from going through the formality of shaking hands with you individually, but, as you can see, I cannot yet dispense with my third leg."

Later Wilson would remark to Grayson, "Can you imagine what kind of a hide Lodge has got, coming up here in these circumstances and wanting to appear familiar and talk with me?"

The days wound down and President-Elect Harding and Mrs. Harding visited the White House on March 3 at the invitation of Edith and the president. "My husband was already downstairs to join me in greeting them, and we had tea in the Red Room.... We tried to make things go, but they seemed ill at ease and did not stay long. Mr. Harding sat in an armchair with one leg thrown over the arm."

On March 4, Edith and the president said their goodbyes and then the cars were at the door to take them to the inaugural ceremony. President Wilson was ready in his room when Edith went to find him. "[His] valet held his high hat and gloves and gave him the cane, which, alas, he could not walk without." Then one final snafu occurred.

At the Capitol, the incoming and outgoing presidents mounted the steps together, but arrangements had been made for President Wilson to take an elevator that was out of sight. The assumption was that Harding would take the elevator with him, but at the moment Harding should have gone with Wilson to the elevator he abandoned him. As Edith wrote years later in her memoir, "Mr. Harding alighted from the car and, smiling and waving his hat, ascended the steps, thoughtlessly leaving my husband to drive on alone. Our car followed quickly and Mrs. Harding fairly raced up the steps. How I longed to follow the lonely figure making his painful way through the lower entrance."

The president's final duty was to adjourn Congress. It was Senator Lodge who presented a formal report. The Detroit *Free Press* of March 5, 1921 reported this final encounter, which Edith recorded in her memoir. "Through a day that had taxed the president's broken physical powers greatly, he came smiling and with whimsical, humorous twist to his comments...A moment later someone touched him on the arm to call his attention to the fact that Senator Lodge had arrived. Mr. Wilson turned toward the man who led the fight against the Treaty. His face lost its smile as he listened to the Senator's formal report and there was in his own tone a touch of cool formality as he said: 'I have no communication to make; I appreciate your courtesy; good morning.'"

This was the last official duty of the Wilsons. Dr. Grayson, Joseph Tumulty, Edith, the president, and two Secret Service men left the building. Woodrow and Edith drove to their home on S Street in Washington to begin a new life.

# THIRTY-FIVE

# MERCILESS TO THE END

## 1923

THE SUMMER OF 1921 WAS HOT IN WASHINGTON AND EVEN
hotter in the White House where open liquor bottles lay about on
tables. President Harding said prohibition was for the people, but
upstairs spittoons now graced poker tables and cigar-chomping men
referred to the president's wife as "Ma." President Harding played
golf and had sex with his mistress in a White House closet. The
Harding administration represented a break with the old world that
had moved on with the Wilsons. The war had not worked out. There
was no payoff for all that carnage and now people just wanted to
forget. President Harding was a man who lived in the present with
no knowledge of or interest in the past.

Sometimes things got out of hand in the new White House. One
visitor reported seeing President Harding choking the director of the
Veterans Bureau in the Red Room, screaming, "You yellow rat! You
double-crossing bastard!" Everything was for sale, for a price. Henry
Cabot Lodge was one of the first senators invited to the White House

to shake hands with President Harding for the press. The pictures made front-page news.

When the Wilsons turned on to the street of their new home in Washington, they saw an incredible site. People had gathered on S street all the way down. They cheered when the car turned the corner in an outpouring of enthusiastic affection. The Wilsons went in and began living as Mr. and Mrs. Wilson, private citizens. It was what Edith had always wanted.

She had set up the new house to approximate the president's old routine. "Both the Doctor and I feared the result of so many changes for our invalid..." Edith had never referred to Woodrow Wilson as an invalid in her memoir until he was out of the White House. It was a slip-up in a masterful portrayal of a man by his wife. In a letter to Mrs. Trask dated May 27, 1920, Edith once again confirmed her real view of the president. "We had no idea that you too were so ill—but rejoice that with the coming of spring and sunshine you are climbing slowly back to life again. My own dear invalid is doing the same—and our hearts are filled with thanksgiving."

Historical documents give us only a few glimpses under the covers, but Edith Wilson did see her husband after his stroke as an invalid, and an invalid was not a president.

Admiral Grayson stayed on as Wilson's doctor. Edith hired Isaac and Mary Scott from Virginia to care for her husband. The Wilsons got up at seven and breakfasted together. Then they went downstairs and worked on the mail. Wilson got exercise by walking up and down the hallway. Then he went upstairs and shaved and dressed for lunch. They saw visitors until three and then took a ride.

The ex-president had purchased the old Pierce-Arrow touring car from the White House and had it painted in Princeton colors. Woodrow ate by the fire in the library and sometimes Edith read to him or they watched a moving picture show in the library. Saturday nights they went to the theater. The first time after they left the White House, Woodrow and Edith entered the theater and people rose and clapped and cheered. At the end of the play, *Abraham Lincoln*, they gave Woodrow a standing ovation.

One Saturday night, one of the actors stopped the play and spoke to the audience. "My only boy was killed in the war," he said, "and not in words can I express how much I miss him." He then looked up to where Woodrow Wilson was sitting with Edith. "But one of the greatest casualties this war has produced is the distinguished man who is in this audience tonight." The audience wept and jumped to their feet and cheered for the crippled man sitting quietly in seat U-21 with his wife beside him.

And then Edith had to take over the mantle of power once more. Wilson's old secretary Tumulty had been on the outside of politics since the Hardings took over and had sent over several overtures to the president. Looking to get back into the political limelight, he asked the former president if he might send a message to the National Democratic Club of New York, which was holding its annual Jefferson banquet.

Tumulty then could assert he was still an insider and capable of getting a former president to sanctify the proceedings. Wilson declined to give him any sort of message. "I feel that a message...would be quite meaningless unless I made it a serious expression of my views and feelings about the national situation, and I do not feel that the occasion is an especially appropriate for breaking my silence."

But Tumulty persisted and called Edith the next day.

"Next morning, Mr. Tumulty telephoned me," she would write later. "'Mrs. Wilson,' said he. 'Can't you get the Governor to send a letter to this dinner in New York?' My reply was, 'Why Mr. Tumulty, he answered your letter yesterday; haven't you got it?' In a very fretted tone he replied: 'Oh yes I got it, but I think it is very important he should write this letter; and won't you persuade him to do it?'"

Edith's reply was firm.

"No, Mr. Tumulty, you know him well enough to know that when he has thought a thing out and decided it there is no use to continue argument; and besides, I thoroughly agree with him."

Tumulty persisted and asked for a meeting with Wilson. Edith relented and the old secretary and the ex-president met at 3:00 p.m. They spoke briefly and when Edith asked if he had mentioned the request, Wilson replied, "No, I am glad to say he had the good taste not to mention it."

The next day the papers carried a message from Woodrow Wilson given at the banquet: "Say to the Democrats of New York that I am ready to support any man who stands for the salvation of America, and the salvation of America is justice to all classes." Edith wrote in her memoir, "My husband was thunderstruck. Reading the article, he learned a message had been read at the Jefferson banquet...purporting to be from [him]."

Joe Tumulty had created the message and hoped it would restore his political wind. Woodrow dictated a letter immediately: "I am deeply distressed to find that in all the papers that contain an account of the dinner in New York last night a statement that a telegram was read that was said to be from me...." Tumulty's secretary called the next day and requested an immediate appointment with Wilson. "Why, there is no urgency about this, Mr. Johnson," Edith replied. "The doctors think it is better Mr. Wilson see no one at night, but Mr. Tumulty can come in any time tomorrow..."

Edith went to her mother's house, where her brother Wilmer told her he had come from Tumulty's office. "You never saw anybody in such a distraught state in your life. He asked me to see if you could help him."

"What about?" Edith asked.

"That telegram Mr. Wilson is supposed to have sent to that dinner in New York. Tumulty tells me it was written by him. He says he was so convinced that Mr. Wilson ought to send a telegram that after seeing him on Friday, he thought there could be no harm.... So Tumulty is in this position: either he has to admit that he faked the message—for the *New York Times* is insisting on an explanation—or get Mr. Wilson to assume the responsibility."

Her brother explained Tumulty had come to the house on S Street and begged Wilmer to tell Edith that "'For God's sake help [him]'—for he says, if this is published it will ruin him and disgrace his wife and little children."

Edith replied that her husband would never say he sent a telegram. There was some back and forth in the papers until Wilson sent a final message to the *New York Times*. "I write to say there is no doubt about the matter. I did not send any message whatever to that dinner nor authorize anyone to convey a message."

Joe Tumulty was effectively disgraced and wouldn't see the president again. Woodrow Wilson was on his deathbed when Tumulty asked to see him one last time. The request came to Edith on the day before Wilson died. She didn't reply. It was only through Dr. Grayson that Joe Tumulty was invited to the funeral. Edith was merciless to the end.

# THIRTY-SIX

# A BROKEN PIECE OF MACHINERY

## 1924

THEY CLOPPED ALONG IN THE PARADE. A MAN SLUMPED DOWN IN a top hat pulled in a carriage behind two uniformed black grooms. The woman beside him was in a fur coat and they looked out of place among the cars. It was a vision of the past. People started to realize who it was and began to cheer and then they rushed into the street.

Edith and Wilson had received an invitation from the War Department to attend the ceremony of the Unknown Soldier at Arlington. When they went to the procession they found their place taken and were forced to the back. "A police sergeant conducted us to the place where the procession was forming..." Edith wrote. "The procession began to move and rather than be left out we wedged our carriage into the line as best we could..."

So the ex-president and his wife were at the back of the line in their old Victoria. At first no one noticed the two people with the African Americans sitting up top in the carriage. But slowly people started to notice the top hat and the pince-nez glasses. The crowd began to cheer. "His obscure position in the parade seemed to emphasize the reception the people gave their wartime chief," Edith later noted. "Breaking barriers, the crowds poured into the street."

Woodrow Wilson had become the bellwether to something decent and moral as the twenties lit up like a rocket and F. Scott Fitzgerald proclaimed, "America was going on the greatest gaudiest spree in history." The Jazz Age Fitzgerald would christen was swirling around the old man in the top hat behind the horse drawn carriage. People just wanted to see what they were losing one more time.

Then in a touching homage, people started migrating to S Street. Thousands of people gathered up and down the street. When Wilson appeared at his door they cheered for ten minutes. "Leaning hard on his cane, the former President walked down the five front steps of his house in order to greet three disabled veterans.... Hundreds of children waited as well, one of whom handed him a letter, which said, 'Young as we are we have learned to admire you and the great principles for which you stand.'"

Wilson managed to speak in a low voice.

"I wish that I have the voice to reply and to thank you for the wonderful tribute you paid me. I can only say God bless you."

A man shouted. "Long live the best man in the world!"

The crowd wept and tears flowed from Wilson's eyes. Trembling, he reached for Edith's hand. Like most of the crowd, she cried as well.

In the summer of 1923, President Harding had a heart attack and died in his hotel suite in San Francisco. Calvin Coolidge became president after taking the oath of office by lamplight in his Vermont home. Wilson, Edith, and Grayson rode in an open car in the funeral procession. People all along the route took off their hats as the Wilsons passed.

The summer of '23 was exceptionally hot and Edith wasn't feeling well. "...everyone told me I looked worn out. The fact is that I felt my splendid health deserting me, and could hardly drag myself around." Dr. Grayson advised her to get away before she had a "complete breakdown." Edith went to visit friends for a week in Mattapoisett, Massachusetts. Grayson stayed with Wilson.

When Edith returned she found a changed man. Her husband had aged and grown more depressed. He was having trouble seeing and reading had become almost impossible. The progressive hardening of the arteries complicated by lack of movement had progressed.

On Armistice Day, Woodrow spoke to America on a new device that was wired into his library. "Mr. Wilson spoke at 8:30 in the evening," Edith later wrote. "When the hour came he put on his dressing gown and descended to the library.... His head ached so he could scarcely see the words on the typed pages before him. I stood behind the microphone with a carbon copy of the address in my hand, ready to prompt him should he lose his place." The radio address was hailed as a success, but Wilson was in low spirits.

In January 1924 Edith came down with grippe and for five days was sequestered in her room. Woodrow came to her door when he could and spoke through the wood. Dr. Grayson was planning to go to South Carolina for a vacation, but Edith was concerned. Letters to which Wilson would dictate replies lay on his bedside table. Edith asked Grayson if he thought her husband was getting sicker.

"No," the doctor replied. "If I did, I would not leave him, and if you want me to give up the trip, I will; but I think you are mistaken."

Edith went to her husband's room and found him with his head bowed. She asked him if he felt badly.

"I always feel badly now, little girl, and somehow I hate to have Grayson leave."

"He is still downstairs. Let me run and tell him, and he will stay." Woodrow caught her hand.

"No, that would be a selfish thing on my part.... It won't be very much longer, and I had hoped he would not desert me; but that I should not say, even to you."

January 29 was a bad night. Edith telegraphed Grayson to return and sent for Doctors Ruffin and Fowler. Grayson examined him on January 31 and stayed the night. In the morning he said his systems were shutting down. Wilson steadily declined as newspapers carried the news of his impending death. His kidneys began to fail and Woodrow Wilson looked up at Grayson.

"I am ready," he said. "I am a broken piece of machinery. When the machinery is broken..."

In the end, Edith held his right hand, his daughter Margaret, his left. Dr. Grayson held his wrist and monitored his pulse. His last whispered word was "Edith."

At 11:15 a.m. Sunday, February 3, 1924, Woodrow Wilson died. Gene Smith writes in *When the Cheering Stopped* of the scene outside the house. "Outside, the crowds gathered after church. The street was closed to all traffic by the police and was entirely silent save for occasionally the voice of a child too young to understand why the hundreds stood voiceless. Among them was Mrs. Minnegerode Andrews who passed out slips of paper upon which was written, 'Peace on earth, good will toward men.'...When the last of the slips was out of her hand, she stepped off the sidewalk and in Sunday finery, she sank to her knees in the cobblestone gutter...All around her men and women went down, the men taking off their hats. The policemen and the reporters turned away, unwilling to stare at this."

The morning milk wagons did not go down the street. Dr. Grayson came out and read a statement to the press. "Mr. Wilson died at 11:15 this morning. His heart action became feebler and feebler and the heart muscle was so fatigued that it refused to act any longer. The end came peacefully."

A reporter shouted out.

"Was Mrs. Wilson in the room when he died?"

"Yes," Grayson replied. "She was right there."

# THIRTY-SEVEN

# EDITH AT LARGE

## 1924–1961

EDITH TOOK CHARGE OF THE FUNERAL AND DECIDED TO HOLD A short service at the house and then a full service at the Bethlehem Chapel of the National Cathedral. She sat down and wrote a letter to the man she once called a "venomous serpent crawling through dirty paths," Senator Henry Cabot Lodge. "As the funeral is private, and not official one, and realizing that your presence there would be embarrassing to you and unwelcome to me, I write to request that you do not attend."

Lodge quickly wrote back. "You may rest assured that nothing could be more distasteful to me than to do anything which by any possibility would be embarrassing to you."

Then the McAdoos arrived at S Street fresh off the fallout from the Teapot Dome Scandal that had touched the president's son-in-law. The McAdoos huddled in the library with advisors while President Woodrow Wilson lay in state. Edith accused the McAdoos of caring little about her dead husband and only about their political ambitions.

Margaret, the president's daughter, proclaimed her father was in a better place and that everyone should be happy. Margaret would spend the rest of her life joining spiritual groups and looking for her own mystic place in the world.

During the funeral, Edith wept inconsolably, putting down the heavy burden she had lifted when the president fell ill on the train outside Colorado five years before. The mask she had been forced to wear was gone and she was prostrate with grief. After Woodrow Wilson was laid to rest, she went back to S Street.

For a year she stayed in seclusion and was kept busy answering eight thousand telegrams and letters of condolences. She inherited two hundred and fifty thousand dollars from her husband's estate and could use the services of the White House for postage, but this required her to sign every envelope. Congress later passed an act allowing her to use a rubber stamp; it would seem signature scandals plagued Edith all her life.

Edith only appeared in ceremonies that furthered the causes Wilson believed in. "I never gave interviews. I have always felt that the wife of a former president should not speak in public." Edith slowly came back to life and traveled during the twenties and thirties in Europe and once all the way around the world. Henry Cabot Lodge died nine months after Woodrow Wilson and the papers made much of the famous feud between the two men. Edith said nothing about the death of Henry Cabot Lodge. Like all her enemies, he was dead to her already.

Edith got to work on Wilson's letters and finding a biographer. She worked through the Wilson papers and settled on Ray Stannard Baker as her husband's biographer. A literary partnership was formed that would ultimately produce the *Woodrow Wilson Papers*. They worked tirelessly together, and Baker questioned why so many of her notes were in pencil and barely legible. Edith explained that she had made notes by the president's bed on any scrap of paper that was available.

Edith campaigned for Franklin Roosevelt and was a frequent dinner guest. One time Roosevelt asked her if she liked the wine glasses and told Edith he got them off the *George Washington*. Edith then told Roosevelt that when the *George Washington* was being broken up, Secretary Daniels offered her husband the desk he used during the crossings. The president said he couldn't take it because it belonged to the government, when in fact it had been a gift to Wilson from Rodman Wannamaker. When told this, Wilson said he would like the desk, but Daniels had to call back and say it had disappeared.

"We never found out what happened to it," Edith told him.

At this point President Roosevelt roared with laughter.

"I can tell you. I have it. And what's more, you're not going to get it away from me."

Edith looked the president in the eye.

"You're nothing but a common thief."

Their friendship endured, but Edith could hold a grudge like no other.

Then the books started to come out. Colonel House published his book, *What Really Happened at Paris: The Story of the Peace Conference.* This so infuriated Edith that she began writing her own. The mission of her book, *My Memoir,* was to establish her steward-ship role. It was a tightrope walk that painted "a team approach" to many problems. But Edith couldn't hide the fact that Woodrow Wilson was an invalid after 1919.

The restraint in Edith's prose is evident throughout the book and she operated according to the same guiding principle she did in the White House. If something made the president look bad then it would not be written. Nothing would stress the president in her book, because the villains were clearly defined. Like the correspondence tossed aside to be opened thirty years later, Edith didn't write about the events or people she did not deem worthy.

Much of *My Memoir* is a walk among the magnolias with impressions of a woman who found herself at the center of power and feted by the kings and queens of Europe. It contains a great deal of fluff, but the truth seeps out and at its center is a woman doing her best to keep her husband alive and run a country.

In 1939, *My Memoir* was published and Edith was floored by its success. "I wrote the first part of my book on the train," she said later. "I was so mad after reading Colonel House's book that I just started to write furiously." Edith received forty thousand dollars for the first serial rights from the *Saturday Evening Post*. The *New York Times Book Review* said it was a book that "humanizes the president without detracting from his dignity...curiously enough [the book] is the first volume of memoirs ever written by the wife of an American president."

Edith didn't like many of the books published about her husband. Edith Gittings Reid published *Woodrow Wilson: The Caricature, the Myth, and the Man*. The book bothered Edith because it ignored her, characterizing her simply as Woodrow's second wife. Historians' minimization of Edith's role in the White House would become a trend. Edith didn't care for Ike Hoover's *Forty-Two Years in the White House* for a different reason: because she thought it made her husband look enfeebled.

The 1940s brought a movie about Wilson, in which Geraldine Fitzgerald played the first lady. Edith attended the premier. The film was ultimately disappointing for many who felt it was too "Hollywood." Edith never commented on the film nor would she accept the fifty thousand dollars offered her, instead donating it to a charity.

After the Japanese bombed Pearl Harbor, Edith sat next to Eleanor Roosevelt as President Franklin Roosevelt declared war on the Japanese. Jonathan Daniels, Josephus Daniels' son, wrote that Edith was "a well preserved still elegantly dressed widow of sixty-nine." Edith was out and about as the country mobilized for war. The former first lady was on buses carrying her own bags and working at the Red Cross once again to do her part for the war effort. She gave up her car during the gas shortage and used her ration book like everyone else.

She had to cut back starting in 1944 as her blood pressure reached 210. She returned to S Street and continued doing her part from her bed. "While I was in bed I cut the ruffles for the curtains and whipped them together.... my Wilcox works like a breeze." President Truman invited Edith to the White House for a victory celebration after the Japanese surrendered. Edith accepted and studied the short man who had been president for only a few months.

A conference in San Francisco to draw up a charter for the United Nations caused Edith's temper to flare when Nell McAdoo released a statement claiming that Woodrow Wilson had said it was better that the United States had not joined the League of Nations. Edith released her own statement.

> Woodrow Wilson would have never made such a statement for it would have reversed everything in his nature and contradicted his life's struggle for the betterment of all people and all nations of the world. What he did say to me and to many of his friends who have spoken of it since then— perhaps it was better that the American people did not join the League of Nations just to follow him, but that they join from their own convictions that they could not stay out, and that conviction would come through the tragic loss of young lives, for in another generation the World War would be followed by another one even more terrible.

Time moved on and people around Edith started to go. Her mother died in 1933. Admiral Grayson continued in the service of presidents and died suddenly at the age of fifty-nine. Edith's brothers, Wilmer and Randolph, died in 1951. Her siblings Wilmer, Randolph, and Gertrude had moved in with her at S Street.

Edith was invited to the White House by every successive president. On January 28, 1954, Edith wrote about sitting next to Richard Nixon at a dinner. "I sat next to him poor thing, he dropped the chili sauce all down his shirt front and on his waistcoat. Mrs. Eisenhower and I took a napkin and ice water and got it nearly all off." She was elated when John Kennedy was elected and never forgot that he had chosen Woodrow Wilson as one of the subjects in his book, *Profiles in Courage*.

In 1961 few people noticed the woman in the back row on the president's platform during Kennedy's inauguration. It was sixteen degrees and bright sunshine. The small woman sat quietly and warmed herself from a small flask of bourbon. She then rode up Pennsylvania Avenue next to Eleanor Roosevelt in an open car. When the driver suggested they put up the top against the cold, Edith immediately complained.

"Open all the windows. I'm stifling!"

There was a luncheon party at Edith's home for Jackie Kennedy, who was late in arriving. Edith was the all-time champion bridge player among presidents' wives. She liked to go up to New York for theater and she loved cars. She took friends around in a sleek black Buick and still went on the long country drives she had enjoyed with Woodrow. She read voraciously and hosted holidays and anniversaries in grand style.

In these later years, it would seem Edith was still the progressive woman who had owned an electric, had means, and traveled Europe on her own in 1914. She was still the woman whose beauty had attracted a bereaved president.

To the end, Edith looked much younger than her years. Her loss of hearing caused her to cut down on social engagements, and she developed a tic on her right side. President Kennedy signed into law a commission to provide a memorial to Woodrow Wilson. Edith sat beside the president at the ceremony and he slipped his chair by hers and said, "You just sit right there and we'll sign it." He then gave her the pen, and she smiled and said, "I didn't dare ask you for it."

During Thanksgiving she came down with a cold she couldn't get rid of. By Christmas it was clear her body was beginning to fail from heart disease. Edith died of congestive heart failure on December 28, 1961, the birthday of Woodrow Wilson. The news flashed around the world and messages of sympathy poured in. In a brief flash of illumination, if not perspective, Edith Wilson was described in American and European newspapers as the "First Woman President." It was a title not given to her until she died, and one that would disappear again for many years.

The funeral services were simple and she was buried in the crypt at the west end of St. Joseph's Chapel. Her name was carved into the stone as she was laid to rest next to her husband. In the 1970s people went to the old manse in Staunton, Virginia, to see the birthplace of Woodrow Wilson and all the memorabilia Edith had approved to be presented there. The one thing that was acquired later was the Pierce-Arrow President Wilson bought in 1919 for three thousand dollars. The car weighed an incredible three tons and rumbled along at twenty-five miles an hour, but it was the car of Edith and Woodrow's courtship.

They had taken many drives through Rock Creek Park and out into the Maryland countryside to get away from the world and try to be alone together.

Now they finally were.

# THIRTY-EIGHT

# THE FIRST WOMAN PRESIDENT

## 2016

EDITH WILSON'S PRESIDENCY WAS SHORT—LESS THAN TWO years—but it was groundbreaking. Woodrow Wilson after his stroke could not perform the duties of the presidency and Edith stepped in to fill the role. Edith's guiding principle as president was to keep her husband alive by taking over his job and restricting access to him. Edith's presidency fits the constitutional definitions of the duties of president. The Constitution defines the president's first role as commander in chief of our military. World War I had just ended but the peace had not been settled. Edith was in the middle of the negotiations to get the Treaty of Versailles ratified and to implement the League of Nations with the United States as a member.

The second function of the president is to make sure that the nation's laws are "faithfully executed." Congress passes laws and the president either signs or vetoes them. Bills were signed into law under Edith and it is an open question about who really signed them. But most scholars agree it was Edith guiding the president's hand. The

Volstead Act was vetoed while President Wilson was in the darkest days of his stroke, and legislation became law under Edith Wilson with no signatures. This became a function of her governing; push through whatever could be pushed through.

Another function of the president as defined by the Constitution is to set foreign policy. The biggest foreign policy concern of Edith Wilson's presidency was the settling of World War I. That encompassed the Treaty of Versailles and the League of Nations and the direction of the United States' foreign policy for the next twenty years. Edith had been involved in the war, receiving the news that war had begun and ended as she deciphered top-secret codes. She would continue to decipher code all through her presidency when necessary, and by proxy monitor the foreign policy of the United States. The resulting isolationist policy after the defeat of the League would prove disastrous for the country and the world.

The Constitution also requires the president to appoint key personnel and fill positions by approving ambassadors and cabinet positions. Edith was involved with the shuffling of cabinet members, such as Secretary of Agriculture David Houston, filling diplomatic positions through instructions to Secretary Lansing, and filling the position of Secretary Lane when he left the Department of the Interior. She also made a mark in the positions she chose to leave open and the ambassadors she did not approve.

The next responsibility of the president is specified as presenting the State of the Union to Congress. Edith, with the help of others including Joe Tumulty, had a hand in crafting the "Messages to Congress" and then sending the documents over to Congress. These were primarily crafted by Tumulty, but Edith was the final arbiter as she read everything and chose whether or not to pass documents to the president.

One of the president's final responsibilities is to pardon felons. Eugene Debs was still in jail when the Wilsons left, and Edith made sure President Wilson saw this last bit of presidential duty before he left. In this she had little influence and the president issued few pardons after he became sick. Debs remained in jail.

Edith exercised five out of the six duties of the presidency. But history is not just facts. It is an accumulation of events and circumstances that interact with individuals upon the grand stage of life. Verisimilitude is by definition *that which appears most true*, but it is only through the exigencies of shared experience that we see truth. It is the journey after all and not the destination that matters most.

The unique role of Edith Wilson began before the president had a stroke. She was, in a sense, a *co-president*, assisting the president with daily duties, from decoding top-secret messages to acting as a sounding board to blotting his signatures. When the stroke occurred, Edith stepped into the role and became *the president*. Edith Wilson's memoir argues that she was a "steward" but never a president. She had a legacy to protect and she was fierce in her determination that nothing should tarnish President Woodrow Wilson in office. She kept her promise even after he died.

It is hard for people to believe the United States had a woman president in 1919. Back then, women didn't take over struggling jewelry businesses or buy and drive cars, certainly not women who had only two years of formal education. But Edith Wilson did all of these things. We cannot know exactly what transpired in the Wilson White House, but since communications were by letters, there is a paper trail that gives us an indication. It is in those letters that we see Edith Wilson's involvement in running the United States from October 1919 to March 1921. *Dear Mrs. Wilson* slowly supplanted *Dear Mr. President*. Even the people who were addressing letters to the president knew Edith would be reading them.

The multifarious nature of the letters shows Edith's hand on all the levers of power. The third person referred to in many letters is *the*

*President*, but the person being instructed was *Edith Wilson*. In others, the senders of the letters knew full well that Woodrow Wilson wasn't acting on anything, so they addressed Edith. The following salutations tell the story.

> "*Dear Mrs. Wilson, I submitted the draft of the proposed letter to Sec. Houston.*"
> "*Dear Mrs. Wilson, Here is a suggestion of a message to Congress...*"
> "*Dear Mrs. Wilson, will you be good enough to speak to the president...*"
> "*Dear Mrs. Wilson, Tomorrow at 12 o'clock the time expires to withdraw petition for candidates.*"
> "*Dear Mrs. Wilson, Will you advise me how the president wishes to [respond to] the attached letter from General Pershing?*"
> "*Dear Mrs. Wilson, Acting Attorney General Ames has just telephoned me that the railroad strike situation is growing more and more serious.*"
> "*Dear Mrs. Wilson, It seems to me that if this statement could be given out tonight and printed in tomorrow's morning papers it would be most helpful.*"
> "*Dear Mrs. Wilson, Work in the Senate today from ten o'clock this hour has not been of any great significance...*"
> "*Dear Mrs. Wilson, Will you kindly read the enclosed letter from Honorable Breckenridge Long relating to Mr. Hapgood's resignation as Minister of Copenhagen?*"
> "*Dear Mrs. Wilson, Day after tomorrow the democratic caucus meets to elect a leader.*"
> "*Dear Mrs. Wilson, On my return to Washington this afternoon Mr. Lansing told of the president's very kind thought and his desire to appoint me as Minister of Switzerland.*"

*"Dear Mrs. Wilson, This matter is so vitally important that I send this letter to you so that you may read it to the president when you think fit."*

*"Dear Mrs. Wilson, Since our talk on Thursday, I have had the present situation very deeply in mind, I have the feeling that all the president went to France to fight for...is being swept away."*

*"Dear Mrs. Wilson, The psychological moment is approaching when the president could strike with great force along the lines suggested in the letter to Senator Hitchcock."*

*"Dear Mrs. Wilson, It now appears that without any initiative on the part of the president, efforts are being made in the Senate to reach a compromise on the Peace Treaty."*

*"Dear Mrs. Wilson, This matter was discussed at a conference between the Attorney General and Director General Hines. They both feel the president ought to accede to the request of the Commission."*

*"Dear Mrs. Wilson, Please don't think I am trying to crowd you or to urge immediate action by the president..."*

*"Dear Mrs. Wilson, When you get a chance to talk to the president, will you please tell him that Senator Hitchcock sent for me yesterday..."*

*"Dear Mrs. Wilson, Enclosed please find the draft of a letter which might be addressed to me if it meets with the president's approval."*

These directives (and many others) were addressed to Edith Wilson and not the president, reflecting the reality that, after Woodrow's stroke, all power flowed through Edith. The best proof that Edith took over the reins of the presidency is that she does not appear in the *Papers of Woodrow Wilson* at all before October 3, 1919. But after the debilitating stroke of October 3, Edith Wilson begins to appear in official correspondence and this increases with time. If Edith wasn't the president, then why were White House communications directed to her? The answer is that everyone knew who was running the United States from 1919 to 1921.

Edith had excellent training. Her husband had included her in almost every major decision, from his reelection to his declaration of war to turning the United States into a juggernaut of power and negotiating the peace to end that war. Woodrow Wilson valued his wife's opinion in the most crucial legislation that cost him his health and then his life, the League of Nations. Edith counseled him in Paris and then called the shots on the crucial campaign to get the treaty ratified.

Edith governed by access under the covenant that it was better for her to make a decision than her husband. If someone asked Tumulty, House, or Grayson who the president was during those years, inevitably they would answer Edith Wilson.

Even though Dr. Dercum gave her the mandate, the men around the president saw Edith as the logical person to keep the White House running as smoothly as possible. And they were right, because Edith had worked so closely with the president, she was the best-qualified candidate to step into the presidential shoes.

And Edith was formidable. She had her husband's health on her mind at every moment. And fortunately for all concerned, she understood politics better than her husband. Even though Edith Wilson didn't believe in the suffrage movement, she understood it was the future. Alice Paul and the suffragettes made Wilson and Edith aware of what was at stake by their unrelenting campaign, which likely prompted Edith to encourage Wilson to speak to the Congress to pass the Nineteenth Amendment.

In many cases Edith saw the larger issues at play. It was she who told the president not to release a letter criticizing the Republicans and urging Americans to vote for the Democrats in midterm elections during the war. She knew it would hurt the president politically and she turned out to be right.

Some historians have said, "Edith Wilson was *almost* the president." Almost is close enough when your husband is on his back, severely paralyzed, and cognitively disabled. Edith was driving the conspiracy to keep Woodrow Wilson's illness from the world. She knew that if he left the White House, then he probably would have died. What's more, his greatest ambition would have died. The League of Nations wouldn't have had a chance if Wilson left office.

Edith Wilson played a pivotal role in moderating what reached the president and what didn't. For good or bad, the president was outside the bedroom door with all the levers of power during the final negotiations. Edith did what any wife would do whose husband becomes ill and can no longer run the family business; she stepped in and ran it herself. Women all over America on farms and in business had been doing this for decades when their husbands became ill or were injured. They simply learned what they had to; like Edith, many had on-the-job training.

It just so happened that the farm Edith stepped in to run was the Executive Branch of the government of the United States. She had done it when her first husband died and left her with a jewelry company in debt. Edith could have liquidated the company, but she didn't. She didn't turn from her duty then nor did she turn when the president of the United States became permanently incapacitated.

Edith stayed up night after night, working on official documents, decoding top-secret diplomatic codes, approving who would and would not see the president, negotiating with senators, appointing cabinet members, diverting correspondence, composing statements, and signing documents. All the while she was trying to make sure her husband would live to see another day. It was heroic.

And now, at the time of this writing, just under a hundred years later, we are faced again with the prospect of our first woman president. Edith Wilson was never nominated, she was never on any ballot, she never took the oath of office, but she did carry the burden of presidential power from 1919 to 1921. She has never been given credit for stepping in during a national emergency and steering the ship of the United States through turbulent waters.

Edith Wilson never sought any acknowledgment and in fact made a point of saying she was not the president. But she did rule and she found out the limits and the heartbreak of that power. Edith Wilson's presidency should be studied closely by the next woman president. Like the Wright brothers' first experimental flights, it was rough and short, but it left behind experience and much to learn from.

The next flight will be longer and will tell us even more. After all, experience is the best teacher, and Edith Bolling Wilson, when it was all said and done, was our first woman president.

# ACKNOWLEDGMENTS

MANY THANKS TO ELMHURST COLLEGE FOR THE USE OF THE *Papers of Woodrow Wilson* and other sources. Thanks to the great people at Regnery for editing and advice. And to my family for enduring.

# SELECT BIBLIOGRAPHY

Ashby, Ruth. *Woodrow and Edith Wilson*. New York: World Almanac Library, 2002.

Bailey, Thomas A. *Woodrow Wilson and the Great Betrayal*. New York: Macmillan, 1945.

———.*The Art of Diplomacy: The American Experience*. New York: Appleton-Century-Crofts, 1968.

Bailey, Thomas and David Kennedy. *The American Spirit: United States History as Seen by Contemporaries*. Belmont: Wadsworth Publishing Company, 2009.

Baker, Ray Stannard. *American Chronicle*. New York: Scribner, 1945.

Berg, Scott A. *Wilson*. New York: Putnam, 2013.

Birdsall, Paul. *Versailles Twenty Years After*. Crows Nest, Australia: Allen & Unwin, 1941.

Bloom, Harold, ed. *F. Scott Fitzgerald*. New York: Chelsea House Publications, 1985.

Blum, John M. *Joe Tumulty and the Wilson Era*. Boston: Houghton Mifflin, 1951.

Burlingame, Roger, and Alden Stevens. *Victory Without Peace*. New York: Harcourt, Brace, 1944.

Cashman, Sean Dennis. *America Ascendant: From Theodore Roosevelt to FDR in the Century of American Power, 1901—1945*. New York: New York University Press, 1998.

Clements, Kendrick A. *The Presidency of Woodrow Wilson*. Lawrence: University Press of Kansas, 1992.

Coffman, Edward, M. *The War to End All Wars: The American Military Experience in World War I*. New York: Oxford University Press, 1968.

Cooper, John M. *Woodrow Wilson*. New York: Knopf, 2009.

———. *Breaking the Heart of the World: Woodrow Wilson and the Fight for the League of Nations*.

Daniels, Josephus. *The Life of Woodrow Wilson*. Westport: Greenwood Press, 1924.

———.*The Wilson Era*. Chapel Hill: University of North Carolina Press, 1946.

Dodd, William. *Woodrow Wilson and His Work*. Garden City: Doubleday, Page & Company, 1920.

Dos Passos, John. *Mr. Wilson's War: From the Assassination of McKinley to the Defeat of the League of Nations*. Garden City: Doubleday, 1962.

Garraty, John A. *Henry Cabot Lodge: A Biography*. New York: Knopf, 1953.

George, Alexander. *Woodrow Wilson and Colonel House: A Personality Study*. Mineola: Dover Publications, 1964.

Grayson, Cary T. *Woodrow Wilson: An Intimate Memoir*. New York: Holt, Rinehart and Winston, 1960.

Hatch, Alden. *Edith Bolling Wilson*. New York: Dodd, Mead, and Company, 1961.

Heckscher, August. *Woodrow Wilson*. New York: Charles Scribner and Sons, 1991.

Hoover, Herbert. *The Ordeal of Woodrow Wilson*. Washington, DC: Woodrow Wilson Center Press, 1992.

Hulbert, Mary Allen. *The Story of Mrs. Peck: An Autobiography*. New York: Minton, Balch & Company, 1933.

Jaffray, Elizabeth. *Secrets of the White House*. New York: Cosmopolitan Book Corporation, 1927.

Kennan, George F. *American Diplomacy 1900-1950*. Chicago: University of Chicago Press, 1951.

Kennedy, David M. *Over Here: The First World War and American Society*. New York: Oxford University Press, 1980.

Larson, Erik. *Dead Wake*. New York: Crown Publishers, 2015.

Lawrence, David. *The True Story of Woodrow Wilson*. New York: George H. Doran Co., 1924.

Levin, Phyllis L. *Edith and Woodrow*. New York: Scribner, 2001.

Link, Arthur, ed. *The Papers of Woodrow Wilson*. Vol. 63. Princeton: Princeton University Press, 1990.

———. *The Papers of Woodrow Wilson*. Vol. 64. Princeton: Princeton University Press, 1990.

———. *The Papers of Woodrow Wilson*. Vol. 65. Princeton: Princeton University Press, 1990.

May, Ernest R. *The World War and American Isolation*. Cambridge: Harvard University Press, 1959.

McAdoo, William G. *Crowded Years*. Boston: Houghton Mifflin, 1931.

Mcpherson, Stephanie. *Theodore Roosevelt*. New York: Lerner Publishing Group, 2004.

Millard, Candice. *Destiny of the Republic*. New York: Anchor Books, 2011.

Miller, Hope. *Scandals in the Highest Office: Facts and Fictions in the Private Lives of our Presidents*. New York: Random House, 1973.

Miller, Kristie. *Ellen and Edith*. Lawrence: University Press of Kansas, 1991.

Morris, Edmund. *Colonel Roosevelt*. New York: Random House, 2010.

Peterson, James W. *American Foreign Policy: Alliance Politics in a Century of War, 1914-2014*. Vol. 2. New York: Bloomsbury Academic, 2014.

Post, Dr. Jerrold and Robert Robins. *When Illness Strikes the Leader: The Dilemma of the Captive King*. New Haven: Yale University Press, 1995.

Ross, Ishbel. *Power with Grace*. New York: Putnam, 1975.

Safire, William. *Lend Me Your Ear: Great Speeches in History*. New York: W.W. Norton & Company, 2004.

Smith, Gene. *When the Cheering Stopped*. New York: William Morrow, 1964.

Starling, Edward W. and Thomas Sugrue. *Starling of the White House: The Story of the Man Whose Secret Service Detail Guarded Five Presidents from Woodrow Wilson to Franklin D. Roosevelt*. New York: Simon & Schuster, 1946.

Startt, James D. *Woodrow Wilson and the Press: Prelude to the Presidency*. New York: Palgrave Macmillan, 2004.

Striner, Richard. *Woodrow Wilson and World War I: A Burden Too Great to Bear*. Lanham: Rowman & Littlefield Publishers, 2014.

Tribble, Edwin. *President in Love: The Courtship Letters of Woodrow Wilson and Edith Bolling Galt*. Boston: Houghton Mifflin, 1981.

Tucker, Robert. *Woodrow Wilson and the Great War*. Charlottes-ville: University of Virginia Press, 2015.

Tumulty, P. Joseph. *Woodrow Wilson As I Know Him*. New York: Garden City Publishing Company, 1925.

Viereck, George S. *The Strangest Friendship in History*. New York: Liveright Publishing Corporation, 1932.

Walworth, Arthur. *Wilson and his Peacemakers—American Diplo-macy at the Paris Peace Conference*. New York: W. W. Norton & Company, 1986.

Weinstein, Edwin A. *Woodrow Wilson, A Medical and Psychologi-cal Biography*. Princeton: Princeton University Press, 1981.

———. *A Medical Biography*. Princeton: Princeton University Press, 2014.

Weisman, Steven. *The Great Tax Wars: Lincoln to Wilson—The Fierce Battles over Money and Power that Transformed the World*. New York: Simon & Schuster, 2002.

Wilson, Edith B. *My Memoir*. Indianapolis: The Bobbs-Merrill Com-pany, 1939.

# NOTES

**CHAPTER ONE: THE COVER-UP**

1.  Madam, it is a grave situation, Edith Wilson, *My Memoir* (Indianapolis: Bobbs-Merrill, 1939), 289.
2.  We have petticoat government, Ishbel Ross, *Power with Grace* (New York: Putnam, 1975), 218.
3.  I tried to arrange my appointments, Wilson, *My Memoir*, 89.
4.  Breakfast was at eight o'clock sharp, Ibid., 90.
5.  My hands now are so full, Phyllis Lee Levin, *Edith and Woodrow* (New York: Scribner, 2001), 375.

**CHAPTER TWO: A BAD DAY**

1.  Edith, can you come to me, Alden Hatch, *Edith Bolling Wilson* (New York: Dodd, Mead and Company, 1961), 214.
2.  War to End All Wars, H. G. Wells, *Daily News*, Aug 4, 1914.
3.  Entering the car, Wilson, *My Memoir*, 275.
4.  The weather was warm, Ibid., 281.

5. The strain of the trip, Arthur S. Link, ed., *The Papers of Woodrow Wilson*, vol. 63 (Princeton: Princeton University Press, 1990), 518.
6. The Doctor and I kept vigil, Wilson, *My Memoir*, 284.
7. About five in the morning, Ibid.
8. Don't you see that if you cancel this trip, Gene Smith, *When the Cheering Stopped* (New York: William Morrow, 1971), 84.
9. I don't seem to realize it but, Link, *The Papers of Woodrow Wilson*, 63.519.
10. The greatest disappointment, Scott Berg, *Wilson* (New York: Putnam, 2013), 636.
11. She would have to wear a mask, Hatch, *Edith Bolling Wilson*, 214.
12. As crusaders, Berg, *Wilson*, 534.
13. People gathered at the stations, Wilson, *My Memoir*, 285.
14. The president's condition, Link, *The Papers of Woodrow Wilson*, 63.527.
15. The New York Times, Levin, *Edith and Woodrow*, 332.
16. I took steps, Link, *The Papers of Woodrow Wilson.*, 63.533.
17. He shouldn't be bothered with any matters of official, Berg, *Wilson*, 638.
18. Dear Mrs. Wilson, if anything, Link, *The Papers of Woodrow Wilson*, 63.534.
19. This was the only instance, Wilson, *My Memoir*, 286.
20. I had never liked the plausible little man, Ibid.
21. President is again jaded, Link, *The Papers of Woodrow Wilson*, 63.538.
22. I have no feeling in, Wilson, *My Memoir*, 287.
23. I'm going to call Dr. Grayson, Hatch, *Edith Bolling Wilson*, 217.

## CHAPTER THREE: THE FIRST MRS. WILSON

1. splendid mischievous laughing eyes, Berg, *Wilson*, 88.
2. I am quite conscious, Ibid., 89.
3. I had longed to meet, Ibid.
4. From Mrs. Wilson, Levin, *Edith and Woodrow*, 40.
5. an amateur at life, Berg, *Wilson*, 91.
6. As compared, Ibid., 101.
7. Wilson's instinctive timidity, George Viereck, *The Strangest Friendship in History*, 320
8. I do feel, Berg, *Wilson*, 101.
9. Do you think, Ibid., 99.
10. A deep happy peace, Ibid., 120.
11. in all senses, Ibid.
12. I am madly in love, Ibid.
13. When you get, Ibid., 121.
14. I am counting, Ibid., 124.
15. It does not end well, Ibid., 127.
16. the most brilliant, dazzling, Ibid., 128.
17. This was the end, Ibid., 136.
18. Was he joking, Ibid., 147.
19. [We] are making, Ibid., 151.
20. dying by inches, Levin, 32.
21. It is not often, Berg, *Wilson*, 161.
22. Mr. Hibben can, Ibid., 167.
23. I stand a very, Ibid., 169.
24. Why not, Ibid.
25. If I know anything, Ibid.
26. Very well. So be it, Ibid.
27. folly and gross impertinence, Ibid., 176.
28. an apothecary's clerk, Ibid., 131.
29. She catered, Berg, *Wilson*, 302.

30. There is nothing, Ibid., 332.
31. The chief cause, Levin, *Edith and Woodrow*, 48.
32. Let's get out, Berg, *Wilson*, 333.
33. Please take good, Ibid., 335.


## Chapter Four: "The President is Paralyzed!"

1. My first thought was to keep him warm, Wilson, *My Memoir*, 287.
2. My God, the President is paralyzed!, Link, *The Papers of Woodrow Wilson*, 634.
3. The symptoms indicate that, Edwin Weinstein, *A Medical Biography* (Princeton: Princeton University Press, 2014), 357.
4. in a condition, Berg, *Wilson*, 642.
5. He looked as if he were dead, Link, *The Papers of Woodrow Wilson*, 63.634.
6. During the first phase, Bert E. Park, "The Aftermath of Wilson's Stroke", *PWW*, 63.526
7. How can that be, Wilson, *My Memoir*, 289.
8. Madam, it is a grave situation, Ibid.
9. Every time you take him a new anxiety or problem, Ibid.
10. Had he not better resign, Ibid.
11. No…Not if you feel equal to what I suggested, Ibid., 289.
12. What this country really needs is a good five cent, Ross, *Power with Grace*, 202.
13. He has the utmost confidence in you, Wilson, *My Memoir*, 289.
14. So began my stewardship, Ibid.
15. Conferred with Tumulty, Link, *Papers of Woodrow Wilson*, 63, 547.
16. The President is a very sick man, Ibid., 63, 544.
17. Admiral Grayson said, Ibid., 63, 550.

18. I talked to Admiral Grayson, Weinstein, *Woodrow Wilson: A Medicinal and Psychological Biography*, 361
19. President is seriously ill, Link, *Papers of Woodrow Wilson*, 63, 560.
20. Hope that President Wilson, Ibid. 63, 561.
21. President Wilson 'may live', Ibid. 63, 563.
22. What we have been afraid of, Ibid. 63, 566.
23. That the President's mind, Ibid. 63, 569.
24. I studied every paper, Wilson, *My Memoir*, 289.
25. The only decision that was mine was what was important, Ibid.
26. In insisting that she never made a decision, Berg, *Wilson*, 643.
27. Edith Wilson did not become as some have asserted, Ibid.
28. Case of removal, Death, Resignation, Ibid., 644.

## CHAPTER FIVE: A MODERN WOMAN

1. Who is that beautiful woman, Levin, *Edith and Woodrow*, 52.
2. So Father kept the watch at night, Wilson, *My Memoir*, 19
3. If you basked in the light of, Ibid., 6.
4. We were the best friends, Ibid.,18.
5. When we had been married, Ibid.
6. The library was fitted out as an, Hatch, *Edith Bolling Wilson*, 53.
7. a most immaculate person, Ibid., 69.
8. was immediately faced with the decision, Ibid., 22.
9. I made him manager, without bond, Ibid.
10. My own part was small for it consisted, Ibid.
11. 80,000, Levin, *Edith and Woodrow*, 70.
12. My dear doctor, I am not a society person, Wilson, *My Memoir*, 53.
13. We are not going back to your house, Ibid., 56.

## CHAPTER SIX: LESS IS MORE

1. Some of the symptoms, Smith, *When the Cheering Stopped*, 105.
2. All sorts of rumors, *The New York Times*, October 6, 1919.
3. He might live five minutes, five months, or five years, Hatch, *Edith Bolling Wilson*, 222.
4. All sorts of rumors, Viereck, *The Strangest Friendship*, 305.
5. restive…and particularly anxious to see several Democratic Senators, Ibid.
6. Details of Illness Kept from Cabinet, Ibid., 306
7. You read the newspapers, Ibid., 307
8. Under instructions, Ibid., 304
9. The President is a very sick man, Smith, *When the Cheering Stopped*, 222.
10. Never was deception, Link, *The Papers of Woodrow Wilson*, 634.
11. The President had a restless, Smith, *When the Cheering Stopped*, 100.
12. Democratic leaders are seriously, Viereck, *The Strangest Friendship*, 309
13. Together they carried the secrets, David Lawrence, *The True Story of Woodrow Wilson*, 299
14. If the Congress, Levin, *Edith and Woodrow*, 353.
15. Tell Mr. Barnes, Ibid., 355.
16. Her high intelligence and her extraordinary memory, Ross, *Power with Grace*, 204.
17. Cabinet Decides to Act, Viereck, *The Strangest Friendship*, 309.
18. If the President is kept, Ibid. 309-310.
19. Any disease that had, Ibid. 310
20. With the exception, Ibid. 310
21. It was learned, *The New York Times*, November, 1, 1919.

22. Between September 30, Levin, *Edith and Woodrow*, 357.
23. Cincinnati, New Orleans and Texas, Ibid.
24. It is explained, Viereck, The Strangest Friendship, 311.
25. The President's condition, Ibid., 309
26. The President had a satisfactory, *The Papers of Woodrow Wilson*, 63.556
27. The fact that you have not told him, Kristie Miller, *Ellen and Edith Woodrow Wilson First Ladies*, Kristie Miller, 194.
28. While Wilson was on his back, Viereck, *The Strangest Friendship*, 319.
29. It was she who acted, David Lawrence, *The True Story of Woodrow Wilson*, 288.
30. an acute period of his illness, Joseph Tumulty, *Woodrow Wilson As I Know Him* (New York: Garden City Publishing Company, 1925), 438.
31. I am not interested in the President of the United States, Ross, *Power with Grace,* 204.
32. I was informed that, Link, *Papers of Woodrow Wilson*, 63. 586.

## CHAPTER SEVEN: TEDDY AND WOODROW

1. It takes more than a bullet to stop a Bull Moose, Stephanie Mcpherson, *Theodore Roosevelt* (New York: Lerner Publishing Group, 2004), 95.
2. Roosevelt appeals to their imagination, Berg, *Wilson* (New York: Putnam, 2013), 238.
3. The pygmy hasn't any chance in America, Link, *The Papers of Woodrow Wilson*, 25.192.
4. There is nothing but the work for me, Levin, *Edith and Woodrow*, 51.

## CHAPTER EIGHT: ATTACK FROM WITHIN

1. Every paper, Hatch, *Edith Bolling Wilson*, 225.
2. I just decided, Levin, *Edith and Woodrow*, 352.
3. Yesterday I sent over, Link, *The Papers of Woodrow Wilson*, 63.618.
4. Mr. Lansing should have retired long ago, Wilson, *My Memoir*, 300.
5. I had talked with him so much, Hatch, *Edith Bolling Wilson*, 226.
6. Mr. Lansing, the Constitution is not a dead letter, Joseph Tumulty, *Woodrow Wilson as I Know Him*, 443.
7. You may rest assured, Ibid. 444.
8. And I am sure the Doctor Grayson, Ibid.
9. Dr. Grayson, we wish to know, Ibid., Smith, *When the Cheering* Stopped, 99.
10. The President had a good night, Ibid., 100.
11. While one might excuse, Kenneth R. Crispell & Carlos F. Gomez, Hidden Illness in the White House, 72.
12. Wilson's paternal regard, Josephus Daniels, *The Life of Woodrow Wilson*, 342.

## CHAPTER NINE: THE ARDENT LOVER

1. This was the accidental meeting, Wilson, *My Memoir*, 56.
2. The two gentlemen, Ibid.
3. The President seemed very tired to me, Ibid., 57.
4. That night he told me of the unusual, Ibid.
5. All Southern children were taught, Ibid., 58.
6. The Civil War had ended, Ibid.
7. The evening ended all too soon, Ibid.
8. When problems confronted him, Ibid. 58-59.
9. She's a looker, Berg, *Wilson*, 359.

10. He's a goner, Ibid., 359.
11. Almost as soon as they were gone, Wilson, *My Memoir*, 60.
12. Oh you can't love me, Ibid., 61.
13. 'Yes,' he said, 'I know,' Ibid.
14. Your dear love fills me with a bliss, John Milton Cooper, *Woodrow Wilson* (New York: Knopf, 2009), 283.
15. Ever since you went away, Ibid., 284.
16. Cousin Woodrow looks really ill, Wilson, *My Memoir*, 61.
17. I was beginning to feel like a criminal, Ibid., 62.
18. Ah, my precious friend, Cooper, *Woodrow Wilson*, 284.
19. Here stands your friend, Ruth Ashby, *Woodrow and Edith Wilson* (New York: World Almanac Library, 2005), 22.
20. dream that her dear, Levin, *Edith and Woodrow*, 75.
21. Much as I love your delicious, Ibid.
22. How I wish I could really help you, Ibid., 76.


CHAPTER TEN: "THE WHOLE BODY WILL BECOME POISONED"
1. Well, Mrs. Wilson, Wilson, *My Memoir*, 291.
2. He was physically, almost, Link, *The Papers of Woodrow Wilson*, 63.634.
3. He had changed from a giant, Link, *The Papers of Woodrow Wilson*, 63.635.
4. I had a hard time, Link, *The Papers of Woodrow Wilson*, 63.619.
5. Mrs. Wilson is of a much stronger character, Ibid., 63.621.
6. Let me have those, Smith, *When the Cheering Stopped*, 108.
7. The President did not have, Hatch, *Edith Bolling Wilson*, 230.
8. This is the situation, Wilson, *My Memoir*, 291.
9. Then we will not operate, Ibid.
10. Dr. Young followed me, Ibid.
11. You understand Mrs. Wilson, Ibid.

12. My own life seemed suspended, Ibid., 292.

## CHAPTER ELEVEN: CHRISTMAS ON THE BOTTOM OF THE OCEAN

1. The isolation made the U-boat, Erik Larson, *Dead Wake* (New York: Crown Publishers, 2015), 214.
2. The United States is remote, *North American Review* 201 (1971): 237.
3. take any steps that might be necessary, Robert Tucker, *Woodrow Wilson And the Great War* (Charlottesville: University of Virginia Press, 2015), 96.
4. a forest of masts, Larson, *Dead Wake*, 229.

## CHAPTER TWELVE: "A SMALL-CALIBER MAN"

1. A small-caliber man, Levin, *Edith and Woodrow*, 341.
2. she would let him know, Smith, *When the Cheering Stopped*, 129.
3. 'All right,' said his secretary, Ibid.
4. I cannot continue my speech, Ibid., 130.
5. No politician ever exposes himself, Levin, *Edith and Woodrow*, 342.
6. I cannot continue my speech, Smith, *When the Cheering Stopped*, 130.

## CHAPTER THIRTEEN: "WE SHALL BE AT WAR WITH GERMANY WITHIN A MONTH"

1. We spoke of the probability, Larson, *Dead Wake*, 227.
2. Suppose they should sink, Ibid., 227.
3. The torpedo itself, Ibid., 240.
4. Olive Bernard saw, Ibid.
5. Thousands of rivets and steel plates, Ibid., 248.

6. The ship was sinking, Ibid., 264.
7. plunged forward like a knife, Ibid., 277.
8. We shall be at war, James W. Peterson, *American Foreign Policy: Alliance Politics in a Century of War, 1914-2014*, vol. 2 (New York: Bloomsbury Academic, 2014), 73.

## CHAPTER FOURTEEN: EDITH AND MAJOR CRAUFURD-STUART

1. Oh, but he must not go, Wilson, *My Memoir*, 293.
2. Of course, my husband, Ibid., 294.
3. I am very glad, Smith, *When the Cheering Stopped*, 115.
4. My, what a magnificent bed, Ibid.
5. This is the bed that, Ibid.
6. If Mrs. Wilson had shown, Link, *The Papers of Woodrow Wilson*, 64.239.
7. If the President, Ibid., 64.360.

## CHAPTER FIFTEEN: THE GARFIELD PRECEDENT

1. My God! What is this, Candice Millard, *Destiny of the Republic* (New York: Anchor Books, 2011), 153.
2. Taking on the role, Ibid., 179.
3. Brown personally took, Ibid., 172.
4. The Constitution was of no help, Ibid., 253.
5. The young man divided, Ibid., 256.
6. During all this terror, Ibid.
7. Bliss permitted no one, Ibid.,193.

## CHAPTER SIXTEEN: CUPID'S TRIUMPH

1. There are some things, Link, *The Papers of Woodrow Wilson*, 33. 111.
2. Every soft creature, Berg, *Wilson*, 362.

3. My happiness absolutely depends, Link, *The Papers of Woodrow Wilson*, 33.126.
4. the country was horrified, Berg, Wilson, 362.
5. The United States must consider, Ibid., 363.
6. The example of America, Hatch, *Edith Bolling Wilson*, 19.
7. That was probably the most unfortunate, Berg, *Wilson*, 364.
8. I never again recovered, Ibid.
9. If I had said, Berg, Ibid.
10. I could go to Congress, Ibid., 365
11. Mr. Bryan, Berg, Ibid., 366
12. The night was clear, Wilson, *My Memoir*, 63.
13. Good; for I hope, Ibid.
14. Take it sir and thank God, Ibid.
15. But he is only a clerk, Ibid., 64.
16. Hurrah old Bryan is out, Levin, *Edith and Woodrow*, 86.
17. You are oh so fit, Ibid., 87
18. awful deserter, Berg, *Wilson*, 368.
19. You are a fencer worthy, Levin, *Edith and Woodrow*, 87.
20. that if he [Bryan] were left, Ibid.
21. For God's sake, Ibid., 371.
22. You owe it to yourself, Ibid.
23. I know…that I am asking, Link, *The Papers of Woodrow Wilson*, 33.279
24. After a quick tour, Levin, *Edith and Woodrow*, 136.
25. a drab faded woman of middle age, Levin, *Edith and Woodrow*, 350.
26. What do you think, Berg, *Wilson*, 371.
27. Cornish is a charming spot, Wilson, *My Memoir*, 71.
28. brought the banishment, Berg, *Wilson*, 372.
29. I felt so queer, Levin, *Edith and Woodrow*, 103.
30. whatever is mine is yours, Ibid.

## CHAPTER SEVENTEEN: THE PETTICOAT GOVERNMENT

1. We have petticoat government, Ross, *Power with Grace*, 218.
2. Please don't think I am trying, Link, *The Papers of Woodrow Wilson*, 64.204.
3. Things are going well, Viereck, *The Strangest Friendship*, 323.
4. You are wondering why I wanted to see you, Ibid., 324.
5. Please give my greetings to the President, Ibid.
6. That is very interesting, Ibid.
7. Mrs. Wilson said that, Ibid.
8. She then asked, Ibid. 325.
9. My Dear Mr. Jones, Link, *The Papers of Woodrow Wilson*, 64.232
10. I, myself, never made a single, Cooper, *Woodrow Wilson*, 357.
11. Tumulty wrote the message, Ibid., 415.
12. I never liked Tumulty, Hatch, *Edith Bolling Wilson*, 65.
13. Finally, when it could no longer, Link, *The Papers of Woodrow Wilson*, 63.636.
14. Thank you for your offer, Ibid. 63.593.
15. My separation from Woodrow, Viereck, *The Strangest Friendship*, 5.
16. Mrs. Wilson is keeping me, Smith, *When the Cheering Stopped*, 124.
17. The President says he, Ibid.
18. I am not interested in the President, Steven Weisman, *The Great Tax Wars: Lincoln to Wilson—The Fierce Battles over Money and Power that Transformed the World* (New York: Simon & Schuster, 2002), 340.
19. Dear Mrs. Wilson, I hope you will let the President, Link, *The Papers of Woodrow Wilson*, 214.
20. Dear Mrs. Wilson, will you kindly read, Ibid., 147.
21. Dear Mrs. Wilson, This matter is, Ibid., 64. 353.

22. Dear Mrs. Wilson, I know the President, Ibid. 64. 355.
23. Dear Mrs. Wilson, Will you please, Ibid. 64, 397.
24. Dear Mrs. Wilson, I do not know, *PWW: 1919-1920.,* 419.
25. Dozens of appointment-to-office, Smith, *When the Cheering Stopped,* 123.
26. when you think fit, Smith, Ibid.,124.
27. Dear Mrs. Wilson, Ibid, 125.
28. Over the wide left margins, Ibid.
29. The president says, Ibid.
30. When you think an opportune time, Levin, *Edith and Woodrow,* 358.
31. The President says it is impossible, Ibid.
32. The President is in such a condition, William Gill, *Trade Wars Against America,* 79.
33. The President says he does not know enough, Levin, *Edith and Woodrow,* 360.
34. I venture to suggest, Ibid.
35. The President says please inform, Ibid., 361
36. Dear Mrs. Wilson, I leave it, Ibid.
37. The President says he agrees, Ibid.
38. I just had nothing to do, Ibid., 362.
39. The President says he cannot do anything, Ibid., 363.

## CHAPTER EIGHTEEN: THE OTHER WOMAN

1. she was the companion I want, Levin, *Edith and Woodrow,* 111.
2. Though I tried to keep, Wilson, *My Memoir,* 74
3. And so, little girl, I have no right, Ibid., 75.
4. I put my arms, Ibid.
5. I'm so glad, Berg, *Wilson,* 374.
6. vulgar marriage, Levin, *Edith and Woodrow,* 141.

7. From an obscure position, Ibid., 141-142.
8. there was something personal, Berg, *Wilson,* 374
9. a passage of folly, Ibid., 375
10. When he was gone, Wilson, *My Memoir,* 76.
11. The dawn has come, Ibid., 76.
12. Without even shaking hands, Ibid., 77.
13. Then I remembered what, Ibid.
14. The curtains were drawn, Ibid., 78.
15. No word was spoken, Ibid.
16. I think I am rarely a coward, Ibid.


CHAPTER NINETEEN: MR. AND MRS. PRESIDENT
1. Oh you beautiful doll, Smith, *When the Cheering Stopped,* 26.
2. When Wilson proposed, Levin, *Edith and Woodrow,* 404.
3. My house was turned over, Wilson, *My Memoir,* 85.
4. I could not ask his wife, Ibid., 84.
5. they were sailing in, Ibid.
6. I walked straight, Ibid.
7. Why not wait and, Ibid., 85.
8. This letter goes to him, Ibid.
9. Yes, I was afraid of, Ibid.
10. The President reached my house, Ibid.
11. oyster patties, boned capon, Berg, *Wilson,* 381.
12. We had a lovely drive, Wilson, *My Memoir,* 86-87.
13. The railway car was, Ibid., 87
14. We decided to get out, Ibid.
15. The old tree which was, Ibid.


CHAPTER TWENTY: THE LEAGUE FIGHT
1. He was too refined, Cooper, *Woodrow Wilson,* 383.
2. I never expected to hate, Berg, *Wilson,* 612.

3.  The United States is the world's best hope, William Safire, *Lend Me Your Ear: Great Speeches in History* (New York: W.W. Norton & Company, 2004), 315.

4.  I do not propose, Alexander George, *Woodrow Wilson and Colonel House: A Personality Study* (Mineola: Dover Publications, 1964), 277.

5.  The increasing demands, Wilson, *My Memoir*, 273.

6.  Picture the situation when my husband was stricken, Thomas Bailey and David Kennedy, *The American Spirit: United States History as Seen by Contemporaries* (Belmont: Wadsworth Publishing Company, 2009), 274.

7.  Admiral Grayson had no access to the truth, William Allen White, *Woodrow Wilson: The Man, his Times, and his Task*, 453.

8.  My dear Mrs. Wilson, great progress, Link, *The Papers of Woodrow Wilson*, 64.37.

9.  Dear Mrs. Wilson, will you get the following, Ibid., 64.42.

10. I beheld an emaciated old man, Cooper, *Woodrow Wilson*, 542.

11. Not forty-five out, John Arthur Garraty, *Henry Cabot Lodge: A Biography*, 377-378.

12. President will Pocket Treaty, Link, *The Papers of Woodrow Wilson*, 64.45.

13. Mr. Lansing told me pathetically, Ibid., 64.365.

14. Tumulty phoned that the President, Ibid., 64.50.

15. The psychologic manifestations, Ibid., 64.525.

16. That is the trouble, Ibid., 64.321.

17. My dear Mrs. Wilson, Ibid., 64.58

18. There were the Irreconcilables, Smith, *When the Cheering Stopped*, 112.

19. You can never know how long, Link, *The Papers of Woodrow Wilson*, 64.88.
20. Your conscience will be clear, Herbert Hoover, *The Ordeal of Woodrow Wilson* (Washington, DC: Woodrow Wilson Center Press, 1992), 285.
21. May I trouble you again, Link, *The Papers of Woodrow Wilson*, 64.95.
22. On the one hand your loyalty, Ibid., 64.96.
23. Wilson's emotions were unbalanced, Cooper, *Woodrow Wilson*, 544.
24. You haven't come to talk compromise, Smith, *When the Cheering Stopped*, 119.
25. eating into my soul, Levin, *Edith and Woodrow*, 379.
26. in desperation, Wilson, *My Memoir*, 296.
27. Little girl, don't you desert me, Ibid., 297.
28. Better a thousand times, Levin, *Edith and Woodrow*, 379.
29. and I would never, Wilson, *My Memoir*, 297.
30. Dear Senator, you were good enough, Link, *The Papers of Woodrow Wilson*, 64.58.
31. half a loaf is, Levin, *Edith and Woodrow*, 379.
32. better a thousand times, Ibid.
33. All the more reason, Wilson, *My Memoir*, 379.
34. I feel like going to bed, Hatch, *Edith Bolling Wilson*, 238.
35. If I were not a Christian, Ibid.

## CHAPTER TWENTY-ONE: MRS. EDITH GOES TO WASHINGTON

1. Very few husbands, Hatch, *Edith Bolling Wilson*, 225.
2. The president now took to rising, Berg, *Wilson*, 389.
3. From my vantage point, Wilson, *My Memoir*, 91.
4. We talked of books, Ibid.
5. Played golf with W., Hatch, *Edith Bolling Wilson*, 61.

6. You don't know, Berg, *Wilson*, 390.
7. There won't be any war, Ibid., 393.
8. Unless the Imperial Government, Ibid., 396.
9. Accompanied by two, Wilson, *My Memoir*, 96.
10. Let's go back again, Ibid., 97.
11. I have that honor, Ibid.
12. One reckless commander, Cooper, *Woodrow Wilson*, 310.

CHAPTER TWENTY-TWO: CITIZEN KANE
1. Upon arrival we changed, Link, *The Papers of Woodrow Wilson*, 63.636.
2. For the first time, Ibid., 64.50.
3. The question as to, Ibid., 64.123.
4. If there ever was a man, Ibid., 63.636.
5. Even newspapers ardently opposed, Wilson, *My Memoir*, 298.
6. Dear Mrs. Wilson, I am sending, Link, The Papers of Woodrow Wilson, 64.72
7. Dear Mrs. Wilson, I have completed, Link, *The Papers of Woodrow Wilson*, 64.90.
8. This message's references, Cooper, *Woodrow Wilson*, 546.
9. A fine piece of political work, Link, The Papers of Woodrow Wilson, 64.123
10. There has been a great deal, Ibid.
11. In the signature, Ibid., 64.125
12. Dear Admiral, Ibid., 64.127
13. Albert Fall engineered, Wilson, *My Memoir*, 298

CHAPTER TWENTY-THREE: THE SNOWS OF SIERRA NEVADA
1. He kept us out, Berg, *Wilson*, 411.
2. America First, Ibid., 397.
3. think first, Ibid.

4. That summer of 1916, Wilson, *My Memoir*, 102.
5. The days were never long enough, Ibid., 102.
6. The first impression, Ibid., 103-104
7. We were three days, Ibid., 105.
8. The president is under terrific strain, Ibid.
9. As Mr. Wilson spoke, Ibid., 105-106.
10. fifteen hundred strong, Ibid., 107
11. We had a large table, Ibid.
12. I write to refresh, Ibid., 108
13. Instead of speaking softly, Berg, *Wilson*, 411.
14. He kept us out of the war, Ibid.
15. evolutionary ostrich, Ibid.
16. ignoble shirking of responsibility, Ibid.
17. There we spent, Wilson, *My Memoir*, 111.
18. I tried to picture, Ibid., 112.
19. I never felt that we could win, Ibid.
20. What we are electing, Sean Dennis Cashman, *America Ascendant: From Theodore Roosevelt to FDR in the Century of American Power, 1901—1945* (New York: New York University Press, 1998), 149.
21. would have no right, Cooper, **Woodrow Wilson**, 356
22. I began to speculate, Wilson, *My Memoir*, 112
23. What a delightful pessimist, Ibid., 113.
24. Why he is not defeated!, Ibid., 114.
25. Impossible, Ibid.
26. Well Tumulty, Berg, *Wilson*, 414.
27. I found real consolation, Wilson, *My Memoir*, 114.
28. I am doubly thankful, Ray Stannard Baker, *Woodrow Wilson: Facing War*, 296.
29. Well little girl, you were right, Wilson, *My Memoir*, 116.
30. She had just talked, Ibid.

31. Shall we wake father?, Ibid.
32. Well, tell him when he wakes up, Berg, *Wilson*, 415.
33. Thursday, Got up at 8, Wilson, *My Memoir*, 117-118.
34. I suppose the suspense, Ibid., 118.
35. They all told of new gains, Ibid.

## CHAPTER TWENTY-FOUR: A SMELLING COMMITTEE

1. A smelling committee, Hatch, *Edith Bolling Wilson*, 233.
2. When the Senate Committee, Levin, *Edith and Woodrow*, 389.
3. Fall asked, Smith, *When the Cheering Stopped*, 133.
4. Well senator, Ibid.
5. Senator Fall entered, Wilson, My Memoir, 299.
6. If agreeable, I wish Mrs. Wilson, Smith, *When the Cheering Stopped*, 134.
7. You seem very much engaged, Wilson, *My Memoir*, 299.
8. I thought it wise, Ibid.
9. I have a copy, Smith, *When the Cheering Stopped*, 134.
10. I hope the Senator, Ibid.
11. I have been praying for you, Wilson, *My Memoir*, 299.
12. which way senator, Hatch, *Edith Bolling Wilson*, 234.
13. You have just left a man, Smith, *When the Cheering Stopped*, 134.
14. The president looks much better, Link, *The PPW*: 1919-1920, 131.
15. assured the reporters, Wilson, *My Memoir*, 299.
16. Senators see President, Link, *The Papers of Woodrow Wilson*, 64.129.
17. Well the president received Senator Fall, Ibid., 64.139.

## CHAPTER TWENTY-FIVE: THE SHADOW OF WAR

1. Tell that to the marines, Berg, *Wilson*, 416.

2. Up at 7:30 Brooks, Wilson, *My Memoir*, 118.

3. was a little moth-eaten, Berg, *Wilson*, 417.

4. This was the first time I felt certain, Wilson, *My Memoir*, 119.

5. My husband, too, Ibid., 120.

6. But a graver problem, Ibid.

7. Foreseeing an inevitable crisis, Joseph Tumulty, *Woodrow Wilson as I Know Him* (New York: Doubleday, 1921), 146.

8. Detestable suffragettes, Hatch, *Edith Bolling Wilson*, 80.

9. My dear one felt, Wilson, *My Memoir*, 120.

10. Woodrow still not well, Ibid., 121.

11. I am convinced the president's, Cooper, *Woodrow Wilson*, 365.

12. as an administrator, Ibid., 365.

13. I am not sure, Cooper, *Woodrow Wilson*, 363-364.

14. Two days later, Wilson, *My Memoir*, 123.

15. The heavy escort, Ibid., 130.

16. We are provincials no longer, Hatch, *Edith Bolling Wilson*, 97.

17. create a peace, Link, *The Papers of Woodrow Wilson*, 40.535.

18. my husband considered, Wilson *My Memoir*, 122.

19. What's wrong Woodrow?, Hatch, *Edith Wilson*, 94.

20. The German government has announced, Ibid.

21. It means war, Hatch, *Edith Bolling Wilson*, 94.

22. I felt a sense of impending climax, Wilson, *My Memoir*, 128.

23. Within an hour, Ibid.

24. March 13, 1917, Ibid., 131.

25. March 14, Ibid.,

26. March 15, Ibid.

27. If he [Wilson] does not go, Baker, Woodrow Wilson, 533.

28. The shadow of war, Wilson, *My Memoir*, 132.

29. grave questions of national policy, Ibid.

30. The night of March 31st, Hatch, *Edith Bolling Wilson*, 98

31. She [Edith] sat upstairs, Ibid.
32. She took it and went, Ibid.
33. On this day while he worked, Wilson, *My Memoir*, 132.
34. Troops were standing, Wilson, *My Memoir*, 132-133.
35. There is one choice, Richard Striner, *Woodrow Wilson and World War I: A Burden Too Great to Bear* (Lanham: Rowman & Littlefield Publishers, 2014), 105.
36. the ultimate peace of the world, Ibid.
37. vindicate the principles of peace, Cooper, *Woodrow Wilson*, 387.
38. Mr. President, you have expressed, Baker, *Woodrow Wilson*, 515.
39. Stand by me Edith, Ross, *Power with Grace*, 94.


### CHAPTER TWENTY-SIX: THE COAL STRIKE AND PALMER RAIDS

1. Palmer said Judge Anderson, Link, *The Papers of Woodrow Wilson*, 64.141.
2. President Makes Proposal, Ibid., 64.142.
3. Dear Mr. Tumulty, the president says will you see, Ibid., 64.145.
4. Dear Mrs. Wilson, I have re-read the statement, Ibid.
5. Not to the let the country see red, Levin, *Edith and Woodrow*, 417.


### CHAPTER TWENTY-SEVEN: THE WAR TO END ALL WARS

1. I want to stand by my country, Norma Smith, *Jeanette Rankin, America's Conscience* (Helena: Montana Historical Society Press, 2002), 113.
2. There the day began at five, Wilson, *My Memoir*, 134.
3. Edith Benham, Wilson, *My Memoir*, 135.
4. Only under government administration, Berg, *Wilson*, 443.
5. The cabinet ladies and I, Wilson, *My Memoir*, 135.

6. We set forth to church, Ibid.
7. I know that the emotional drain, Wilson, *My Memoir*, 134.
8. What do you suggest?, Hatch, *Edith Bolling Wilson*, 104.
9. I'll get Grayson, Ibid., 105.
10. The president came out, Ibid.
11. I was not hurt, Ibid.
12. A tall western boy, Hatch, *Edith Bolling Wilson*, 108.
13. Always there were figures, Wilson, *My Memoir*, 144.
14. they would both look, Ibid., 145.
15. Now I'll show you how to do a jig, Ibid.
16. No matter how foolish the skit, Ibid.
17. When shearing time came, Ibid., 160.
18. Do you think it's dying?, Hatch, *Edith Bolling Wilson*, 110.
19. Ordinarily the president's, Wilson, *My Memoir*, 150.
20. The situation was graver, Ibid.
21. Next day came a cable, Ibid., 151.
22. Don't bother over that, Ibid., 152.
23. We had gone over every word, Ibid., 154.
24. With victory an accomplished fact, Ibid.
25. The president's words, Levin, *Edith and Woodrow*, 204.

## CHAPTER TWENTY-EIGHT: SUNSET BOULEVARD

1. Dr. Grayson spent the night, Smith, *When the Cheering Stopped*, 137.
2. On sunshine days, Link, *The Papers of Woodrow Wilson*, 63.637.
3. Mr. Wilson will eat Christmas dinner, Levin, *Edith and Woodrow*, 395.
4. In his wheel chair, Smith, *When the Cheering Stopped*, 138.
5. My tour of inspection, Ibid.

## CHAPTER TWENTY-NINE: ALL QUIET ON THE WESTERN FRONT

1. Please leave out of your vocabulary, Link, *The Papers of Woodrow Wilson*, 43.430.
2. Taking soundings?, Hatch, *Edith Bolling Wilson*, 113.
3. I asked him to come in, Wilson, *My Memoir*, 155.
4. Suppose you tell him, Ibid.,155.
5. Well Edith tells me, Ibid.
6. Here is glorious news!, Hatch, *Edith Bolling Wilson*, 123.
7. In ordinary times, Tumulty, *Woodrow Wilson as I Know Him*, 332
8. I would not send it, Levin, *Edith and Woodrow*, 217.
9. That message, Hatch, *Edith Bolling Wilson*, 131.
10. All the negotiations, Wilson, *My Memoir*, 169.
11. We'll go, Hatch, *Edith Bolling Wilson*, 124.
12. I wish I could, Wilson, *My Memoir*, 170.
13. This is your task, Ibid.
14. My recollection is that, Ibid.

## CHAPTER THIRTY: JUDAS

1. milk, butter and sausages, Smith, *When the Cheering Stopped*, 140.
2. On March 4th my secretary, Wilson, *My Memoir*, 302.
3. At first I hardly knew, Ibid.
4. Having tackled, Ibid.
5. I am seriously thinking, Dr. Jerrold Post and Robert Robins, *When Illness Strikes the Leader: The Dilemma of the Captive King* (New Haven: Yale University Press, 1995), 88.
6. The president looked old, Hatch, *Edith Bolling Wilson*, 239.
7. He permitted himself, Link, *The Papers of Woodrow Wilson*, 63.637.
8. Mr. Lansing should have retired, Wilson, *My Memoir*, 300.

9. As soon as the President became ill, Ibid.
10. the League Covenant, Daniels, *Life of Woodrow Wilson*, 148.
11. Lansing is insulted daily, Link, *The Papers of Woodrow Wilson*, 64.243.
12. I don't know how, Ibid., 64.179.
13. Dear Mr. Secretary, Ibid. 64.366.
14. My Dear Mrs. Wilson, I am in receipt, Link, *The Papers of Woodrow Wilson*, 64.316.
15. Is it true as I have been told, Hatch, *Edith Bolling Wilson*, 240.
16. It is true, Ibid.
17. The most charitable opinion, Link, *The Papers of Woodrow Wilson*, 64.385.
18. Sen McCumber said, Ibid., 64.428.
19. It was the wrong time to do the right, Berg, *Wilson*, 667.
20. The president as you see, Link, The Papers of Woodrow Wilson, 64. 389.
21. I cannot permit to pass, Ibid. 64.409.
22. The president delivered, Ibid. 64.415.
23. I begged Mr. Wilson, Ibid. 64.417.
24. The diseased arteries, Link, *The Papers of Woodrow Wilson*, 64.433.
25. We have been repeatedly assured, Smith, *When the Cheering Stopped*, 144.
26. It is unthinkable that a sane man, Ibid.
27. Like a sleep princess, Ibid.
28. They ask in stage whispers, Ibid., 145.
29. One of the foremost statesmen in Washington, Levin, *Edith and Woodrow*, 429.
30. Nothing but the greatest deference, Ibid.
31. I hate Lansing, Smith, *When the Cheering Stopped*, 144.
32. First, the President was incapacitated, Ibid.

33. Look how strong I am!, Ibid.

## CHAPTER THIRTY-ONE: THE SUFFRAGETTES

1. While my husband, Wilson, *My Memoir*, 113.
2. I am tied to a conviction, Berg, *Wilson*, 487.
3. Women do not really need the suffrage, Ibid., 488.
4. Suffrage for women will make absolutely no change, Ibid.
5. Mr. President, how long, Ibid.
6. Miss Paul, an ethereal-looking Quaker, Ross, *Power with Grace*, 308.
7. One bitterly cold day, Wilson, *My Memoir*, 125.
8. We, the women of America, Berg, *Wilson*, 489
9. They certainly seem bent, Ibid.
10. I was indignant, Wilson, *My Memoir*, 138
11. I am here to watch you, Ibid., 43.
12. For years there was uncertainty, Ross, *Power with Grace*, 308
13. Hundreds of women, Ibid., 314
14. He [the president] told me that we had made a fearful blunder, Ibid., 318.
15. I was blazing with anger, Ibid., 316.
16. I felt that since no president, Ibid., 318.
17. It is high time, Ross, *Power with Grace*, 319.
18. Who was the real president, Ibid., 321.
19. If anyone had even a remote right, Robert Bender, *Colliers*, vol. 65, 197.

## CHAPTER THIRTY-TWO: OUR OWN COUNTRY

1. In a minute, Wilson, *My Memoir*, 172.
2. Your [message] upsets every plan, Levin, *Edith and Woodrow*, 228.

3. It is not too much, Link, *The Papers of Woodrow Wilson*, 53.352.
4. The American Armies, Berg, *Wilson*, 525.
5. I could not bear him, Levin, *Edith and Woodrow*, 240.
6. All noticed that [Mrs. Wilson] was constantly, Ross, *Power with Grace*, 151
7. I don't want to get mad, Lawrence, *The True Story of Woodrow Wilson*, 259
8. The grinding work, Wilson, *My Memoir*, 233.
9. When we first reached Paris, Ibid.
10. In the circumstances, Ibid., 238.
11. We had been told, Ibid.
12. It was a great moment in history, Ibid, 239.
13. Every day we would go, Ibid., 240.
14. No ma'am, cause I know, Ibid.
15. The president turned to Lodge, Ibid., 241.
16. If the Foreign Relations Committee, Ibid., 242.
17. Very well, I consider that, Ibid.
18. Certainly the facts justify, Ibid.
19. I went out to the dining room, Hatch, *Edith Bolling Wilson*, 170.
20. her fingernails were black, Levin, *Edith and Woodrow*, 257.
21. I opened the door, Wilson, *My Memoir*, 245-246.
22. House has given away, Ibid., 246
23. on the sad day, Levin, *Edith and Woodrow*, 295.
24. We went about on tiptoe, Wilson, *My Memoir*, 249.
25. The president was sicker, Link, *The Papers of Woodrow Wilson*, 64.633.
26. Brains of the commission, Wilson, *My Memoir*, 250.
27. Colonel, have you been reading, Ibid.
28. The colonel's face, Ibid., 251.

29. Yes, all that is true, Wilson, *My Memoir*, 274.

## CHAPTER THIRTY-THREE: DEAD AS MARLEY'S GHOST

1. President Will Never Recover, Link, *The Papers of Woodrow Wilson*, 64.432.
2. The president's stroke, Link, *The PWW: 1919-1920*, 432.
3. Technically we are still at war, Link, *The Papers of Woodrow Wilson*, 64.433.
4. No longer an independent human being, Berg, *Wilson*, 682.
5. The Woodrow Wilson who lived on, Ibid.
6. My Dear Mrs. Wilson, day after tomorrow, Link, *The Papers of Woodrow Wilson*, 64.273.
7. bounds of executive authority, Link, *The Papers of Woodrow Wilson*, 64.274.
8. Personally I do not accept, Smith, *When the Cheering Stopped*, 141.
9. If there is any doubt, Ibid.
10. I have the feeling that all the president, Hoover, *The Ordeal of Woodrow Wilson*, 287
11. I had a long talk with Mrs. Wilson, Link, *PPW: 1919-1920*, 320.
12. People in the future will forget, Hoover, *The Ordeal of Woodrow Wilson*, 288.
13. Should the American government, Link, *The Papers of Woodrow Wilson*, 64.345.
14. President Wilson contracted a cold, Ibid., 64.351.
15. The poor president, Ibid., 64.360
16. I challenge the following, Smith, *When the Cheering Stopped*, 142.
17. Had Lord Gray ventured upon, Levin, *Edith and Woodrow*, 412.

18. If I accept them, Smith, *When the Cheering Stopped*, 148.
19. I am willing to compromise on anything but, Link, *The Papers of Woodrow Wilson*, 64.321.
20. If we must go to the American people, Ibid., 64.387.
21. Tumulty tried so hard, Ibid., 64.638.
22. Dear Mrs. Wilson, Director of Railroads Hines, Ibid., 64.391.
23. Dear Mrs. Wilson, I went over the railroad situation, Ibid., 64.396.
24. Dear Mrs. Wilson, will you please have the president mark accepted, Ibid., 64.397.
25. I will not play for position, Smith, *When the Cheering Stopped*, 148.
26. There is a strong disposition, John Milton Cooper, *Breaking the Heart of the World: Woodrow Wilson and the Fight for the League of Nations*, (Cambridge: Cambridge University Press, 2010), 33.
27. Any reservation seeking, Ibid., 346.
28. I never leave except for an hour, Smith, *When the Cheering Stopped*, 149.
29. has strangled his own child, Levin, *Edith and Woodrow*, 437.
30. As dead as Marley's ghost, Smith, *When the Cheering Stopped*, 149.
31. Doctor, the devil is a busy man, Hatch, *Edith Bolling Wilson*, 238.
32. I sat with him miserably fumbling, Smith, *When the Cheering Stopped*, 151.
33. If only I were not helpless, Smith, Ibid.
34. My conviction is that Mr. Lodge, Wilson, *My Memoir*, 303.

CHAPTER THIRTY-FOUR: ON THE ROAD

1. President Wilson went motor riding today, Link, *The Papers of Woodrow Wilson*, 65.41.
2. President Wilson took his fourth automobile ride, Ibid.
3. And so he was driven through Washington, Smith, *When the Cheering Stopped*, 146.
4. You see Edith, they still love me, Levin, *Edith and Woodrow*, 444.
5. Dear Mrs. Wilson...what should the postmaster, Link, *The Papers of Woodrow Wilson*, 65.122.
6. Dear Mrs. Wilson, I do not know how the president feels about, Ibid., 65.117.
7. I am wondering if in view, Ibid., 65.180.
8. I don't know whether it is warm or cold, Levin, *Edith and Woodrow*, 438
9. Dear Mrs. Wilson, Acting Attorney General, Link, *The Papers of Woodrow Wilson*, 65.175.
10. I believe you know, Ibid., 65.324.
11. He doesn't know, Smith, *When the Cheering Stopped*, 159.
12. The first lady could go straight, Ibid., 160.
13. His mind is not like of old, Link, *The Papers of Woodrow Wilson*, 65.550.
14. Lunched with Polk, Ibid., 65.343.
15. Mr. Wilson desires a third term?, Smith, *When the Cheering Stopped*, 161.
16. He fervently believes, Ibid.
17. I have always admired, Hatch, *Edith Bolling Wilson*, 243.
18. I hobble from one part of the house, Berg, *Wilson*, 694.
19. He more easily loses control, Ibid.
20. Gentlemen, I hope you will excuse me, Ibid., 695.
21. Can you imagine, Ibid.
22. My husband was already downstairs, Wilson, *My Memoir*, 316.

23. His valet held, Ibid., 318.
24. Mr. Harding alighted, Ibid.
25. Through the day had taxed, Ibid., 319.

## CHAPTER THIRTY-FIVE: MERCILESS TO THE END

1. Ma, Smith, *When the Cheering Stopped*, 198.
2. You yellow rat!, Ibid., 199.
3. Both the doctor and I feared, Wilson, *My Memoir*, 321.
4. We had no idea that you, Link, *The Papers of Woodrow Wilson*, 65.332.
5. My only boy was killed, Berg, *Wilson*, 717-718
6. I feel a message, Wilson, *My Memoir*, 333.
7. Next morning, Mr. Tumulty telephoned me, Ibid.
8. No Mr. Tumulty, Ibid.
9. No, I am glad to say, Ibid., 334.
10. Say to the Democrats of New York, Cooper, *Woodrow Wilson*, 587
11. My husband was thunderstruck, Wilson, *My Memoir*, 334.
12. I am deeply distressed, Ibid., 335.
13. Why there is no urgency, Ibid.
14. That telegram Mr. Wilson, Link, *The Papers of Woodrow Wilson* 336.
15. For God's sake help him, Wilson, *My Memoir*, 337.
16. I write to say there is no doubt, Ibid., 338.

## CHAPTER THIRTY-SIX: A BROKEN PIECE OF MACHINERY

1. A police sergeant conducted, Wilson, *My* Memoir, 330-331.
2. His obscure position. Ibid., 331
3. America was going on the greatest, Harold Bloom, ed., *F. Scott Fitzgerald* (New York: Chelsea House Publications, 1985), 81.
4. Leaning hard on his cane, Berg, *Wilson*, 716.

5. I wish that I have the voice, Ibid.
6. Long live the best man, Ibid.
7. everyone told me I looked, Wilson, *My Memoir*, 351.
8. Mr. Wilson spoke at 8:30, Ibid., 355.
9. No, If I did, I would not leave him, Ibid., 359.
10. I always feel badly, Ibid.
11. No, that would be a selfish thing, Ibid.
12. I am ready, Smith, *When the Cheering Stopped*, 238.
13. Outside, the crowds gathered after church, Ibid., 242.
14. Mr. Wilson died at 11:15, Ibid., 244.
15. Was Mrs. Wilson, Ibid.

## CHAPTER THIRTY-SEVEN: EDITH AT LARGE

1. Venomous serpent, Levin, *Edith and Woodrow*, 267.
2. As the funeral is private, Cooper, *Woodrow Wilson*, 597
3. You may rest assured, Levin, *Edith and Woodrow*, 492
4. I never gave interviews, Hatch, *Edith Bolling Wilson*, 266.
5. We never found out, Ibid., 271.
6. I can tell you, Ibid.
7. I wrote the first part of my book, Ibid., 272.
8. Humanizes the president, Ibid., 273.
9. a well-preserved still elegantly dressed, Miller, *Ellen and Edith Woodrow: First Ladies*, 255.
10. While I was in bed, Hatch, *Edith Bolling Wilson*, 273.
11. Woodrow Wilson would have never made such a statement, Ross, *Power with Grace*, 304.
12. I sat next to him poor thing, Ibid., 327.
13. Open all the windows, Hatch, *Edith Bolling Wilson*, 275.
14. You just sit right there, Ross, *Power with Grace*, 343.
15. I didn't dare ask you, Ibid.

## CHAPTER THIRTY-EIGHT: THE FIRST WOMAN PRESIDENT

1. steward, Wilson, *My Memoir*, 289.
2. Dear Mrs. Wilson, I submitted the draft, Link, *The Papers of Woodrow Wilson*, 65.282.
3. Dear Mrs. Wilson, here is a suggestion, Ibid., 65.128.
4. Dear Mrs. Wilson, will you be good enough, Ibid., 68.176.
5. Dear Mrs. Wilson tomorrow at 12, Ibid., 65.145.
6. Dear Mrs. Wilson will you advise me, Ibid., 65.146.
7. Dear Mrs. Wilson, Acting Attorney General Ames, Ibid., 65.175.
8. Dear Mrs. Wilson it seems to me, Ibid., 65.564.
9. Dear Mrs. Wilson, Work in the Senate, Ibid, 64.58.
10. Dear Mrs. Wilson, Will you kindly read the enclosed letter, Ibid.
11. Dear Mrs. Wilson, Day after tomorrow the democratic, Ibid., 64.273.
12. Dear Mrs. Wilson, On my return to Washington, Ibid., 64.350.
13. Dear Mrs. Wilson, this matter is so vitally important, Ibid., 64.353.
14. Dear Mrs. Wilson, Since our talk on Thursday, Ibid., 64.326.
15. Dear Mrs. Wilson, the psychological moment, Ibid., 64.287.
16. Dear Mrs. Wilson, It now appears, Ibid., 64.276.
17. Dear Mrs. Wilson, This matter was discussed at a conference, Ibid., 64.246.
18. Dear Mrs. Wilson, Please don't think I am trying to crowd you, Ibid., 64.204.
19. Dear Mrs. Wilson, When you get a chance to talk to the president, Ibid., 64.203.
20. Dear Mrs. Wilson, Enclosed, please find the draft of a letter, Ibid., 64.50.

# INDEX